From Mesopotamia to Modernity

From Mesopotamia to Modernity

Ten Introductions to Jewish History and Literature

edited by

Burton L. Visotzky

The Jewish Theological Seminary, New York

and

David E. Fishman

The Jewish Theological Seminary, New York

Westview Press
A Member of the Perseus Books Group

Copyright © 1999 by Burton L. Visotzky and David E. Fishman

Published in 1999 in the United States of America by Westview Press, 5500 Central Avenue, Boulder, Colorado 80301-2877, and in the United Kingdom by Westview Press, 12 Hid's Copse Road, Cumnor Hill, Oxford OX2 9JJ

Find us on the World Wide Web at www.westviewpress.com

Library of Congress Cataloging-in-Publication Data
From Mesopotamia to modernity : ten introductions to Jewish history and literature / edited by Burton L. Visotzky and David E. Fishman.
    p.   cm.
    Includes bibliographical references and index.
    ISBN 0-8133-6716-6 (hc) — ISBN 0-8133-6717-4 (pbk).
    1. Jews—History.   2. Judaism—History.   3. Jewish literature—History and criticism.   4. Jews—Intellectual life.   I. Visotzky, Burton L.   II. Fishman, David E., 1957–
DS117.F77   1999
909'.04924—dc21   99-22787
                                                                        CIP

The paper used in this publication meets the requirements of the American National Standard for Permanence of Paper for Printed Library Materials Z39.48-1984.

10   9   8   7   6   5   4   3

Contents

Introduction

BURTON L. VISOTZKY AND DAVID E. FISHMAN

THE EXPLOSIVE GROWTH OF JEWISH STUDIES PROGRAMS in American universities is testimony to the acceptance of Judaism as part of the fabric of modern American life. In the Jewish community itself, the question is no longer, "Am I a Jew first or an American first?" Rather, Jews in America express their patriotism and American identity through a broad range of Jewish religious identities. This identification leads them to explore Jewish history and literature in the institution that they consider the key to their success as Americans—the university. Furthermore, Christians show a keen interest in the academic study of the religion that was the source of their own. Particularly since World War II, an ever growing interest in the Judaism of Jesus has gripped Christian scholarship. As a result, Jewish studies courses in universities are populated by both Jews and Gentiles.

The plethora of course offerings on Judaism, particularly on an introductory course level, has been hampered by the lack of a textbook that attends to both the history and the literature of the Jews. Perhaps uniquely among peoples, the history of the Jews is ineluctably entwined with its literature. The people of the book is also the people of linear history; therefore, the history and literature of the Jews form the woof and warp of the fabric of Jewish civilization. There are works that address Jewish history. Likewise, there are books that survey Jewish literature. This book attempts, for the first time, to encompass both aspects of Jewish civilization in its pages.

In order to do so, this textbook consciously eschews the treatment of what might be deemed "current events" in its pages. For the most part, both the history and the literature considered do not go beyond the advent of the State of Israel, just following World War II. There are a variety of reasons that we editors have chosen to end the text short of our own era. First, it seemed unlikely that there could be any sense of objectivity writing about events (or books) that we ourselves were part of. Second,

1

readers will notice an absence of separate chapters on modern Israel, American Jewry, and the Holocaust. We are aware of the ubiquity of individual course offerings on each of these topics in American university curricula. In other words, we chose not to include in our introductory textbook those topics that we knew were most likely to be presented in discrete courses.

Readers might notice other lacunae in our choices for this book. Women's studies has grown to be a particularly important discipline on American campuses, no less so in Jewish studies. Yet we have neither devoted a separate chapter to nor particularly emphasized feminist views in our various chapters. There is no negative judgment of women's studies in this choice, quite the contrary. Our very first chapter, on the central work of Jewish literature, happily employs feminist readings as a strategy for reading the Bible. But we have tried to avoid privileging one discipline over any other. As such, women's studies takes its place among the other academic disciplines employed by the scholars here assembled. Indeed, where appropriate, authors write explicitly about each disciplinary approach in order to educate students about the various methodologies employed.

Readers will find, then, a variety of methods throughout the range of chapters. Primarily, of course, the disciplines of history and literature are the focal points of this collection.

General surveys of both history and literature in virtually every area of Jewish civilization have been presented. In some instances, broad brush strokes suffice, particularly where there is a great swathe of history covered in a given period, or where the literature is either obviously central (e.g., the Bible) or overwhelmingly plentiful (e.g., modern literature). In some cases the chapters are more encyclopedic, particularly when the authors were aware of a lack of such an exhaustive overview (e.g., rabbinic literature).

The differences in style and content reflect the individual tastes of the authors, each an expert in her or his own field. This latitude of style was promised to the authors, as is appropriate for recognized scholars. At the same time, these scholars were asked to limit idiosyncratic content and to be representative of their discipline as a whole. We trust that readers find the result is a unique textbook in its survey of both Jewish literature and Jewish history. This duality reflects, perhaps, a peculiarity of Jewish studies: Literature holds such a central position that historic eras are often referred to by the books written in them.

It is not unusual to find a Jewish studies course on the biblical era, which is to say the period from approximately 1500 B.C.E. to approximately 400 B.C.E. That broad millennium is represented par excellence in the Jewish library by the Hebrew Bible. Any student of history will understand that covering more than a thousand years by focusing on the literature of one unique anthology is an unusual approach to the subject. Furthermore, to reduce a thousand years of literature to one canonical work is equally unusual. Yet in Jewish studies, the power of the biblical canon is so great, and the paucity of other works so notable, that the earliest era of Israelite development is necessarily represented in this volume by a chapter on the Hebrew Bible.

The opening chapter is meant to introduce the novice to the various genres of literature contained within the Hebrew Bible while at the same time covering its major historic periods. Because of the enormous concentration of time and topics in the chapter, this approach steers a middle course through the debates among modern scholars on methods of Bible study and the meaning of the canon to historians and religion scholars alike. The chapter takes the neophyte through the basics of biblical history and literature together. At the same time, the scholar in those fields will appreciate how Ora Horn Prouser has carefully balanced her exposition to include the range of viewpoints in the academy on this essential work and historic period.

To introduce the student of Judaica to approaches that will persist throughout the rest of the chapters in this book, there is a section on methodology at the end of the chapter on the Hebrew Bible and a section on academic study in the rabbinic literature chapter. The intention is to make the student aware of the options that scholars choose as they approach their various subjects. Consciousness of method should allow the student to critique both the primary materials cited as well as the analyses that will be found in this book and throughout the field of Jewish studies.

As the biblical era drew to a close, Hellenism began to make its impact. The Greek-speaking world stretched from the islands of the Mediterranean in the west all the way east to India. Central to the geography of the Hellenistic world conquered by Alexander the Great was the Land of Israel, the Holy Land of the Jews and the Bible. Further east, the Jews who first suffered and then flourished in the Babylonian Exile lived their lives in full cognizance of the Hellenistic revolution in culture, language, and thought. So although the Bible looms large for the early period, works preserved in Hebrew, Aramaic, and Greek offer further evidence for the Hellenistic period of Jewish history. These varied literary works, considered in Chapter 2 by Albert Baumgarten, teach us a great deal about both the history and the thought of the Jewish communities of that postbiblical period.

These works of Jewish Hellenistic literature are important because there is otherwise a paucity of historic material on Judaism in that period. Yet it is the period in which much of later Jewish thought took its first shape. Moreover, it was in the Hellenistic era that the synagogue and other Jewish institutions that still persist found their origins. The chapter includes a discussion of literature up to the destruction of the Jerusalem Temple in the year 70 of the common era. Among the literature of this latter part of the Hellenistic period are the Dead Sea Scrolls. The library of the sectarian community that produced those scrolls has been much studied since its discovery in the middle of the twentieth century and has shed great light on early and middle Judaism and the origins of Christianity.

Following the consideration of the literature of the Hellenistic period comes a brief survey in Chapter 3 of the history of the Hellenistic and Roman periods. This era is seminal in Jewish history, for it marked the end of the Jerusalem Temple cult, and the successive rule of Greeks, Romans, and Christians over the Jews in the Land of Israel. In Chapter 3, Shaye J. D. Cohen sketches the history of the Jews under Greek and Roman rule. He focuses on the Jewish wars against Rome and the consequences of the losses of those wars. Although the chapter relies on Greek and Latin as well as Hebrew and Aramaic sources, it narrows its focus to the advent and growth of rabbinic Judaism.

The literature of the rabbinic movement in both the Land of Israel and Babylonia is the subject of Chapter 4, by Burton L. Visotzky. A broad survey of rabbinic literature covering almost a millennium carries readers through the consequences of Rome's destruction of the Jerusalem Temple and the concomitant emergence of the synagogue as the decentralized institution of Jewish life. The various genres of the literature are considered, and some of the issues in the modern study of this varied library of works are discussed. The broad sweep of years covered in rabbinic literature necessitates a survey approach. The reader will note the exclusion of nonrabbinic literature. Although such literature exists, particularly in Greek, but also in Hebrew and Aramaic, the wealth of rabbinic material and limits of space necessitated the narrower focus. In this chapter, as in most of the others, the methodologies of research considered and the approaches taken represent the historic mainstream of scholarship. Recent trends and as-yet-unproven methods have been eschewed in favor of the classical methods pioneered by European scholars well before World War II. These methods are still reliably, if not exclusively, employed in the academy.

The literature of the rabbis was revolutionary in that it transformed Judaism from a cultic religion centered in a place (the Jerusalem Temple) into a religion of study. The priest gave way to the rabbi-teacher, who embodied a portable sanctuary. The broad range of the literature these men produced is considered in its evolution. As time passed and outside influences changed the shape of rabbinic literature from its dialectic and Hellenistic modes, new influences from Christianity and Islam and particularly Arabic literature began to hold sway. The literature of the rabbis became poetry, philosophy, legal codes, and mysticism.

Of course, this literature was not created in a vacuum, and the rabbis and sages who produced medieval literature often partook of the secular world. The broad expanse of medieval Jewish history is considered by Robert Chazan in Chapter 5, a survey of the outside forces and internal institutions of Jewry. The focus of this chapter is European history. Although it would be possible to write a history of the Jewish East, not only the area under Islam, but also the area east of the Holy Land, this book keeps its gaze primarily upon Europe. The choice of Eurocentric history allows an examination of the interplay of Christianity, Islam, and Judaism. It also betrays the background of both the scholars who wrote these chapters and our expected readership.

The literature of the medieval period includes, however, both works written in lands where Arabic held sway as well as in lands where Latin ruled. The Jewish library remained primarily Hebrew and Aramaic, but works in Arabic, Latin, Judeo-Arabic, and Ladino are considered in the "Medieval Jewish Literature," Chapter 6, by Raymond P. Scheindlin. Here, the distinction between secular and religious literature can be first observed, particularly in works of Jewish poetry composed under Muslim rule. Thus the very definition of Jewish literature expands from religious volumes to all works composed by Jews. The debate about what constitutes "Jewish literature" began in the medieval period but has continued to the present day.

Although an important component of medieval Jewish literature, Jewish philosophy is treated separately in Chapter 7, by Warren Zev Harvey. Like much other medieval Jewish literature, the philosophic works written by the Jews of the Middle Ages betray distinct outside influences, particularly from Aristotelian philosophy as it reached the Jews through the Arabic-speaking world. But the philosophy of the medieval Doctors of the Church also had its influence. These sources of fructification wedded with traditional Jewish thought, particularly the notoriously unsystematic, organismic rabbinic thought, to produce a new flowering of literature. The power of medieval Jewish philosophy was such that it continued to hold sway even through the Enlightenment.

In addition, medieval Jewish mysticism is considered in Chapter 7. This mysticism was largely ignored in the nineteenth century, but in the twentieth century a rebirth of interest led to a rediscovery of many, many medieval mystical texts. Previously the province of a rarefied group of mystical practitioners, medieval mystical literature is now studied by scholars. The academic study of medieval mysticism has shed much light on what were previously considered esoteric and aberrant texts. The consideration of medieval Jewish mystical literature among the works of medieval and modern Jewish literature appropriately places these works in their broader Jewish context for student and scholar alike.

The conventions adopted for this volume's treatment of the Middle Ages were also observed for the modern era. In Chapter 8, "Modern Jewish History," the focus remains on Jewry in the West, centered upon Europe. David Fishman's survey of Jewish history in this period includes, of course, careful consideration of the rise of American Jewry. The other pole of Jewish history in the post-European context is the establishment of the State of Israel. These two communities have been central to Jewish consciousness and identity in the latter half of the twentieth century. The chapter considers both the internal forces in Jewish life and interactions with the broader world.

We reserved a separate chapter, Chapter 9, for the history of Soviet Jewry. The history of Russian Jewry is so important to the broader history of the Jews in the twentieth century that it deserves a separate treatment. American Jewry and Israel have been written about extensively, but the history of Jews in the former Soviet Union, the third-largest Jewish community of the twentieth century, is virtually unknown to American readers. The oppression of Soviet Jewry and the subsequent exodus of Russian Jews were closely followed by a rebirth of Judaism within Russia. Although this situation is still in flux, the importance of the history of Soviet Jewry to the American audience must be recognized. Zvi Gitelman has undertaken an exposition of these events.[1]

In Chapter 10, the final chapter of the book, David Roskies considers modern Jewish literature. Again, as with the medieval period, a heuristic distinction can be made between secular and religious writing. Here literature in the broad range of modern languages, including Hebrew, Yiddish, English, and Russian, is treated. This chapter breaks new ground in pointing to the subversive effect that literature plays within the Jewish community in particular and in the society at large. As a whole, Roskies casts a broad net in an attempt to capture modern Jewish literature. The enthusiasm of the author is a direct challenge to the reader to taste the fruits of this rich menu of works.

Indeed, our intention is to share the enthusiasm of the contributing scholars for the works and history they discuss. Jewish history and literature cover a broad swathe of time and territory. It would be impossible for one volume, even many volumes, to capture the breadth and depth of Jewish civilization throughout the ages. Since this is a volume of "introductions," there is a marked distinction among the various styles of each author presenting his or her area of interest. Although authors were requested to offer a somewhat encyclopedic overview of their area of study, individual tastes and theories do surface. The scholars represented here, each a recognized expert in his or her niche of Judaica, offer an individual overview of Jewish history and literature for each period.

This book is an introductory volume. Readers are encouraged to read further and, we hope, be infected by the enthusiasms of each author. To that end, we have included a "Suggested Readings" section at the end of each chapter. Thus, students will have the opportunity to broaden their horizons and scholars will have a clue to the sources and authorities that support the theories of each chapter. We hope this introduction will in some small way capture the vast riches of Jewish history and literature. As a famous tale in rabbinic literature tells it: "All the rest is commentary. Go now, study."

Notes

1. It is noted with pride that most of the authors in this volume have taken an active role in the rebirth of Jewish life in the former Soviet Union. All but one of the contributors to this book have taught classes in Moscow. Indeed, this work was first commissioned as a volume for Russian students and published there. The current textbook has been thoroughly revised for our American audience.

1

The Hebrew Bible

ORA HORN PROUSER

THE HEBREW BIBLE, a book valued and treasured by varied groups of people, is also referred to as the "Old Testament," or the "Tanakh." Each designation makes a specific theological statement. The Hebrew term "Tanakh" is used to refer to roughly the same books known to Christians as the "Old Testament." The term "Old Testament" implies that there is a "New Testament" that supersedes it, a theological assertion once at the core of Christianity. The ordering of the books in the "Old Testament" supports this theology. The books are arranged more or less chronologically, except for the prophetic books, which are all at the end, highlighting the Christian reading of the prophets as revelations of the coming of Jesus. The term "Hebrew Bible" refers to the same group of books as the "Tanakh," in the traditional Jewish order.

"Tanakh" is actually a Hebrew acronym composed of initials for the original tripartite division of the Hebrew Bible, which differs from the Christian ordering. The Hebrew Bible consists of three sections: Torah (Pentateuch), Nevi'im (Prophets), and Ketuvim (Writings). The three divisions differ in content and style, and each will be treated in this chapter.

There are many different methodologies used to understand and interpret the biblical text. They range from traditional religious commentaries to modern historical and literary analyses. Each methodology differs in its approach to the text, thus deriving additional meanings from the Hebrew Bible.

Torah

The Torah, also called the Pentateuch, or Five Books of Moses, begins with the creation of the world and then follows a particular genealogical line as it develops from family, to clan, to nation. It is significant that the

Torah, although it is primarily interested in the People of Israel, begins with the Creation of the world. Many issues of relevance to the study of the Torah are raised in the description of Creation. The Torah begins with two different Creation stories. The first, found in Genesis 1, portrays an orderly, perfectly planned Creation.

> When God began to create heaven and earth—the earth being unformed and void, with darkness over the surface of the deep and a wind from God sweeping over the water—God said, "Let there be light"; and there was light. God saw that the light was good, and God separated the light from the darkness. God called the light Day, and the darkness He called Night. And there was evening and there was morning, a first day.[1] (Gen. 1:1–5)

By means of artful word repetition, the most important elements of this chapter of Genesis are stressed. God created the world by word alone in an orderly, thought-out manner. Humankind was the climax of this creation. God was pleased with every step of the creation, and especially with the cumulative achievement. Like the Cosmos it describes, the first chapter of Genesis is crafted in a highly orderly manner. The first three days establish the precise pattern for what will be created on each of the remaining three days. The creation of the light on the first day parallels the fourth day's creation of the luminaries. The second day's creation, the sky, is filled with birds on the fifth day. The land, on which the Divine Creator put the finishing touches on the third day, is occupied by animals and humans on the sixth day. The creation of the Sabbath, however, is beyond this structure. It stands out on a thematic and structural level, which emphasizes its unique importance.

Genesis 1 presents the world as we would ideally like to perceive it. Genesis 2, however, conveys a very different portrayal of creation. It lacks the repetitive style and vocabulary that gave such a reliable order to Genesis 1. Chapter 2 mirrors the world more as we experience it. There the Creation was not planned out to perfection. The process reflected no specific order and contained elements of trial and error.

> The Lord God formed man from the dust of the earth. He blew into the nostrils the breath of life, and man became a living being. The Lord God placed a garden in Eden, in the east, and placed there the man whom He had formed. . . . The Lord God said, "It is not good for man to be alone; I will make a fitting helper for him." (Gen. 2:7–8, 18)

In this second chapter, God created a man, placed him in a garden, and then added other creations to satisfy the man's needs. A major need noted by God was for companionship. God created the animals to be partners with man, but they were not appropriate. Finally God created the woman out of the man's rib.

The fact that the Bible begins with a doubling of the creation story is a significant statement about the genre of the book. Although it is possible to explain the repeated creation as coming from two different sources (this will be discussed), it still behooves us to make sense of the text in its present form. The text can be understood if one keeps in mind that the Bible is not a history book, even though there is a significant amount of historical information within it. Rather, the Bible is a theological work dealing with issues such as Israelite heritage, chosenness, an understanding of God. History is a means of transmitting that information because history is God's arena for action. Thus, the doubling of the creation stories indicates that the Bible is a theological masterpiece explaining God and humankind's place in the world.

There are significant differences between the two creation stories, including the order and method of creation, especially as they relate to the humans, the place of humankind within creation, the characterization of God, and more. Genesis 1 portrays an organized world with a transcendent God, whereas Genesis 2 presents a world in progress with a more immanent God. The juxtaposition of the two chapters can be understood as an attempt to satisfy humankind's need for both sides of God; an all-powerful God, who creates a perfect world, and a more intimate God, who is concerned for a human's loneliness.

The creation of the woman differs significantly in the two narratives as well. In Genesis 1 the man and the woman are created simultaneously, whereas in Genesis 2 the woman is created second, and using a part of the man's body. Classical readings of the Bible have long inferred an inferior status for women based on the creation story in Genesis 2. More recently, as many newer methodologies, including literary and feminist criticism, have been brought to bear on the biblical text, it has become clear that more egalitarian readings are possible. For example, it has been suggested that just as humans are considered the pinnacle of creation in Genesis 1, because they are created last, when all is ready for them, so too, because of the timing of her arrival, the woman in Genesis 2 should be considered the high point of creation. Others have read creation out of the man's body as an attempt to imitate the female ability to reproduce. Although these points may be argued, it is clear that assumptions about the Bible's view of women based on the process of creation are tenuous at best.

Thus, from a brief perusal of the creation story, one may learn about the genre of the Torah, begin to understand the relationship between God and humankind, and evaluate the various characterizations of God.

The theme of creation is revisited several times in the Torah. One important element of creation is the fruitfulness of humans and animals in filling and inhabiting the world (Gen. 1:28). This motif is repeated after the flood, when Noah and the animals are similarly encouraged to be fruitful and to inhabit the earth (Gen. 8:17). The imagery of creation is also used to refer to the creation of the Israelite people. God promised Abraham several times in Genesis that he and his descendants would be fruitful and would multiply vastly. There are further allusions to the creation of the world in Exodus 1:1–10, the story of Moses' birth. Moses was described as "goodly" by his mother, using the same words with which God characterized every day of creation. In addition, to save him, Moses' mother placed him in a *teba*. Although this word is often translated as "basket," a more precise translation is "ark," as it is the same word used to describe Noah's vessel. These allusions point to parallels between the creation of the world and the birth of Moses. The creation of the Israelite people, which begins in Exodus, can be compared in importance to the creation of the world. Both are purposeful divine acts of tremendous consequence.

Another important motif is that of chosenness and election. God chooses and rejects individuals in the Torah, often for no apparent reason. Initially, God chose Abel and rejected Cain (Gen. 4). This choice had devastating consequences for both individuals. Perhaps in imitation of God, parents in the book of Genesis choose favorites from among their children. Sarah chose Isaac, Isaac favored Esau, Rebecca favored Jacob, and Jacob chose Joseph. In the majority of the patriarchal narratives, it was the matriarch who decided which son should receive the blessing to carry on the covenantal line. Although it was the father who had the power to pass on this blessing, it was often the mother who engineered the situation so that her favored one, who was also God's chosen, was the recipient. For example, Sarah arranged to have Ishmael banished from their home, and Rebecca directed Jacob to deceive his father into thinking he was Esau. In each case, the matriarchal role was essential to the appropriate carrying on of the covenantal line.

Throughout the Hebrew Bible, God continues to choose some individuals over others in the selection of Moses, Joshua, individual judges, Samuel, Saul, and David. In some cases this state of chosenness lasts for a person's lifetime, and in some situations the favoritism is transferred to the individual's descendants. For example, Samuel was chosen by God to be a prophet, and his special position lasted throughout his lifetime but was not transferred to his children. David was chosen by God to be king, and by his merit, the Davidic line retained the monarchy for almost 500 years. However, God rejected people as well. Saul was chosen by God to be king, but when he subsequently disobeyed God's orders, God rejected him.

These cases of chosenness among individuals highlight the idea of the election of the Israelite people. God chose the Israelite people from among all others to be God's "chosen people." This involves both added benefits and added responsibility. The Israelites were the recipients of God's special care, protection, and concern. At the same time, however, they were designated to be "a light unto the nations." Their status obligated them further to follow God's commandments and directions as a model to the world. God's election of the Israelite people caused them hardship and pain at times, but never completely obscured the rewards reaped through chosenness. In addition, the state of being chosen was wholly dependent upon God's will and whim. This supports the tremendous emphasis in the Bible on God's strength and the need to appreciate the extent of God's power and humankind's dependence upon its divine benefactor.

To the reader of the Bible, some of God's choices seem arbitrary and difficult to understand. Certain patterns do, however, emerge. One consistently repeated theme is the elevation of the younger son. According to ancient Near Eastern and biblical law, the eldest son inherits the major portion of his father's property, and is the true and blessed heir of the family. The narrative biblical texts, however, do not follow that pattern. For various reasons and by various means, the eldest was generally eliminated and the younger son received the blessing and became the true heir. This can be seen very clearly throughout the book of Genesis. In the first set of siblings, Abel was killed, Cain was banished, and it was the youngest son, Seth, who continued the family line traced by the Bible (Gen. 4–5). In the patriarchal narratives, Isaac inherited the patriarchal blessing from Abraham after Abraham's elder son, Ishmael, was banished (Gen. 21). Isaac's younger son, Jacob, inherited the patriarchal blessing by stealth (Gen. 27–28). Jacob's oldest son, Reuben, was passed over for the patriarchal blessing perhaps because he engaged in illicit relations with his father's concubines (Gen. 35:22; 49:4). It was one of the younger sons, Judah, who became the ancestor of King David and of the southern tribe that maintained its identity even after the destruction of the Temple and the Babylonian Exile. This pattern continues throughout the Bible. Moses was younger than his brother, Aaron, who served as his aide. King David was the youngest in his family. Solomon was among the younger sons of David.

The consistency of this pattern leads the reader to question the whole institution of inheritance through the older son. One way of interpreting this persistent theme is as a pointed presentation of Israel's place in the ancient Near East. Israel was a very small country compared to the major powers of the day. Except for the brief period of united monarchy in the time of David and Solomon, Israel and later the divided kingdoms of Israel and Judah were minor players in the international arena. Eventually they lost their land altogether and their populations were exiled to Babylonia. Throughout these periods, however, Israel considered itself to be God's chosen people. The dissonance caused by this contradiction led to the idea of the ascendancy of the younger son. Although logic and societal norms dictated that the older son would inherit, appearances can be deceiving. Just as it was the younger, weaker son who inherited his father's blessing (or became prophet, priest, or king), the smaller, weaker people would remain heir to God's covenant and blessing. Things are not as they appear to be. This was a message of great hope to the Israelites at every stage in their history.

This theme goes hand in hand with the theme of deception in biblical narrative. Throughout the Bible we see individuals achieve their goals by means of deception. In most of these cases, not only are the biblical heroes not condemned, but they are lauded and rewarded for their cleverness. A clear case is that of Jacob's deceiving his father into blessing him instead of his brother Esau (Gen. 27). Rebecca was both the mastermind and the behind-the-scenes actor in this scheme. The narrative is fraught with questions about Esau's worthiness and character, as well as Isaac's level of awareness of what was being done. Some read Esau as an unworthy son, and others understand Esau as a loving, obedient son who became a tragic victim. Isaac, too, can be read as innocently blessing Jacob, since he was unaware of the scheme, or as a conscious or unconscious coconspirator who wanted to bless Jacob without openly rejecting his beloved Esau. Rebecca can be understood as a conniving wife with her own agenda or as a loving wife who helped her husband to accomplish what seemed too difficult for him to do alone. Regardless of the accepted reading, Jacob received the blessing and was not punished for his actions. Rebecca too suffered no consequences for her part in the scheme. Jacob did need to leave home, but that was not banishment in any way.

Jacob, probably the strongest of the patriarchs as the father of the twelve sons who would become the twelve tribes, received the covenantal blessing through stealth. The lack of recrimination can be understood as a further statement of the understanding of Israel in the ancient world. In biblical narrative, deception seems to be a legitimate tool for the weak to use against stronger powers. The ancient Israelite audience probably was amused and encouraged by the thought that there are many ways to achieve one's goals. Israel, as a weaker country, could not accomplish much through outright means against the stronger powers. However, the message inherent in biblical narrative is that there are alternative means to be used in order to succeed. Israel could find its way in the ancient world with the dual hope that the smaller can be the chosen one and that there are many routes to strength and success.

Although today we may be able to look at this narrative and analyze the predominant literary motifs and themes, historically, Jacob's deception has been a difficult one for Jewish commentators. The characterization of Jacob as lying and deceptive was used in anti-Semitic circles to reinforce the caricature of the sneaky, lying Jew. In order to deal with this situation, some medieval Jewish commentators went to great lengths to interpret the text in such a way as to make Jacob an honest man.

In modern times there is no need, we hope, to save Jacob from anti-Semitic readers. We still have the problem of reading biblical ethics. How does one learn ethics from the Bible, and what should be done with portions of the Bible that encourage behavior that can be morally wrong? These questions go beyond issues of deception, to larger matters such as violence and the treatment of women. At times, these difficult passages, through deeper analysis or deconstruction, can be found to have alternative readings that argue against the violence or the immoral behavior depicted. There are actions in the Bible, however, that might cause the reader to want to state publicly that this behavior can no longer be considered acceptable. The issue of the ethics of reading is coming into the fore in biblical studies, and as it is pursued further, there is a chance that new answers and directions will be found. Deception in biblical narrative, however, does not need to be a major theological problem. These narratives should be read as providing a mixture of hope and humor to a people, small in number, yet covenantally promised a special portion.

Israelite hope in response to national adversity was extended through other biblical themes as well. The divine deliverance of the people from Egypt in the book of Exodus is probably the climactic moment of the Torah. Throughout the book of Exodus the Israelites are, for the first time, presented as a people, not simply a single family line. That is the fulfillment of God's blessing to Abraham: that his "descendants would be as great as the stars in the sky." This newfound national standing, however, raised new issues of relationships with outside cultures. It was the first time the Israelites could be considered a major threat, which led to their enslavement and poor situation in Egypt. At this point, God forged a new relationship with the Israelites as well. In order for God to free them from oppression and return them to their land, God needed to be reestablished as the omnipotent deity (Exod. 6:6–8).

Neither the Israelites nor the Egyptians believed, at first, in God's power over the Pharaoh. God's divine power was proven to them in a steady stream of miraculous events. Magical acts were followed by ten major disasters, which affected only the Egyptians, not the Israelites. Through these disasters, God's supremacy over the Pharaoh and the Egyptian deities, along with God's intense faithfulness to the Israelites, was displayed. All areas considered under the aegis of the Egyptian deities, such as fertility, nature, water, life, and death, were claimed by God. In Israel's escape from Egypt, God's parting of the sea added additional miraculous elements. The combined effect of all these miracles illustrated God's supremacy over the natural world and over all earthly powers, as well as over all human pretenders to divinity. In the process, God also became known as the redeemer from slavery and injustice, the God of the oppressed. The relationship between God and Israel became one of protection and guidance on God's part, with grateful indebtedness expected from the Israelites.

This powerful view of God and of the relationship between God and Israel is a major theological focus of the Torah, and of the Bible as a whole. Many narrative texts refer back to the Exodus. Legal texts often give the Exodus as the explanation of specific laws or as the motivation to obey the law. This idea of precedence begins in the Ten Commandments and continues through laws pertaining to slaves, foreigners, festivals, and more.

> Bear in mind that you were slaves in the land of Egypt and the Lord your God redeemed you; therefore I enjoin this commandment upon you today. (Deut. 15:15)

The Exodus from Egypt also serves as the model for all future redemptions. The prophets of the Babylonian Exile often allude to the Exodus in describing God's future redemption of the Israelites from exile. For example, the sixth-century prophet known as Deutero-Isaiah described Israel's future return from Babylonia, using images from the Exodus story:

> Go forth from Babylon, flee from Chaldea! Declare this with loud shouting, announce this, bring out the word to the ends of the earth! Say: "The Lord has redeemed His servant Jacob!" They have known no thirst, though he led them through parched places; He made water flow for them from the rock; He cleaved the rock and water gushed forth. (Isa. 48:20–21)

The Exodus symbolizes God's protective care over Israel as well as the indebtedness of the Israelites toward God.

This persistent relationship of chosenness and obligation is a major portion of two other foci of the Torah: covenant and law. God made several covenants with human beings, covenants that cover different groups and different situations. God's first covenant was with Noah, his family, and all living things present on the ark (Gen. 9:8–17).

> And God said to Noah and to his sons with him, "I now establish My covenant with you and your offspring to come, and with every living thing that is with you—birds, cattle, and every wild beast as well—all that have come out of the ark, every living thing on earth. I will maintain My covenant with you; never again shall all flesh be cut off by the waters of a flood, and never again shall there be a flood to destroy the earth." (Gen. 9:8–11)

After the flood, in an unconditional covenant, God promised that the world and its inhabitants would never again be destroyed by a flood. God's all-inclusive covenant with life on earth is followed soon afterward by another unconditional covenant with one group of humans, Abraham and his descendants (Gen. 15:7–21).

> On that day the Lord made a covenant with Abraham saying, "To your offspring I assign this land, from the river of Egypt to the great river, the river Euphrates." (Gen. 15:18)

The most important covenant God made with the Israelites was the Sinai covenant. This covenant differed in that it was conditional, placing obligations on the Israelites. God's continued election and protection of the Israelites were directly tied to the Israelites' moral, cultic, and civil behavior. A unique aspect to this covenant is that it was between God and all the Israelites. Although God's earlier covenant with Abraham referred to his descendants, the covenant itself was between God and Abraham. At Sinai, however, Moses was the facilitator and intermediary, but the covenantal parties were God and the Israelites en masse.

> Moses went and repeated to the people all the commands of the Lord and all the rules; and all the people answered with one voice, saying, "All the things that the Lord has commanded we will do!" (Exod. 24:3)

Further on in the Bible, God made an unconditional covenant with David (2 Sam. 7:12–16). After God promised David to be with him throughout his reign, God added that David's son and his descendants would rule forever under God's protection as well.

> Your house and your kingship shall ever be secure before you; your throne shall be established forever. (2 Sam. 7:16)

This promise was not dependent upon the descendants' proper behavior, but was simply a grant to David. After Solomon's death, the Israelite empire was split into two separate kingdoms, Israel in the north, and Judah in the south. According to the Bible, the small state of Judah was preserved as a separate entity only because of God's promise to David. Even if individual kings did not seem to be deserving of the privilege, the Davidic line continued for almost five hundred years, until the fall of Judah in 587/586 B.C.E.

Just as the Bible is clear regarding what God promised the Israelite people, the responsibilities of the Israelites are delineated as well. Major portions of the Torah consist of the legal, cultic, and ethical obligations of the

Israelites. The laws in the Torah are portrayed as coming directly from God, and failure to obey the law was a direct rebellion against God. The middle of the five books in the Torah is Leviticus, which contains a large portion of the legal texts, both civil and cultic. The very placement of the book highlights the central role of law in the Torah. The laws are not simply an accompaniment to the narrative text but are, rather, at its very core.

It is significant that biblical law rested on God's authority. Although there are cases in the Bible in which individual laws were enacted by kings, the overwhelming sense is that God was the source of the law, adding weight to the Israelites' sense of obligation to observe the laws. It was an essential part of their covenantal obligation, and their observance or nonobservance of the law had direct consequences for their daily lives. Observance of the law ensured the fulfillment of God's covenantal obligations, including enough rainfall, peace, and the presence of God in their community. The continued survival of the Israelite people rested on their covenantal relationship with God and the fulfillment of the responsibilities that this covenant placed on its respective parties.

After the Israelites had left Egypt and established their covenantal relationship with God at Mount Sinai, they experienced an extremely formative period. The Israelites developed from a group of runaway slaves to a community in covenant with God ready to conquer the Land of Israel. This time period was characterized on one level by a close relationship between the Israelites and God. As they traveled, God continuously led them with a pillar of fire or a pillar of smoke (Exod. 13:21–22). They could always sense God's presence in their community. However, as this transitional time was difficult, the people were querulous and rebellious. The difficulties of desert wandering led the Israelites to complain about scant water, food, and loss of a settled life (Num. 11, 16). Their lack of faith in God's ability to successfully lead them in conquering the Land of Israel ultimately caused God to punish those who had left Egypt by condemning them to live out their lives wandering in the desert without entering the Promised Land (Num. 13–14).

At times both God and Moses despaired of being able to transform the Israelites into a unified, God-fearing community. On several occasions God threatened to wipe out the whole nation and save only Moses, from whom would come a new "chosen people." Moses repeatedly interceded on the people's behalf by reminding God of the covenants made with the patriarchs. Perhaps more important, Moses asked God what the other nations would think of God if the Israelites all died in the desert. Time and again God relented and saved the Israelites, though punishing them for their acts of rebellion. Moses also lost faith in the people at several points, claiming that the burden of "carrying" the Israelites through the desert was just too great. In response to Moses' despair, God showed a protective nature to the Israelites and offered Moses additional help and support structures to enable him to lead the people.

By the end of the book of Deuteronomy, the Israelites were poised to enter the Promised Land. Moses gave a lengthy farewell speech in the book of Deuteronomy, reminding the people of their obligations to God and to each other. He recounted their wilderness experience, warning them to follow God's laws in order to be able to retain the land that God was giving them (Deut. 5–8). He transferred his leadership to Joshua, his successor who had been chosen by God, before all of the Israelites (Num. 27:18–23; Deut. 34:9). There was no doubt that Joshua was continuing Moses' work and that he had been invested with Moses' authority. This sense of continuity was an essential element of the people's ability to develop and to conquer the Land of Israel.

The Former Prophets

The Torah ends with the death of Moses and the Israelites poised on the border of Canaan, ready to enter the land. The section of the Bible called the Prophets continues where the Torah left off. It begins with the book of Joshua, which describes the conquest of the land of Canaan (which then becomes Israel) by the Israelites, ably led by Joshua. God continued to be actively involved with the Israelites, helping them to win their battles against the settled Canaanite peoples.

The book of Joshua describes the Israelites' conquest of the Land of Israel as a series of successful military battles against major cities. The Israelites were ordered by God to annihilate the Canaanite people totally. This entailed killing every human being and animal and burning the land. All booty was forbidden to the people and left "for God." God ordered a "Holy War" against the Canaanites. It is reported that the Canaanites had sinned to the point where the land was "vomiting them up," and now it was time for the Israelites to dispossess them of the land. These battles were not decided by numbers of soldiers or sophistication of weaponry. God determined who the winners were to be. Only when the Israelites sinned did God cause them to lose in battle.

It seems unlikely that the Israelites coming out of the desert would be able to conquer the Canaanite cities, which were so much more technologically advanced. The Bible, however, compensates for this situation by depicting each battle fought using quite unconventional tactics. In the most famous such battle, the conquest of the city of Jericho, the Israelites marched around the city once a day for six days. On the seventh day, they marched around the city six times, and on the seventh time, blew their horns and created a very loud ruckus, causing the walls of the city to fall down. In fighting other cities, the Israelites used military strategies such as attacking at night or splitting the camp into two and trapping the enemy between them. According to the book of Joshua, the Israelites conquered all of Canaan and divided the land among themselves as directed by God.

The next book of the Bible, the book of Judges, paints a different picture. In this book, the Israelites were living in Canaan/Israel but were constantly having difficulty with their non-Israelite neighbors. This is a direct contradiction of Joshua, in that it is clear in Judges that the peoples of the land were not all conquered and destroyed. This contradiction has been studied by many scholars who have tried to understand the settlement of the Israelites in Canaan from a historical perspective. Some scholars support the picture of the Israelites conquering the land in a series of lightning attacks, as portrayed in the book of Joshua. Others favor a more moderate approach, closer to the book of Judges. Rather than seeing a desert people easily conquering a strong, settled city-state, some scholars favor an immigration model of conquest. Perhaps the Israelites moved into the unoccupied hill country of Canaan and settled there while growing and becoming stronger. As they grew, they needed more room, and over a long period of time, they began to fight with their Canaanite neighbors until they ultimately conquered the whole land. Unfortunately, there is no unequivocal archaeological or extrabiblical evidence to validate one theory or the other. Until such evidence is found, we will not be able to integrate fully the books of Joshua and Judges from a historical standpoint.

There is much to be learned, however, from the theological message of the book of Judges. A cyclical pattern exists in the book: The people would sin, causing God to place them under the oppression of a neighboring people. After some time, the people would repent, crying out to God to help them. God would send a savior, who would lead the people in battle and overthrow the oppressor. After a period of peace, the cycle would begin anew. Each of these leaders was unlikely in some regard, fighting with smaller numbers against greater tribes. This inequality helps to reinforce the role of God in human affairs. The message that is repeated many times is that if the Israelites obeyed God's law, they would live in peace and prosperity; if they displeased God, they would fall under the oppression of foreign peoples.

Another repeated theme, related to the previous one, in the book of Judges is that many of these difficulties occurred because there was no king in the land and every person anarchically did what was right in his or her own eyes (e.g., Judg. 17:6; 18:1; 19:1; 21:25). The reader of the book of Judges begins to sense that if only there were a king, none of these problems would exist. As one continues into the books of Samuel, the situation becomes more ambiguous. The text vacillates between promonarchic and antimonarchic agenda. When the people requested a king, Samuel responded with a long diatribe about the evils of kingship. Immediately thereafter, God ordered Samuel to heed the people's request and anoint a king, chosen by God. Saul was chosen and proceeded to act as both a successful king, saving Israel from warring enemies, and as a negative character, issuing foolish orders and disobeying God's and Samuel's instructions. This tension continues throughout biblical literature. At times, the monarchy is portrayed as appropriate and the king as God's chosen one. God's special relationship with David is a clear example of that pattern. Elsewhere, however, the idea of a monarchy is abhorrent, since God is the Israelites' "king," and thus an earthly king is unnecessary.

The stories of Saul and David are cases for understanding the theme of chosenness in the Bible. Saul was originally chosen by God and described in very complimentary terms. He had tremendous physical stature, was a good, brave man, cared for his family, and valued God's word as expressed through a prophet. Not long after he was anointed king, however, he was rejected by God. The reason given for this rejection was a lack of obedience to God's directions as expressed through the prophet Samuel (1 Sam. 15). Saul was ordered to destroy the Amalekites, killing all living things according to the rules of holy war. Instead, he spared the king and the choice animals. Although those actions were clearly in violation of the ban, he was not the first to make accommodations to his situation. In the book of Joshua, when the Israelites destroyed Jericho, they saved the family of Rahab, who had protected their spies. That too was theoretically in violation of the ban but was not considered a punishable act by God. In addition, David, God's chosen, committed such serious sins as adultery and murder but was not removed from kingship. Thus, unanswered questions throughout Samuel are why Saul was chosen and then rejected and why David was chosen but never rejected. As was seen earlier, God's reasons for choosing and rejecting are not necessarily made clear. Perhaps, just as all the older sons were eliminated in the book of Genesis, so too Saul, of such great stature, was like an older son who must be considered and eliminated before choosing the shorter, younger, David.

David was a successful ruler who transformed Israel into one of the stronger empires of his time. He also was faithful to God and God's laws, as communicated to him through the prophets. At times, it is difficult to get a clear picture of David's character. He was a very politically savvy individual who seemed to know intuitively the route to kingship. He ingratiated himself to many, alienated those whom he had to, and managed to distance himself from much of the violence and killing that helped to solidify his monarchy. At the same time, he is portrayed as righteous and God-fearing. When David did commit sins, he accepted God's judgments and punishments. However, many of David's actions become very hard to evaluate. Was he mourning for Saul and Jonathan because he was truly sad, or was it a political act? Did he really love Jonathan or did he recognize that the route to kingship must necessarily involve the king's son? Questions like those abound in David's life, and the text supports conflicting readings of David's character.

David's son Solomon also had a lengthy reign and managed to keep the empire strong. He expanded international relations, which were beneficial for cultural and literary development within ancient Israel. Solomon also engaged in grandiose building projects, the most important of which was the building of the Temple in Jerusalem. The Temple became Israel's most holy place of worship and sacrifice. All of this building, however, placed a tremendous financial strain on the people of the kingdom. They were taxed to pay for the projects, and they needed to contribute labor as well. This led to a significant amount of discontent among the populace.

Upon the death of Solomon, his son informed the people that he would continue and intensify the demands that his father had put upon the Israelites. This caused a large part of the country to secede, establishing a separate state. The majority of the land, ten of the twelve tribes, broke off to form the northern Kingdom of Israel. The tribes of Judah, David's home tribe, and of Benjamin, which was only a tiny remainder of a tribe at this point, became the southern Kingdom of Judah. The tribes never again were a united monarchy, existing instead as two separate entities, at times allies, but occasionally warring with each other.

The Kingdom of Israel was the larger of the two lands. This proved both an asset and a liability. It was a stronger kingdom in possession of more territory than its neighbor Judah. However, the size of its territory and population led to a much more heterogeneous population, and thus more internal strife. No one dynasty ruled Israel for any significant period of time. Rather, there were recurrent eras of usurpation, revolt, and civil war. Israel's territory included part of the main trade routes between Egypt and Mesopotamia. This location led to external difficulties and struggles with greater foreign powers. In addition, the Temple, the center of Israel's religious life, was in the south, in the Kingdom of Judah. The first king of Israel attempted to rectify the situation by creating two alternative centers of worship in the north. Those sites were denounced by the south as idolatrous and were evidently never accepted by the Israelite people on a par with the Temple in Jerusalem.

Judah was much smaller than Israel both in territory and in population. This relative size was beneficial because it meant that Judah had a much more homogeneous population. The Davidic dynasty was able to reign for hundreds of years until the fall of the kingdom. Geographically, Judah was out of the way of the main trade routes, which made it a less likely target of expansionist kingdoms.

These differences between the lands led to different developments, successes, and failures. In the international world, Israel was far stronger and more important than the small Kingdom of Judah. However, Judah's inner strength enabled it to exist 134 years longer than Israel. The Kingdom of Israel fell to the Assyrians in 721 B.C.E., and Judah was conquered by the Babylonians in 586 B.C.E. The people of Israel were exiled by the Assyrians; they assimilated into the Assyrian culture and were not heard from again. The Judaeans, however, retained their identity throughout their exile in Babylonia until they were able to return to their land, around 70 years later. Several factors contributed to this situation, the most important of which was the role of the prophets.

Latter Prophets

Although various forms of prophecy existed in Israel from early times, prophecy reached its height from the eighth century through the sixth century B.C.E. In this period, we see what is known as "classical prophecy," and the prophets are called "latter prophets." This terminology is to distinguish them from the "former prophets," also known as "preclassical prophets." The former prophets were those who appear in the books of Judges, Samuel, and Kings, proclaiming God's word, performing miraculous, seemingly magical acts. They interacted primarily with the government, informing the kings of God's desires and warnings.

The latter prophets, in contrast, were called by God to deliver one or more messages to the Israelites. This could be a temporary calling or a lifetime vocation. Prophets were not paid by those to whom they prophesied. They were not available to the people at all times to answer specific questions. Rather, these prophets were at God's beck and call, performing God's work, and bringing God's message to the Israelite people. For example, in the eighth century, Amos, chronologically the first of the classical prophets, described his mission to Amaziah the priest:

> I am not a prophet and I am not a prophet's disciple. I am a cattle breeder and a tender of sycamore figs. But the Lord took me away from following the flock, and the Lord said to me, "Go prophesy to my people Israel." (Amos 7:14–15)

The prophets worked alone, and in general had very lonely lives. They delivered unfavorable messages to the Israelites and thus were often the objects of physical and emotional abuse. Nevertheless, the prophets carried on their work, conveying God's message to the Israelite people.

These prophets spoke in universal tones. They understood the Israelite God to be the sole God of the world, controlling all peoples. They also presented a new understanding of what God desired from people. They explained that God did not want the people merely to obey the ritual laws, worshipping exclusively through proper sacrifices and Temple service. Although that was important to God, it was more important that the people lead moral and ethical lives. The prophets declared that ritual acts were essentially meaningless if performed by those leading unethical lives. They even raised the importance of moral laws to the point of saying that the people would be punished with the destruction of the state for the omission of ethical acts. The eighth-century prophet Micah made this clear when he stated:

> He has told you, O man, what is good,
> And what the Lord requires of you;
> Only to do justice
> And to love goodness
> And to walk modestly with your God.
> (Mic. 6:8)

The prophets preached against idolatry and sin, but always included morals and ethics on a par with rituals. Although later Christian interpretation embraced the prophetic books as reflecting a rejection of ritual law, it is important to understand that the prophetic works were not abandoning ritual and cultic worship of God. Rather, they were claiming that those modes of worship are essential, but cannot survive in a vacuum. They must be accompanied by appropriate moral and ethical behavior.

The prophets acted as social critics, accusing the Israelites of abandoning the poor and the needy. They emphasized the need to support and provide for those in society who were without protection, such as widows and orphans. Individual prophets lashed out at the Israelites for the large gap that they saw between the rich and the poor. The Israelites should have considered the situation untenable and acted to realign the balance of wealth. Although these prophetic messages are standard ethical messages, it is very significant that the prophets included this type of condemnation in their words to the Israelites. The inclusion of social criticism makes clear that God's demands on humankind include not only cultic and sacrificial responsibilities but also both personal and communal ethical behavior.

The latter prophets were continuously warning the Israelites that if they did not change their ways, God would destroy their land. They preached this to the people of Israel, whose kingdom was ultimately destroyed in 721 B.C.E. They then preached to the citizens of Judah, pointedly adding that they should learn from Israel's mistakes and fate. The people in general, though, did not heed the prophets' words. This sounds difficult for the modern reader to understand, since the Judaeans had already seen that the fall of the north had been prophesied, and that it came about. However, it must be borne in mind that even though the words of these prophets were immortalized by the Bible, there were other prophets circulating at the time, many of whom were equally convincing, but misguided "false prophets." From the people's point of view, though, it was not clear which prophets were true and which were false. Opposing prophecies sounded similar in style, and prophetic competitors accused one another of fraud. It is only human to want to believe good news. Therefore, the job of the biblical prophets was difficult at best.

When the Babylonians conquered Judah and destroyed Jerusalem in 587–586 B.C.E., they destroyed the Temple that had been built by King Solomon. By this point, the Temple was considered the only legitimate place to sacrifice to God. An intricate set of laws involving ritual purity was legislated about the Temple and the Israelites' relationship with God. Thus, the fall of the Temple was not simply the razing of a holy site, but the destruction of a way of life. It would seem natural for the Israelites to respond like others in the ancient world, understanding the destruction as the fall of their God to the Babylonian god, and therefore assimilating into Babylonian religion. That did not happen, because of the efforts of the prophets. They taught the Israelites to understand the fall of Jerusalem as a punishment for their sins.

Instead of viewing the Israelite God as powerless against the Babylonian god, the prophets claimed that God had controlled the Babylonians and used them to punish the Israelites. The prophets also advised the Israelites to continue to worship their God in Babylonia and repent over their past sins in order to be returned to Israel. The Israelite God was the God of the world and could be worshiped on foreign soil. This new theological approach allowed the Israelites to remain loyal to God while in exile and to retain their identity as a people and as a religion. The prophets saved the Israelites from being absorbed and helped them to retain a unique identity. While the exiles were in Babylonia the prophets also prepared them to return to Judah and to rebuild their Temple and their land. The sixth-century prophet Ezekiel, who lived in exile in Babylonia, instructed the exiles not to believe those who told them that they no longer had a land or a God.

Thus said the Lord God: "I have indeed removed them [the Judaeans] far among the nations and have scattered them among the countries, and I have become to them a diminished sanctity in the countries whither they have gone. . . . I will gather you [the exiles] from the peoples, and assemble you

out of the countries where you have been scattered, and I will give you the
Land of Israel." (Ezek. 11:16–17)

God promised that although the exiles had no Temple in which to worship, and although they were not in the Land of Israel, the God of Israel was with them in Babylonia. In Babylonia they could not achieve the holiness they experienced in Jerusalem, but God was still with them.

A closer look at the life of one prophet, Jeremiah, sheds light on the difficult issues of biblical prophecy. Jeremiah's prophetic career unfolds in Judah in the late seventh and early sixth centuries, immediately before and during the destruction of Jerusalem by Babylonia in 587 B.C.E. Jeremiah was called by God to be a prophet as a young man. God informed him that he had been chosen even before birth to be a prophet. Although Jeremiah complained to God of his inadequacies, it was clear that he had no choice but to obey God's orders. God warned him from the beginning that his task would be difficult, but that God would be there to save him throughout.

> *So you, gird up your loins,*
> *Arise and speak to them*
> *All that I command you.*
> *Do not break down before them,*
> *Lest I break you before them.*
> *I make you this day*
> *A fortified city,*
> *And an iron pillar,*
> *And bronze walls*
> *Against the whole land—*
> *Against Judah's kings and officers,*
> *And against its priests and citizens.*
> *They will attack you,*
> *But they shall not overcome you;*
> *For I am with you—declares the Lord—to save you.*
> *(Jer. 1:17–19)*

Jeremiah faithfully preached the divine message to the people, accusing them of ignoring God and warning them of the coming destruction. At the same time, he performed another essential duty of a prophet: intercession on behalf of the people before God. He continuously prayed to God to forgive the Israelites and not to punish them so severely. This form of arguing with God should not be considered a rebellion against God, but rather a fulfillment of God's wishes. God's love and mercy were weighed against a contrasting capacity for anger and a sense of justice. God knew that the Israelites should be punished for their sins but called upon the prophets to pray for the people and to forestall the divine punishments. In fact, Jeremiah interceded for the people so often that at times God was compelled specifically to direct him not to do so.

> As for you, do not pray for this people, do not raise a cry of prayer on their behalf, do not plead with Me; for I will not listen to you. Don't you see what they are doing in the towns of Judah and in the streets of Jerusalem? . . . Assuredly, thus said the Lord God: My wrath and My fury will be poured out upon this place, on man and on beast, on the trees of the field and the fruit of the soil. It shall burn, with none to quench it. (Jer. 7:16–17, 20)

Jeremiah is a particularly interesting prophet because of his strong emotional nature. His prophetic career and its requirement that he constantly rebuke the people made him feel isolated from the Israelite community. They, in turn, often treated him very poorly, to the point that he needed to go into hiding to save his life. Similarly, despite his closeness with God, he sensed a distinct separation between himself and the Divine due to his constant intercession on behalf of the people, and his belief that God did not protect him sufficiently or as promised. This led to intense isolation and sorrow; on several occasions Jeremiah broke down and attempted to reject his prophetic calling. Each time, though, Jeremiah recovered, and God took him back. Human pain and anguish, however, were very real in the life of a prophet.

> *O Lord, you know—*
> *Remember me and take thought of me,*
> *Avenge me on those who persecute me,*
> *Do not yield to your patience,*
> *Do not let me perish!*
> *Consider how I have borne insult*
> *On your account.*
> *When Your words were offered, I devoured them;*
> *Your word brought me the delight and joy*
> *Of knowing that Your name is attached to me,*
> *O Lord, God of Hosts.*
> *I have not sat in the company of revelers*
> *And made merry!*
> *I have sat lonely because of Your hand upon me,*
> *For You have filled me with gloom.*
> *Why must my pain be endless,*
> *My wound incurable,*
> *Resistant to healing?*

You have been to me like a spring that fails,
Like waters that cannot be relied on.
(Jer. 15:15–18)

Although Jeremiah gave voice to his sorrow more than other prophets, it should be assumed that his was not a unique situation. Prophetic activity had repercussions on very personal areas of the prophets' lives, keeping them from living the "normal" lives they might otherwise have pursued.

Although much of what is read in the prophetic books consists of condemnation, calls to change and repent, and threats, there is also prophetic consolation and comfort. This is seen very clearly in the second half of Isaiah.

The book of Isaiah is generally understood as being the work of either two or three different prophets. First Isaiah is composed of chapters 1–39. The prophet Isaiah lived during the second half of the eighth century, a dating based on his interactions with eighth-century kings, such as Ahaz and Hezekiah. He counseled them during some very difficult times in Judaean history. During Isaiah's years as prophet, Israel attacked Judah in an attempt to overthrow Assyrian domination, in what is known as the Syro-Ephraimite War; Assyria conquered Israel; and Judah became a vassal state. In the midst of these events, Isaiah dealt directly with the Judaean king, expressing God's word, encouraging appropriate responses, and trying to keep Judah from suffering a fate similar to that of Israel. Isaiah encouraged neutrality vis-à-vis other nations, with an emphasis on correcting Judah's internal failings. For a time, the kings did not heed his directions and Judah became a smaller, weaker, vassal state under Assyrian domination.

The second half of the book of Isaiah reflects a much later time period. Chapters 40–55, known as Deutero-Isaiah, are words of comfort and consolation addressed to an exiled Judaean people. In these chapters, the prophet addresses the exiles, explaining to them the reasons for the destruction, reminding them of God's love and of their chosen status, and encouraging them with thoughts of their future return to Judah. Finally, chapters 55–66 are known as Trito-Isaiah, reflecting the postexilic life of the Jews after they returned to Judah. The division between Deutero-Isaiah and Trito-Isaiah is not too clearly defined, and some scholars view the two sections as the work of the same prophet, beginning his work in Babylonia and finishing it after returning with the exiles to Judah. Others consider Trito-Isaiah a disciple of Deutero-Isaiah. Although there is some continuation of theme and imagery from one section to the next, the prophets are separated from each other in both time and space. The cumulative work of the various prophets in Isaiah expresses in microcosm the Judaean experience in both internal and external struggle, through destruction and exile, and, finally, rebuilding.

Ketuvim

The third division of the Hebrew Bible is known as the "Ketuvim," the "Hagiographa," or the "Writings." As may be inferred from these terms, this diverse section of the Hebrew Bible is significantly more difficult to characterize. Several different genres of literature are contained in the Ketuvim, including poetry, wisdom literature, narrative, and history.

The largest corpus of biblical poetry exists in the Ketuvim, specifically in the book of Psalms. This book involves psalms written and used for many different occasions. There are psalms of petition, asking something of God, such as direct help and salvation from enemies (e.g., Pss. 3, 5, 42). Psalms of thanksgiving (e.g., 30, 32, 41, 92) acknowledge God for blessings in general or for specific acts of kindness. Psalms of lament (e.g., 44, 60, 90) and psalms of praise (e.g., 8, 100, 146) also respond to specific occasions, as well as to more general situations. Whatever the original setting of the psalms, most are written in such a way that they can be used for varied occasions by different groups of people. Many of these were probably used in liturgical settings in the ancient world, and some are still repeated in worship today.

Biblical poetry has a variety of characteristic features. The most distinguishable trait is that of parallelism. In general, poetic lines contain two phrases that repeat, state opposites, or most commonly, reiterate with small changes of nuance. For example, in Psalm 51:3 the author first asks God for mercy, appealing to God's faithfulness, and then appeals to God's compassion.

> *Have mercy upon me, O God, as befits your faithfulness;*
> *In keeping with your abundant compassion, blot out my*
>   *transgressions.*

When appealing to God's faithfulness, or devotion, the author hints at God's past dealings with the Israelite people and their covenantal relationships. Perhaps the author could receive mercy for the sake of his ancestors. God's compassion, however, is a trait totally within the divine character. The author adds that if he does not deserve mercy because of past transgressions, he is still appealing to God's inherent sense of compassion. Thus, although these two lines appear to make the same point twice, the differing nuances present in the wording make this far from a simple repetition.

This small section of the psalm exhibits another important literary device. The lines are chiastic in structure, which means that the second part of the verse uses the reverse order in its parallel statement. Thus, both the first clause of the first line and its parallel, the second clause of the second line, ask God to act in a certain way. Similarly, the second clause of the first line and the first clause of the second line both give the reasons why God should respond to the psalmist. Chiastic structure abounds in biblical literature, adding literary artistry and poetic strength to the verses.

Whereas Psalms is a book usable for many different occasions, two other examples of biblical poetry in the Ketuvim each focus on one situation. One of these, the Song of Songs, is a collection of love poetry between a man and a woman. The man and woman describe each other's beauty, delight in their love, and long for each other when they are apart. The book teems with imagery of the natural world, including both flora and fauna, which leads the reader to see the love portrayed as an inherent part of the natural world. It is striking to have a book celebrating physical love so explicitly as part of the biblical canon. The traditional Jewish interpretation of the book is allegorical, referring to the love between God and the Israelite people. This interpretation has enabled the book to be accepted by those who might otherwise be scandalized by descriptions of the beauty of physical love. However, others interpret the book as beautiful love poetry, either a collection of unrelated poems or almost a drama played out in poetry.

One very beautiful analysis of the book involves an intertextual reading of the Song of Songs and the Garden of Eden narrative in Genesis 3. According to this interpretation, everything that went wrong between man and woman in the Garden is righted in the Song of Songs. Both stories focus on a garden and life among much flora and fauna. In both stories the focus is on love and not marriage and procreation. Most significantly, the rare word for "desire" or "lust" is repeated in both stories in opposite contexts. In Genesis 3:16 the woman is told that her lust will be for her husband, but he will rule over her. In Song of Songs 7:11, however, the woman proclaims that she is her beloved's and his lust is for her. Thus we have come full circle, and relationships have been repaired. Desire and lust can be reciprocal, without one partner needing to rule over the other.

Several books in Ketuvim are poetic in style but should be considered wisdom literature. Classical wisdom literature teaches that by leading a righteous, faithful, disciplined, and prudent life, one may achieve success. However, sin will always lead to punishment and failure. The book of Proverbs makes this abundantly clear.

> *He who lives blamelessly will be delivered,*
> *But he who is crooked in his ways will fall at once.*
> *He who tills his land will have food in plenty,*
> *But he who pursues vanities will have poverty in plenty.*
> *A dependable man will receive many blessings,*
> *But one in a hurry to get rich will not go unpunished.*
> . . . .

He who trusts his own instinct is a dullard,
But he who lives by wisdom shall escape.
He who gives to the poor will not be in want,
But he who shuts his eyes will be roundly cursed.
(Prov. 28:18–20, 26–27)

Wisdom literature is instructional in tenor, teaching people the proper way to lead a successful life. Parts of the book of Proverbs are written in a didactic style, words of advice given from a father to a son. In this context, the author is trying to teach younger people what he has learned from his life. The information given is not book learning, but rather life experience.

As can be expected, the approach to life taught by wisdom literature is not always affirmed by daily experience. In theory, people find comfort in stating that righteous people are rewarded and sinners are punished. However, in reality, life does not consistently work that way. Righteous people suffer along with the unrighteous. Two expressions of this reality exist in the Bible. The books of Ecclesiastes and Job both contradict the conclusions of classical wisdom literature as expressed in the book of Proverbs. In Ecclesiastes and Job, the authors attempt to understand how God can allow evil to befall those who are in no way deserving of punishment. They come to the conclusion that there are many elements of the world that are incomprehensible to human beings.

In the book of Job, God responded to Job's complaints that he was being punished when he never sinned, and that he was suffering undeservedly. God claimed that Job was speaking from a human perspective, which was, by nature, limited in scope. The divine view is inscrutable.

Where were you when I laid the earth's foundations?
Speak if you have understanding.
Do you know who fixed its dimensions
Or who measured it with a line?
Onto what were its bases sunk?
Who set its cornerstone?
(Job 38:4–6)

Only a divine being could comprehend God's plans for the world, and it was presumptuous of Job to think he had the right or the ability to understand God's actions. While God's speeches are very enigmatic, it seems that God is affirming that there is a plan for the world, but that it is not necessarily human centered. The world is full of many species of flora and fauna, all of which are of concern to God and thus affect divine actions.

One fascinating interpretation of the book of Job understands this dynamic somewhat differently. Rather than reading God's speeches as describing a just and planned-out world that is beyond human comprehension, perhaps the answer is that God is not just. Although elsewhere in the Bible, Israel would receive that precious commodity, rain, only when observing God's laws, in Job it is observed that God causes it to rain on uninhabited places. If rain is the classic sign of reward and punishment, why would God waste rain on places where people do not exist to enjoy it? Thus, perhaps the world is not based on principles of reward and punishment and on divine justice. Whereas in Proverbs wisdom is God's first creation, in God's speeches in Job, the sea monsters are among God's first creations. The question that then arises is, if divine justice is taken out of the equation, why observe God's laws, and why lead a moral life? The answer, according to this interpretation, is that one must lead a moral life because it is the right thing to do.

Early Israelite thought favored collective responsibility, and thus an innocent person could be punished by God because of the sins of his or her community or ancestors. As this belief waned and innocent people were still seen to suffer, a new understanding needed to be reached. Thus, Job came to say that we do not understand the world, and perhaps there is no divine justice as we have understood it. Nevertheless, one must lead a moral and ethical life because that is what humans as moral beings should do.

The book of Ecclesiastes differs somewhat in that it is a first-person account of a man who has lived the "life of wisdom" and found that it did not work. This book is a direct attack on the philosophy espoused by the book of Proverbs. It disputes the basic premises of classical wisdom thought and comes to startling conclusions. According to his experience, the author perceives that nothing is determined by one's proper or improper behavior. "A season is set for everything, a time for every experience under heaven" (Eccles. 3:1). These "times" will occur regardless of human behavior; they are not rewards or punishments. Though occasionally he contradicts himself, claiming that God will hold each person responsible for his or her actions, the thrust of the book is that people need not live a certain way in order to influence God's determinations. "There is nothing worthwhile for a man but to eat and drink and afford himself enjoyment with his means" (Eccles. 2:24).

The varied nature of the material in the Ketuvim, the Writings section of the Bible, is made very clear in the juxtaposition of the pessimism and futility of Ecclesiastes with the happiness and hope of Ruth and Esther. Those two books are narratives that both center on the lives of women. The book of Ruth is an idyllic story tracing the life of a family that endured hardship and death and, finally, birth and happiness. Two women struggled against hunger and death to attain the basic needs of life. Not only were they were successful in surviving, but Ruth's child became the ancestor of King David.

The book of Esther is set in Persia and describes the attempted destruction and the ultimate salvation of the Jewish people. Esther managed to save the Jewish population of Persia through a combination of good fortune, cleverness, and bravery. It is noteworthy that in both Ruth and Esther God is not a visible actor. God is not even explicitly mentioned in the Hebrew book of Esther. Although this can be understood in many ways, it seems to point to an emphasis on human action in the world. God works behind the scenes, but humans need to initiate activities and take responsibility for themselves and their people. Significantly, it is the women who act and attain success and good fortune through their bravery, cleverness, and initiative. Just as in the beginning of the Bible, the matriarchs ensured that God's chosen sons would inherit the blessing, so too toward the end of the Bible, when God's direct presence is not felt, it was the women who ensured that Israel would survive and that future generations would carry on with appropriate leaders.

Methodology

Since the Hebrew Bible is of such importance to such large numbers of people, it is natural that it is approached with different assumptions and varied methodologies. Rabbinic, or classical Jewish, interpretation of the Torah assumes that the Bible is divine in origin. This leads to a belief in the historical validity of the Bible. The desire to derive moral and didactic lessons even from the placement of single letters and words is a reflection of the perfection and divinity ascribed to the Bible.

Two main methods within this school are *peshat* and *derash*. The *peshat* is the contextual meaning of the text: the plain sense of the words. *Derash*, in contrast, is the derived meaning of the text. Often the *derash* attempts to give a moral or didactic understanding of the verses in question. Rabbinic commentators fall into these two main methods of interpretation, with some of them engaging in both. A rabbinic dictum describes the Torah as having "seventy facets." The rabbis saw the beauty, perfection, and completeness of the Torah demonstrated in that the same text sustains so many interpretations. Chapter 4, "The Literature of the Rabbis," discusses these ideas in more detail.

Modern critical studies of the Bible generally include different assumptions and methodologies. In the nineteenth century, Julius Wellhausen theorized that the Torah was not the work of a single, divine author, as was commonly believed. He demonstrated that the biblical text was an artful compilation of the work of several authors or sources. He attributed the texts to four main schools. The "Yahwist" texts, known as "J," are narrative texts that use the divine appellation YHWH, the tetragrammaton, for the name of God. According to Wellhausen, these texts originated in Judah, in the south, in the tenth century. "E" is the "Elohist," who wrote in the north in the ninth century, using the divine name "Elohim." "D" is the book of Deuteronomy from the seventh century. The priestly material is from a priestly school, "P," which emphasized holiness and continuity. Debate continues to rage as to the dating of "P," ranging from the seventh century, preexilic times, to a postexilic period.

This source approach has been beneficial in alleviating issues of contradiction within the biblical text. For example, in the flood story, Genesis 6–9, conflicting accounts are given of the number of animals taken into the ark: one pair of each, or seven pairs each of "clean" animals and one pair each of "unclean" animals. It is very difficult to harmonize the two statements. However, using Wellhausian source criticism, we can attribute the conflicting verses to different sources and remove the contradiction. Knowing the sources is also helpful in understanding the bias and approach of a specific text.

Many scholars, while accepting the premises of source criticism, do not use it as a primary methodology for several reasons. At times the bias of a text, that is, its pro-priestly outlook, is used by modern critics to determine its source, resulting in circular reasoning. Source criticism is also less helpful in understanding the biblical text as a whole than as individual stories. When using this method, scholars separate the pieces of the text in search of original authors, but they rarely put the fragments back together to be understood as a literary unity. While looking for the pre-text, one can lose sight of the text in its present form. Source critics gain insight into the original resources of the biblical "Redactor," and readers are left to marvel at the creative genius that wove the strands into the Bible we know.

Other methodologies used in modern biblical criticism include the comparative approach, which seeks to place the Bible in its ancient Near Eastern context and to use knowledge about these cultures in understanding the biblical text. This contextualization is helpful in understanding historical events, specific words, imagery, legal conventions, poetic and literary devices, and literary themes. Ancient Near Eastern historical texts, such as annals of kings and records of battles, can be used to elucidate not only the general world in which the Israelites lived but also specific events mentioned in the Bible. Certain Israelite and Judaean kings are even mentioned in Assyrian and Babylonian texts as vassals and those who must pay tribute.

Literary epics from the ancient Near East are invaluable sources of imagery, themes, metaphors, and poetic and literary devices, many of which are found in the Bible. These ancient Near Eastern texts are compelling, not only as records of cultural similarities, but even more so in the contrast they provide. Unique elements of Israelite culture can be determined from these comparisons. Analysis of these differences often leads to a better understanding of the revolutionary nature of the Bible. To engage effectively in this type of comparative effort, biblicists study the cultures and languages of the Akkadian, Assyrian, Babylonian, Sumerian, and Egyptian civilizations. Extensive study and background are crucial to the comparative approach to the Bible, but the rewards are commensurate.

Another modern method of studying the Bible is the literary approach. This entails studying the Bible as a piece of great literature: carefully analyzing structure, characterization, word choice, themes, intertextuality, and much more. Close readings of biblical texts often reveal beautiful nuances, symbolism, and imagery within biblical literature that can be missed using other approaches. When literary theory is applied to the Bible, the beauty, richness, and depth of the text come through, showing the Bible to be truly a work of art. Literary interpretation is a very accessible approach in that it requires far less background on the part of the practitioner. Of course, the more familiarity with the biblical text and its milieu, the greater the possibilities for understanding.

A relatively new and exciting method of biblical study is feminist interpretation of the Bible. Using feminist methodology, one may analyze how issues of gender and power impact on the biblical text. Some scholars try to read from a minor female character's point of view in order to gain new perspectives on old texts. Often what needs to be done is to strip away centuries of male-centered assumptions about and interpretations of the text in order to read it anew. This process allows fresh readings of the Bible, which are usually far more positive toward women than the generations of scholarship allow.

Many methods of biblical studies exist; only a small sampling of the major ones have been mentioned here. Perhaps the best approach is one that does not limit itself to a single discipline but seeks to extend and broaden meaning in numerous ways. By gaining perspective on as many facets of the biblical text as possible, students of the Bible most effectively reveal its remarkable intricacies.

Notes

1. Translations of biblical verses are from the New JPS (Jewish Publication Society) translation, *Tanakh: The Holy Scriptures.*

Suggested Readings

Brenner, Athalya, and Carole Fontaine, eds. *A Feminist Companion to Reading the Bible: Approaches, Methods, and Strategies.* Sheffield: Sheffield Academic Press, 1997.

Childs, Brevard. *Introduction to the Old Testament as Scripture*. Philadelphia: Fortress Press, 1979.

Fox, Everett. *The Five Books of Moses*. New York: Schocken Books, 1995.

Friedman, Richard Elliott. *Who Wrote the Bible?* Englewood Cliffs, N.J.: Prentice-Hall, 1987.

Gottwald, Norman. *The Hebrew Bible: A Socio-Literary Introduction*. Philadelphia: Fortress Press, 1983.

McKenzie, Steven L., and Stephen R. Haynes, eds. *To Each Its Own Meaning: An Introduction to Biblical Criticisms and Their Application*. Louisville, KY: Westminster/John Knox Press, 1993.

Pritchard, James B., ed. *Ancient Near Eastern Texts Relating to the Old Testament*. Princeton: Princeton University Press, 1969.

Sarna, Nahum M., and Chaim Potok. *The JPS Torah Commentary*. Philadelphia: The Jewish Publication Society, 1989–1995.

2

Jewish History and Culture in the Hellenistic Period

ALBERT I. BAUMGARTEN

The Political and Legal Context

In the year 539 B.C.E., the Persian king, Cyrus, allowed the Jews, who had been exiled to Babylonia in 586 B.C.E. by King Nebuchadnezer, to return home to Jerusalem. A new era in the history of the Jews of Palestine thus began, one in which they were to live in their own land, but as subjects of a world empire. This situation was to persist until the Jews achieved formal independence under the Maccabees, in 140 B.C.E. Thus, for almost four hundred years, conditions of Jewish life in Palestine were dependent on the arrangements instituted by the empire controlling that part of the world, a role that was to pass from the Persians to the Macedonians at the time of Alexander the Great (333 B.C.E.), and after his death in 323 B.C.E. to his successors, at first Ptolemaic (until the Battle of the Bania in 198 B.C.E.) and later Seleucid.

These successive empires were conservative, and Persian policy, once established, was carried on with little if any change until the end of Seleucid rule. The basic principle of this policy was autonomy. Although the world empire controlled foreign and military matters and collected taxes, local affairs were in the hands of native officials, recognized by the imperial regime and empowered to rule the Jews in its name. The king's law for governing the Jews was Jewish law as interpreted by Jewish religious authority (Ezra 7:25–26).

In effect, the Temple personnel in Jerusalem became imperial officials. As such, they were entitled to compensation, which they duly received

indirectly, in the form of exemption from taxes (Ezra 7:24). As a comple-
ment to these arrangements, the Jews proved their loyalty to the king by
offering a daily sacrifice for his welfare (Ezra 6:9–10; 7:17). This sacrifice
was funded by the king; hence it was not a financial burden on the Jews.
Offering it on the altar, however, was an act of great symbolic meaning, as
it was an acknowledgment of fealty.

In addition to the Temple officials, there was a political ruler, or governor, appointed by the king, of whom Nehemiah is one example. In general, the regime did not encourage the emergence of a strong local political (as opposed to religious) leadership. Effective local power was
concentrated in the hands of the priesthood, so much so that Hecataeus of
Abdera, a Greek describing the Jews in the early Ptolemaic era, wrote that
the Jews were ruled by their high priest and had always been so governed, never having had a king. Hecataeus was obviously wrong, as his
remarks overlook the history of kingship in Israel from Saul, David, and
Solomon until the Babylonian Exile. Nevertheless, Hecataeus's comments
testify to the sense of permanence of priestly rule that he encountered in
Jerusalem. It seemed to him as if things had always been as he knew
them.

The Hellenization of Jerusalem

The conquests of Alexander the Great changed the nature of the interactions between Jews and Greeks. Although there had been some contact
between the two peoples prior to the time of Alexander, his successors
brought many Greeks to live and work in the service of their empires in
the East, thus altering the nature of the connection. Greeks such as
Hecataeus of Abdera began to write about the Jews and their history,
whereas Jews began to learn about the ways Greeks viewed the world. At
first, the Ptolemies many not have been interested in bringing outsiders
into the orbit of Greek culture. Nevertheless, whether actively promoted
by the regime or not, the ways of the foreign rulers began to trickle down
into ever widening Jewish circles.

The book of "the Preacher," Kohelet (Ecclesiastes), is early evidence for
the impact made by Greek ways on Jews of Jerusalem. Although this
book is attributed by the tradition to King Solomon, son of David and
king in Jerusalem (Eccles. 1:1), it can be dated on a linguistic basis to the
Hellenistic period, late in the years of Ptolemaic rule. The most prominent
example of such evidence is the employment of the Persian/Greek word
pardes to mean orchard in Ecclesiastes 2:5. The word acquired that meaning only after it had passed from the Persians to the Greeks in the third
century B.C.E.

The author of Kohelet was a rich man, with an acquisitive attitude typical of the era; he was anxious to accumulate as much property as possible but worried about the meaning of life. For example, he asked whether he would have the opportunity to enjoy his wealth (6:1–2). Would his heir, who inherited his fortune, know how to use it wisely (2:18–19, 21)? The "Preacher" shared some of the traditional values: For example, he urged his reader to be careful in making vows and to fulfill them scrupulously (5:2–5). Nevertheless, he also had corrosive doubts concerning many widely held beliefs. Life, for him, lacked meaning and nature was repetitive (1:9–10). The social order was full of wickedness (3:16; 4:1), and God's justice took too long to punish those deserving chastisement (8:10–17). The same fate affected man and the animals (3:19), the righteous as well as the wicked, the good and the evil, those who sacrificed and those who did not (9:2), and the wise as well as the foolish (2:15–16).

About all the author could recommend was a cautious enjoyment of the pleasures of the world:

> Go, eat your bread with enjoyment, and drink your wine with a merry heart; for God has already approved what you do. Let your garments be always white; let not oil be lacking on your head. Enjoy life with the wife whom you love, all the days of your vain life which He has given you under the sun, because that is your portion in life and in your toil under the sun. (9:7–9)[1]

In its original form (before it was brought more into line with traditional thought by the addition of a new conclusion, 12:9–13), his book ended on the same pessimistic note with which it had begun: "Vanity of vanities, says the Preacher; all is vanity" (12:8; cf. 1:2).

How do those thoughts indicate the Preacher's connection with the Greek world? Despite what is sometimes argued, the pessimistic comments cited were certainly not of Greek origin, as those attitudes had been known in the Near East well before the arrival of the Greeks. One can, for example, compare the Preacher's recommendation to enjoy the pleasure of the world with the following from the ancient Babylonian Epic of Gilgamesh, written centuries before the encounter with Hellenism. Gilgamesh, troubled about the meaning of life, like the author of Kohelet, received the following advice:

> *Thou Gilgamesh, let full be thy belly,*
> *Make thou merry by day and by night.*
> *Of each day make thou a feast of rejoicing,*
> *Day and night dance thou and play!*
> *Let thy garments be sparkling fresh,*
> *Thy head be washed; bathe thou in water.*

Pay heed to the little one that holds onto thy hand,
Let thy spouse delight in thy bosom!
For this is the task of [mankind].

Tablet x, iii, 6–14

At most one can say that pessimistic attitudes, which have existed virtually from time immemorial, may have received some reinforcement as a
result of contact with Greeks.

What then is *decisively* indicative of contact with the world of the
Greeks in Kohelet? Perhaps the clearest example can be found in the attitude toward women:

> I found more bitter than death the woman whose heart is snares and nets,
> and whose hands are fetters; he who pleases God escapes her, but the sinner
> is taken by her. Behold, this is what I found, says the Preacher, adding one
> thing to another to find the sum, which my mind has sought repeatedly, but I
> have not found. One man among a thousand I found, but a woman among
> all these I have not found. (7:26–28)

Put baldly, the author was a misogynist. Unlike other biblical authors, he
did not contrast good women with bad ones, warning his reader to avoid
the latter and seek out the former (cf. Prov. 31:10–31). In his mind, *no*
woman was ever good: The one decent person among a thousand he
found was certainly a rarity, but that one was never a woman. Exceptional as these attitudes were for the world of the Bible, they were typical
of the Greek world of the Hellenistic period, in which the term "misogynist" itself was coined (by the comic poet Menander—end of the fourth,
beginning of the third centuries B.C.E.—as the title of a play). Apparently,
the circumstances that encouraged the emergence of misogyny in Greek
society also were present in Jewish Jerusalem. Hence this thoroughly
"modern" attitude also appealed to the author of Kohelet, and he included it in his work.

Equally indicative are the author's comments on youth and old age.
For example, he urged his reader to enjoy the days of his youth, before
bodily decay impaired his ability to find pleasures in life,

> before the sun and the light and the moon and the stars are darkened and the
> clouds return after the rain; in the day when the keepers of the house trem-
> ble, and the strong men are bent, and the grinders cease because they are
> few, and those that look through the windows are dimmed. (12:2–3)

Here too, the contrast between the perspective of the author and that usually found in the Bible is significant. Old age, in biblical texts, was nor-

mally perceived as a time of blessing and of wisdom. The old should instruct the young concerning the meaning of life, on the basis of their background (see, e.g., Deut. 32:7). In the traditional Greek world, too, parents were normally seen as the repository of knowledge and experience. All this, however, changed among the Greeks with the sophists of the fifth century B.C.E., who could argue—shocking to the ears of conservatives—that a wise son had the same right to beat his foolish father as the father had to chastise his infant son. Old age was thus no longer seen as a blessing, but as a possible burden, or even a curse.

These Greek ideas had permeated upper-class circles in Jerusalem, as represented by the author of Kohelet. In the new world of unabashed acquisition opened up by the Greeks, Jewish society had changed sufficiently to make these new ideas appeal to the elite of Jerusalem. In their eyes, the old man was as likely as not to be perceived as a fool (4:13). As they saw matters, whatever small pleasures might be found in life were no longer necessarily appreciated in old age (12:1).

A Rejoinder—Ben Sira (Ecclesiasticus)

The challenge to traditional beliefs found in the pessimism of Kohelet would not be ignored. A first instance of an attempt to deal with these views can be found in the rabbinic tradition attributed to Simon the Righteous, in all likelihood the high priest who served in Jerusalem at the time of the Seleucid conquest, at the beginning of the second century B.C.E. Simon maintained that the world was sustained by three things: by the Law, by Temple service, and by acts of loving-kindness (Mishnah Abot 1:2). Kohelet, as we have seen, had expressed doubts about the value of observing the Law, declaring that the same fate awaited one who sacrificed as one who did not sacrifice. Social action, for Kohelet, was a matter of enlightened self-interest, at best (Eccles. 11:1–2). In contrast to these attitudes, Simon the Righteous reasserted the traditional understanding of the Law, of the covenant between God and his people, of the value of the Temple service, and of the need for Jews to help each other as a matter of fulfillment of a divine commandment. All these practices, according to Simon, sustained the world: If they were to end, the world would return to a state of chaos.

A more elaborate defense of the traditional worldview in the face of the challenge of Hellenism can be found in the Wisdom of Ben Sira (Ecclesiasticus). This book was not preserved in the canon of the Jews of Palestine, but only in translation, in Greek (and from Greek into other languages, such as Syriac), as part of the canon of the Jews of Alexandria and later of the Roman Catholic church. Thanks to their discovery in the Cairo Ge-

niza, sections of the Hebrew original of this book have been known since
the end of the nineteenth century. In excavations at Masada conducted by
Yigael Yadin from 1963 to 1965, a copy of part of this work, deposited
there before the fall of Masada at the end of the Great Revolt (66–73/4
C.E.), was found. We therefore know the work in the original Hebrew
from manuscripts that cover large portions of the book and can reconstruct the Hebrew for the remaining parts on the basis of the translations.

The author of Ben Sira lived in Jerusalem. He can be dated on the basis
of the translation of his work into Greek, prepared circa 132 B.C.E. by his
grandson. Therefore, the author lived in Jerusalem around 180 B.C.E. His
personal hero was Simon, son of Onias, the high priest of his day (Ben
Sira 50:1), possibly the same person as Simon the Righteous (already
mentioned). It is therefore not surprising to find Ben Sira sharing points
of view with Simon the Righteous.

For Ben Sira, wisdom was intimately connected with the observance of
the Law of God, as all wisdom came from God (1:1). When properly subjugated to the fear of God, the wise person realized that there were limits
to human understanding and did not ask too many difficult questions. He
recognized that he was inadequate to fully comprehend issues that he
was permitted to investigate, hence he did not push to attempt to understand forbidden matters, certainly beyond his grasp:

> Seek not what is too difficult for you, nor investigate what is beyond your
> power. Reflect upon what has been assigned to you, for you do not need
> what is hidden. Do not meddle in what is beyond your tasks, for matters too
> great for human understanding have been shown you. (3:21–23)

Such a wise man would never deviate into error. He would never be
one of those whose "hasty judgment has led them astray, and wrong
opinion has caused their thought to slip" (3:24). He would honor his father (3:1–16). He would fulfill his duties to the poor as a matter of
covenantal obligation (4:1–10). He would rely on the reward of God, even
if it seemed late in coming, putting his trust in God's record over history
in always forgiving and saving the faithful in times of affliction (2:7–11).
He would "fear the Lord and honor the priest, and give him [the priest]
his portion as is commanded" (7:31).

Virtually every assertion on the list above stands in distinct contrast to
a conclusion argued by Kohelet. Ben Sira's most direct challenge to his rival's work can be found in chapter 24. Kohelet had concentrated on the
search for wisdom and its consequences, seeking above all to be wise and
to live his life in accordance with the precepts of wisdom: "And I applied
my mind to seek and search out by wisdom all that is done under
heaven" (Eccles. 1:13). To such seekers, Ben Sira offered his answer of

what is true wisdom. Wisdom, he asserted, was created by God at the beginning of creation. Personified as a woman, she was universal, belonging to every people and nation (Ben Sira 24:1–6). Nevertheless, this wisdom had a special home, decreed by God. Her dwelling was in Jacob, her inheritance was in Israel (24:8). It was there that she ministered before God in his Temple in Jerusalem and found her resting place in Jerusalem (24:10–11). She flourished among the people of Israel (24:13–17).

Lest the reader have missed the point, the author made his conclusion even more explicit. The wisdom that all people sought, which was most consistent with the world as a whole, "cosmic" in the broadest sense of the term, "is the book of the covenant of the Most High God, the law which Moses commanded us as an inheritance for the congregations of Jacob" (24:24). All other peoples may search (possibly in vain) for that wisdom. For Jews it was available in its purest and most divine form in the Torah.

As is the case with many ideologies, the view of what was needed in the present was supported by a historical survey of the past. Ben Sira supplied this element in his world in his chapters in praise of famous men, summarizing the Jewish past from Enoch and Noah to Simon son of Onias of his own day (chapters 44–50). Ben Sira described in loving detail the service in the Temple conducted by Simon (50:5–21). The rule of the Jews by Simon constituted for him the highest fulfillment of all God's blessings in history, with little left to desire. The author therefore concluded his section on Simon by blessing God, "who does great things and exalts our days" (50:22). He prayed (according to the Hebrew original):

> May he give you gladness of heart and grant that peace be in our days in Israel as in the days of old. May his love abide upon Simon, and may he keep in him the covenant of Phinehas; may one never be cut off from him; and as for his offspring, [may it be] as the days of heaven. (50:23–24)

The author's hopes were stated explicitly enough: his aspirations were for the continued rule of the house of Simon, forever. Such was not to be the case, as events would unfold immediately in the next generation.

The Persecutions of Antiochus IV

Relations between Jews and Seleucids began on a note of continuity. At the time of the conquest of Jerusalem by Antiochus III in 198, the essential conditions of Jewish life under the world empires were maintained. Josephus cited provisions of the Seleucid constitution of Jerusalem (*Ant.* 12, 138–144),[2] which continued the basic arrangements laid down by the Persians outlined above. Moreover, as a means of enforcing these regulations, Josephus noted the contents of a decree of Antiochus III controlling access to the Temple in Jerusalem and reinforcing the holy character of the city (*Ant.* 12, 145–146).

Circumstances were not to remain the same under the successors of Antiochus III. The most extreme example of a break with the past was the decrees against traditional Jewish observance promulgated by Antiochus IV in the winter of 168/167 B.C.E. Antiochus IV forbade all regulations that reinforced the differences between Jews and their neighbors, from the calendar and other special practices in the Temple, to food laws and circumcision. Jews would make themselves abominable, unclean, and profane by the standards of the Torah, forgetting the law and abandoning its ordinances (1 Macc. 1:44–49). The motives of Antiochus IV in issuing these decrees remain a subject of intense scholarly debate. Were these acts undertaken at the initiative of Jewish reformers, who wanted to modernize their religion and remove from it all traces of practices which separated Jews from their neighbors, as suggested by Bickerman? Were the Hellenists of Jerusalem, in fact, the instigators of these actions by the king? Alternately, perhaps Hellenization in Jerusalem was not sufficiently advanced by that time for there to be a group "modern" enough to attempt such a program. On that possibility, as suggested by Tcherikover, perhaps the decrees of Antiochus IV were punishment for rebellion. On that view, Jewish Hellenists collaborated with these royal decrees, but they were not at all the initiators of the royal policy. These are two of the leading answers that have been proposed by scholars in this century to resolve the puzzle of why Antiochus IV took the steps he did.

Whatever explanation is adopted, two facts remain clear: first, that some Hellenizing Jews collaborated, at the very least, with the royal decrees; second, that these decrees led to an armed revolt, first raised by Mattathias the Hasmonean, under the command of his son Judah Maccabee. This revolt, taken together with the troubles afflicting the Seleucid empire on other fronts, was sufficiently successful to have the Temple restored to its original worship and purified (1 Macc. 4:36–60; 2 Macc. 10:1–9). This success was memorialized in the holiday of Hanukkah (2 Macc. 1:1–2:18). Furthermore, the decrees of Antiochus IV were annulled, and Jews returned to their former legal dispositions (2 Macc. 11:22–26).

Ultimately, the Hasmonean family, under the leadership of Judah Maccabee and his younger brothers, was to achieve a double goal, both national and familial: By the year 140 B.C.E., the Jews would be independent of all world empires and the high priesthood would be in the hands of their family. This accomplishment was made possible by means of a two-track policy: (1) utilizing the competition between forces contesting for control of the Seleucid empire to obtain the greatest possible privileges for the Jews and the Hasmonean family, and (2) maintaining Roman support for the emerging Jewish state (1 Macc. 8). Thus, a long-term result of the persecutions of Antiochus IV was the achievement of Jewish independence after close to four hundred years of domination by various world empires.

Independence and Its Consequences

The nature of the change that had taken place should not be underestimated. One measure of that transformation is supplied by the Greek translation of Ben Sira 50:24. The Hebrew original of that verse, as we have seen, had been a ringing affirmation of loyalty to the house of Simon son of Onias, and an expression of hope of its continued reign as supplying high priests, for as long as the days of heaven. Events did turn out as Ben Sira had fervently hoped. By 132 B.C.E., when Ben Sira's grandson translated the work into Greek, it was clear that some of Simon's descendants were those who collaborated with the decrees of Antiochus IV. Others had left Palestine to found a rival temple in Leontopolis in Egypt. The high priesthood in Jerusalem was now in the hands of the Maccabees. In light of the situation, what was Ben Sira's grandson to do? If he rendered the original literally, readers of his day would have been aware of the painful contrast between the hopes expressed by his grandfather and the way matters had turned out. It seemed better to the grandson to conceal this awkward situation by modifying the translation. So great had been the changes in the two generations that separated author from translator! Therefore his version is as follows: "May He entrust to us His mercy, and let Him deliver us in our days." This verse was harmless and nonspecific enough to avoid all possible embarrassment to the original author.

For the Maccabees, now ruling the Jews, the political game they were playing was a most dangerous one. In the midst of the intrigues of a disintegrating empire, with rival cliques contesting the right to rule its remaining fragments, the price of backing the wrong contestant was potentially fatal. Some alternate source of power was therefore essential for the ill-fated day when the Maccabees might be on the losing side of the interminable wars of succession. This was the reason that successive Maccabean leaders, from Judah Maccabee on, assiduously cultivated the connection with Rome (1 Macc. 8). Rome was the superpower of the day. Rome's diplomatic backing might prove vital to survival, if the emergent Jewish state were threatened. Roman interests at that juncture favored any group that seemed to be weakening the Seleucid empire, whose remnants were viewed by the Romans as a potential source of a coalition that might threaten Roman conquests; hence the Romans were glad to lend their support to the Jews under the leadership of the Maccabees.

Internally, there were difficulties of another sort. The Maccabees had achieved the high priesthood on the basis of an appointment by Seleucid rulers. What indication did they have that their rule was legal and legitimate by Jewish criteria? True, the Maccabees had loyal Jewish soldiers willing to fight with them, in whose eyes they must have been legitimate rulers, whom they could offer to the Seleucid bidders. Nevertheless, how could Maccabean rule be justified formally in Jewish terms, in particular when it had come at the expense of the reign of the high priestly family of the Oniads, who traced their ancestry back to Zadok, high priest at the time of King David?

One way the Maccabees attempted to deal with this problem was to convoke a national assembly of all the different constituent parts of the people in the early fall of 140 B.C.E. This body probably did not have full freedom to take any decision it chose, and its conclusions must have been largely determined in advance, before its sitting, at the intervention of the ruling family. Nevertheless, the determination of this body gave Maccabean rule a more solid basis in Jewish eyes. Simon, Judah Maccabee's youngest surviving brother and ruler of the Jews at that time, was confirmed as leader and high priest forever, until a trustworthy prophet should arise (1 Macc. 14:41). He was to be governor, in charge of the sanctuary, and obeyed by all; all contracts would be written in his name, and he would be clothed in purple and gold (1 Macc. 14:42–43).

Most interesting of all is the proviso that Simon was to be leader and high priest "until a trustworthy prophet should arise." The meaning of this clause is elucidated by another passage in 1 Maccabees (4:46). At the time of the purification of the Temple the question arose of what to do with the stones of the original altar, which had been defiled by the sacrifices offered on them during the time of the decrees of Antiochus IV. It was clear that these stones could no longer be used and that a new altar must be constructed, but should these old stones be destroyed? On the one hand, they had been defiled, but on the other hand, they had once been holy. The decision taken was to store "the stones in a convenient place on the Temple hill until there should come a prophet to tell what to do with them." Waiting for the decision of a prophet was thus a means of dealing with an insoluble question. Whatever inevitable steps had to be taken in the present could then be taken, but the irresolvable problem in the present was thus bracketed by having a final decision deferred until the coming of a true prophet.

What irresolvable issues might have faced the assembly in 140 B.C.E. that required deferral until the coming of a trustworthy prophet? Perhaps they were the status of Maccabean rule as a whole, the Maccabees' assumption of the office of high priest in spite of the fact that their family had not been in that position previously? Whatever the situation might have been, the decision of the assembly of 140 B.C.E. let the political reality of Maccabean domination proceed with a greater measure of legitimacy, while allowing a small opening to remain—more theoretical than practical, but useful never-theless—for those who might want to express a reservation on this matter.

On the religious front, the Hellenists had abandoned much of tradi-tional Jewish religion as conventionally understood. The challenge posed by their actions seemed serious enough to require a response. Biblical covenantal theology insisted on the belief in one God, and one God only. As had been stressed by Ben Sira, this theology upheld performance of the commandments and reliance on the reward of God, even if the latter might be late in coming. Much of this must have seemed in need of rein-forcement in the aftermath of the decrees of Antiochus IV and their conse-quences. It is therefore not surprising that an institution of whose exis-tence we did not hear before the mid–second century B.C.E. began to take a prominent place in the lives of Jews: the daily recitation in the Temple of a number of biblical passages—Deuteronomy 6:4–9, 11:13–21, and Num-bers 15:37–41, known conventionally as the Shema, the opening word of the series of verses, and the Ten Commandments. This practice was given even higher status by means of the claim that it went back to Moses. Priests in the Temple were thus reminded regularly that their religion promoted belief in only one God, that God rewarded and punished men in accordance with their deeds, and that God had redeemed the Jews from Egypt (a redemption in the past, which also hinted at future re-demption). These priests could then spread these beliefs as part of their regular responsibility for instruction of the people in the ways of God (see, e.g., Ben Sira 45:17).

The context in which this innovation was introduced was a sensitive one. How could one alter the daily ritual in the Temple, where the divine service was essential to maintaining the world order (see the discussion of the statement of Simon the Righteous above)? This dilemma was re-solved in part by attributing the innovation to Moses, but also by a simple practical step: The recitation of the Shema took place away from the sacri-ficial area, in the Chamber of Hewn Stone in the Temple, after the sacrifi-cial rites had been completed unaltered (Mishnah Tamid 4:3). The old was performed without any change, whereas the status of the new was im-plicitly acknowledged by executing it elsewhere in the Temple precinct.

In the end, the institution of the recitation of the Shema was to prove ef-fective and successful. Its opening verses would be so well known by Jews that they would be cited as the most important of the command-ments, according to Jesus in the Gospels (Mark 12:29–31; Matt. 22:37–40; Luke 10:26–27). Even the Dead Sea Scroll sectarians, whose attitude to ward the Maccabees was equivocal at best, adopted it as part of their lives (Qumran Cave 1, *Serah HaYahad* [Rule of the Community] 10, 10–14), and

authors such as Josephus had no doubt that Moses himself had ordered
the Jews to recite the Shema daily (*Ant.* 4, 196).

Independence also had other consequences, not all of which were logically consistent with the steps discussed above. For example, the political
circumstances under which the Maccabees achieved these results were
such that they required the family to become well versed in the surrounding world and its culture. How could one judge which camp to join,
which pretender to back, without some assessment of who was likely to
win the forthcoming contest? How could one reach these judgments
without extensive knowledge of the larger political environment and its
culture? Thus one of the ironies of Maccabean rule was that it led to an extensive Hellenization of its leaders, which also trickled down along various paths to the members of the nation as a whole. This Hellenization can
be seen in any number of aspects, but perhaps the easiest is to point to the
assembly of the people that ratified the rule of Simon and his sons. Such
an assembly had no traditional status in the Jewish polity, but it was a
regular feature of Greek city life. When faced with the necessity of regu-
larizing the rule of the Hasmonean dynasty, use was made of an institution drawn from the world of the Greeks.

Yet another indication of this same tendency can be seen in the reign of
Salome Alexandra (76–67 B.C.E.). In her day, according to Josephus, real
power was in the hands of the Pharisees, and she was idealized by the
rabbis as the embodiment of the ideals of the Torah. Nevertheless, the notion of a queen as sovereign is foreign to the structures of the priesthood
or the monarchy as envisaged in the Bible. What might have been the
source of inspiration for Salome Alexandra's rule? At least one likely possibility is to look to the role of the Cleopatras of Egypt of her day. With
contemporaneous female rulers staking out a position in their own name
in a neighboring place, it is not surprising that Salome Alexandra conceived the notion of being sovereign queen in her own right.

The Maccabees thus were torn in contrary directions, a conflict that
they did not always resolve in a consistent way. Some of their actions in
the aftermath of independence were intended to bolster the traditional
faith, on behalf of which they had fought and come to rule. Others of their
actions were little different than those that might have been taken by their
initial Hellenizing opponents had the latter been victorious. Such, however, were the consequences of independence.

Josephus and Philo

Much of the information in the previous sections comes from 1 and 2 Maccabees, books that were considered sacred by the Jews of Alexandria, hence
preserved in Greek, but not by the Jews of Palestine. Thus the Hebrew orig-

inal of 1 Maccabees has not survived. The time span covered by these books ends with the rise of John Hyrcanus (Hyrcanus I), on the death of his father, Simon Maccabee, in 134 B.C.E., as narrated in 1 Maccabees. From that point until the destruction of the Temple by the Romans in 70 C.E., our principal source of information is the works of the historian Josephus Flavius.

Born to the priestly family in Jerusalem circa 38 C.E., Josephus was a descendant of the Hasmonean family on his mother's side. He received an excellent education, eventually investigating the different Jewish groups and spending three years as the follower of a desert hermit named Bannus. He became involved in the rebellion against Rome in the heady days following the initial victory over Cestius Gallus (fall of 66 C.E.), being appointed as commander of the Galilee by the revolutionary government. Defeated by the Romans, he went over to their side, benefiting from his prediction that the Roman commander Vespasian would become emperor. As a protégé of the house of the Flavians, he spent the remaining years of his life in their service, writing an account of the rebellions, *The Jewish War*—first in Aramaic and then in Greek (only the latter has survived)—after the defeat of the rebels. Addressed at least in part to Jewish readers, this book was intended to dissuade them from taking up arms against Rome. Later in his career Josephus wrote three works: *Antiquities of the Jews*, an account of Jewish history up to the outbreak of the war against Rome; *Life*, his autobiography; and *Against Apion*, a book directed against a well-known anti-Semite from Alexandria; in that book Josephus answered charges that had been directed against the Jews by various ancient authors.

Another major source of information is found in the works of the Jewish philosopher Philo of Alexandria, who lived in Egypt a generation or two prior to Josephus. Philo teaches us most about the Egyptian community, about its intellectual ambitions and social standing. He was a member of the leading Egyptian Jewish family and had received the finest Jewish and Greek education available. His works show a special sensitivity to the problem of living on the interface between two worlds, that is, trying to be loyal to a covenant community while remaining sophisticated intellectually.

In spite of their inevitable focus on the Jewish community in Egypt and its needs, Philo's works teach us a good deal about events in Palestine. We learn much from him, for example, about the attempt by the Emperor Caligula (38–41 C.E.) to introduce his statue into the Temple in Jerusalem, and of the steps taken by the Jews to try to avert the decree.

The Emergence of Jewish Sectarianism

One last phenomenon of Jewish life beginning in the second century B.C.E. deserves attention: the emergence of groups such as Pharisees, Sadducees, Essenes, and the Dead Sea Scroll sect. These parties and sects were to offer alternate ways of being Jewish as responses to the vastly changed conditions of that era. Their proliferation was to be a characteristic of those days, and their conflict an important factor in Jewish history down to the destruction of the Temple by the Romans in 70 C.E.

One of the fundamental characteristics of these groups was that they drew purity boundaries between themselves and other Jews. A member of the Essenes would not eat food prepared by other Jews and might starve to death rather than violate this obligation. A member of the Dead Sea Scroll group had similar restrictions. He was also supposed to have no business dealings with other Jews, except for cash transactions, as only in the latter was the purity barrier between a Dead Sea Scroll sect member and an outsider adequately maintained. What factors in life during the second century B.C.E. might have been responsible for the emergence of these movements, and of such practices?

Complex social phenomena normally require nuanced explanations. Nevertheless, one factor should be stressed. Prior to the crises of the early second century B.C.E., such as the encounter with Hellenization and the reforms of Antiochus IV, the purity barriers erected by Jews had divided them from their non-Jewish neighbors. Much the same dynamic had been taking place between Greeks and natives in Egypt, as we learn from Herodotus. With the onset of the predicaments of the early second century, these barriers were under severe pressure, as the intention of the reforms of Antiochus IV was to prohibit many of the practices that created a divide between Jews and outsiders.

One might have expected that the victory of the Maccabees would lead to a restoration and reinforcement of these divisions. In fact, such was the case, but as we have seen above, *only in part*. Maccabean practice was inconsistent: Their success also resulted in an ever increasing exposure of Jews to the world around them and to the adoption of many "foreign" ways of thought and behavior.

What then were those loyal to the old ways to do? One answer was to form new groups of their own, with firm boundaries surrounding them on which they could rely. New purity regulations would be created, still separating insiders and outsiders, now not on the national perimeter but on that of the new sect, dividing its members and other Jews. The groups that arose in the second century B.C.E.—the Pharisees, Sadducees, Essenes, and the Dead Sea Scroll sect—were joined during the first century C.E. by a number of even newer groups, including the early Christians.

The Pharisees are known to us directly from Josephus, the New Testament, and rabbinic literature. Two points should be stressed about the Pharisees: first, that they supplemented the written law of the Torah with their "tradition," *paradosis* in Greek. This tradition, although not written in the Torah, taught them how to apply its laws and thus was at the heart of their dispute with other groups, who had supplements of their own to fill that role. The tradition of the Pharisees was thus very controversial, a point that emerges clearly from the story told by Josephus (*Ant.* 13, 288–298) concerning the abandoning of the Pharisees for the Sadducees by John Hyrcanus (134–104 B.C.E.), as well as from the debate reflected in the Gospels (Mark 7 and parallels). The Pharisees attempted to bolster their tradition by calling it the tradition of the elders, thus giving it a pedigree going back to the leaders of the nation from the most remote past.

The exact teachings contained in this tradition are poorly known: Perhaps they included the law of abrogation of vows (Mark 7; Mishnah Hagigah 1:8), the basic forms of work prohibited on the Sabbath, and the laws of the festival offering, as well as those on the abuse of sacred property. Consistent with the path that led to the rise of sectarianism as a whole outlined above, as well as reflecting the meaning of their name (separatists), the Pharisees probably kept themselves somewhat apart from other Jews in matters of food and purity. Further details about Pharisaic practice are becoming available as a result of publication of new Dead Sea Scroll texts; hence more information should be known as the project of publishing Dead Sea Scroll material approaches completion.

The tradition of the Pharisees likely served as the basis for the second of their central claims: that they (and only they) knew how to observe the law accurately, strictly, in all of its details (in Greek, the claim to *akribeia*). Against other groups, who almost definitely made similar claims, the Pharisees maintained that only the tradition of the elders that was in their possession was exact. On the basis of comments in Josephus and remarks in Dead Sea Scroll texts, it seems that the Pharisees enjoyed special prestige, and that their claim to preeminence had a distinctive status in the eyes of the people.

The Pharisees are of particular importance for one additional reason. When Jewish life was restored in the aftermath of the destruction of the Temple by the Romans in 70 C.E., the family of Gamaliel and Simon son of Gamaliel, prominent Pharisees in predestruction Jerusalem, came to play the leading role. The Pharisaic way of life thus was a significant component in the mix that was to emerge as Rabbinic Judaism.

In contrast to the Pharisees, who derived new applications of the law by means of interpretation preserved in tradition, the early Christians claimed to be the beneficiaries of a new revelation, a "new" testament. This new revelation had been embodied in the person of Jesus of Nazareth, revealed to all through teaching and miracles during his lifetime and confirmed after his death by the empty tomb where he had been buried (Mark 16).

The Christians would generate many varieties of their group in the generations immediately following the death of Jesus. Some of these would be more insistent on the observance of Jewish law as understood by other Jews, others less so, but many would try to remain in the broad band of movements contained in the Jewish world. With the ultimate dominance of Pauline Christianity, which did not require converts to Christianity from the pagan world to accept circumcision as a condition of entry, and with the intensification of the debate between Jews and Christians, the gap between Jews and Christians began to grow. Ultimately the Christians would find themselves as an independent religion, maintaining their ties to the Hebrew Bible, but insisting that Christianity was the only legitimate fulfillment of the promises of the Bible. Christians both usurped and denied the status of the Jewish people as the group with whom God had established an eternal covenant. A sect within Judaism had become a religion of its own, a new, third way between the realities of Jews and non-Jews.

The path of the Dead Sea Scroll sect was different from that of the Christians: The former were hypernomic, or intensely bound to the Law, and the latter were to become antinomic, or unbound from the Law. Whereas Christianity became an independent religion, the dominant one of the Roman Empire, the Dead Sea community led to a dead end. Nevertheless, the group whose texts have become known to the world thanks to the sensational discoveries in the area of Qumran, by the shores of the Dead Sea, discoveries that began in 1947 and multiplied in the decade thereafter (now first being fully published), has taught us much about the world of ancient Jewish sectarianism. Removed from contact with other Jews as a result of purity and food regulation of the most extreme sort, the Dead Sea Scroll group was also at odds with practices in the Temple. They thus were willing to sever ties with other Jews and with the most central institution in Jewish life of their time in order to remain faithful to the practices they believed correct. Dividing mankind up into "sons of light" and "sons of darkness," they believed that the blessings promised in the Bible were reserved for the former (themselves), whereas all the rest were consigned to eternal punishment by a divine decree that could not be changed.

The Qumran covenanters had little choice but to concede that their understanding of the Torah had not been known in the eras that preceded the emergence of their movement. They could not appeal, as the Pharisees had, to a tradition that went back to the elders of the nation from time immemorial. Authors close to the Qumran sect therefore wrote pseudepigrapha, in which voices of great authority from the past gave an encore of sorts on the stage of history, modifying what they were believed to have said in previous appearances in favor of teachings dear to the heart of the Qumran community. One example of such a text is the Temple Scroll, a new version of God's direct revelation to Moses. As another path to the same objective, the Dead Sea Scroll covenanters also developed the notion of an original esoteric Torah, eventually lost to the nation as a whole, which they (and only they) had been privileged to (re)learn as a result of ongoing revelation. Through these techniques those at Qumran attempted to retain some sort of connection with the past while cutting the connection with the traditional institutions that were widely accepted as representing the national experience. At the same time, the beliefs of the Qumran sect reinforced their own sense of conviction that they were right in holding fast to practices rejected by the nation at large.

The Qumran community was small. Its administrative center has been excavated, and its dining room could seat no more than 120–150 people at a time. Its cemetery contains 1,100 graves, which must spread over the two hundred or so years of the life of the community (ca. 125 B.C.E.–70 C.E.). These figures also suggest that the number of inhabitants at any one time during those years cannot have been high. The way of life advocated by those at Qumran had no significant continuation in the years that followed the destruction of the Temple in 70 C.E. In a sense, Qumran is therefore little more than a footnote to Jewish history. Nevertheless, the opportunity to read documents of Jewish sectarians at firsthand, without the intervention of Josephus or the New Testament, makes these texts a resource of inestimable importance and fascination.

Close to the Dead Sea Scroll community, indeed, to be identified with them in the view of many scholars, were the Essenes, known from the writings of Philo of Alexandria, Josephus, and the Roman author Pliny the Elder. The Essenes, in my opinion, were different from the Qumran covenanters, somewhat closer to the middle of the spectrum. Thus, although the Essenes offered their own purificatory sacrifices and thereby denied the validity of those offered in the Temple, Essenes could be found in Jerusalem in the vicinity of the Temple, unlike their Qumran counterparts off in the desert. Essene rejection of the legitimacy of all that was done in the Temple was not as extreme as that of Qumran members.

Of all the groups under consideration here, the Jerusalem Sadducees were the least sectarian in character, closest to being identified with the ruling elite of the Temple. As Josephus remarked about them, they came from the highest circles of Jewish society of their day (*Ant.* 18, 17). The Sadducees are sometimes maligned as being assimilationists, eager to please the ruling power at the expense of "Jewish" interests. In fact, they were not so. The Jerusalem Sadducees fought for the practices they believed to be correct and took a leading role in the war against the Romans. Their laws were different, and they did not accept the tradition of the Pharisees (*Ant.* 13, 297), but they had an interpretive supplement of their own by which they lived, which taught them how to apply the laws of the Torah, and which they tied to the ultimate source of written authority in the Torah.

Since the discovery and publication of Qumran texts such as *Miktzat Ma'asei Torah* from Qumran Cave 4 (4QMMT), a possible connection between the Sadducees and the Qumran community has been raised and considered at length. Sadducean law, as attributed to them by the rabbis, turns out to have a number of overlaps with the practices approved by the Dead Sea Scroll sect (such as the status required of all those connected with offering and utilizing the ashes of the Red Heifer: Mishnah Para 3:7, 4QMMT B:13–16). What these overlaps teach us about the relationship between the Sadducees and the Qumran sect has been much discussed. How can we identify the members of one group, whose members served in the Temple (Jerusalem Sadducees), with another, which rejected that central institution (Dead Sea Scroll group)? This is an example of one of the questions that would have to be resolved before making a firm identification of the Jerusalem Sadducees with the Dead Scroll sect.

Conclusion

Jewish independence was not to last long, as Roman policy toward the Jews changed, and Roman support, as we have seen, was an essential plank of Maccabean politics. The Romans themselves conquered Jerusalem in 63 B.C.E., inaugurating a new era in Jewish history in which the issue of how to contend with foreign rule under the dominion of a world empire was problematic. This dilemma sparked at least three Jewish revolts, the Great Revolt (66–74 C.E.), the Diaspora Revolt (115–117 C.E.), and the Bar Kokhba Revolt (132–135 C.E.). The period of the Maccabees thus stands as a brief shining moment of seventy-seven years (140–63 B.C.E.), when the Jews enjoyed the blessings and problems of independence. It was the interlude between one era of subjugation and the entrance to yet another.

The issues faced by the Jews during the Hellenistic period as a whole, from the problem of how to retain their identity in the face of a dominant foreign culture to the competition between the various answers to the meaning of being Jewish in changed times, made a major contribution to shaping the nature of Judaism. Ultimately, Rabbinic Judaism emerged as dominant, in the period of the Mishnah and Talmud, from the second century C.E. on. As Rabbinic Judaism had a substantial Pharisaic basis, its victory would not have been possible without the foundations laid in the Hellenistic era.

Notes

1. All biblical translations are from the Revised Standard Version.

2. Quotations from Josephus's *Antiquities of the Jews* (abbreviated in the text as *Ant.*) are from the translation by Ralph Marcus, Loeb Classical Library (Cambridge, Mass: Harvard University Press, 1976).

Suggested Readings

Bickerman, E. J. *Four Strange Books of the Bible*. New York: Schocken, 1967.

Bickerman, E. J. *From Ezra to the Last of the Maccabees*. New York: Schocken, 1962.

Bickerman, E. J. *The Jews in the Greek Age*. Cambridge, Mass.: Harvard University Press, 1988.

Charlesworth, J. *The Old Testament Pseudepigrapha*. Garden City, N.Y.: Doubleday, 1983.

Hengel, M. *Judaism and Hellenism*. Philadelphia: Fortress Press, 1974.

Sanders, E. P. *Jesus and Judaism*. Philadelphia: Fortress Press, 1985.

Sanders, E. P. *Paul and Palestinian Judaism*. Philadelphia: Fortress Press, 1977.

Sandmel, S. *Philo of Alexandria: An Introduction*. New York: Oxford University Press, 1979.

Schürer, E. *History of the Jews in the Age of Jesus Christ*, rev. ed., ed. G. Vermes. Edinburgh: Clark, 1973–1987.

Smith, M. *Palestinian Parties and Politics That Shaped the Old Testament*. London: SCM, 1987.

Tcherikover, V. *Hellenistic Civilization and the Jews*. Philadelphia: Jewish Publication Society, 1959.

Vermes, G. *The Dead Sea Scrolls in English*. Sheffield: JSOT Press, 1987.

3

Judaism Under Roman Domination: From the Hasmoneans Through the Destruction of the Second Temple

SHAYE J. D. COHEN

IT IS IRONIC THAT THE ROMANS entered Judaean politics by invitation of one Jewish faction that was in a power struggle with another. In 76 B.C.E. Alexander Jannaeus, the last great king of the Hasmonean line, died. He was succeeded by his widow, Salome Alexandra, who herself died in 67 B.C.E. The royal couple's two sons, Hyrcanus and Aristobulus, then fought each other for succession to the throne. Both Hyrcanus (usually called by scholars Hyrcanus II) and Aristobulus (usually called by scholars Aristobulus II) appeared before the Roman legate in Syria, each asking to be recognized as the ruler of Judaea. Other Jews appeared as well, asking the Romans to reject the claims of both—by this time many Jews were thoroughly disillusioned with Hasmonean rule.

The Romans at first supported Aristobulus II, but when they realized he was a potential troublemaker, a suspicion amply confirmed by subsequent events, they transferred their support to Hyrcanus II. Aristobulus considered fighting the Romans, but realizing the overwhelming might of Rome and the hopelessness of his situation, he surrendered in 63 B.C.E. to

Chapter 3 was first published as two separate chapters in Herschel Shanks, ed., *Ancient Israel* (Englewood Cliffs, N.J.: Prentice Hall, 1988), and Herschel Shanks, ed., *Christianity and Rabbinic Judaism* (Washington, D.C.: Biblical Archaeology Society, 1992). They have been edited and condensed for use in this volume with the kind permission of the author and publishers.

the Roman general Pompey. The supporters of Hyrcanus opened the city of Jerusalem to the Romans.

But that was not the end of the battle for Jerusalem. Although the city was in Roman hands, many of Aristobulus's supporters garrisoned themselves in the Temple and refused to surrender. After a three-month siege and some fearsome fighting, however, the Temple fell to Pompey's legions (63 B.C.E.).

Pompey's conquest of Jerusalem closed one chapter in Roman-Jewish relations and opened another. A hundred years earlier Judah Maccabee had sought and obtained an alliance with the Romans, who were then just becoming the dominant power in the eastern Mediterranean. At that time, the Romans eagerly supported anyone who would help them weaken the power of the Seleucid kings of Syria. Judah's successors followed the same strategy of seeking Roman support in their struggles for independence from the Seleucids.

Gradually, Rome's power grew; its policy in the region, however, never wavered: Any power that might pose a threat to Roman interests was to be weakened. When the Jews were a useful ally against the Seleucids, they were embraced. When the Hasmonean state expanded, the Romans had no desire to see it become in turn a new threat to Roman interests. By the middle of the first century B.C.E., when the Romans had at long last decided that the time had come to incorporate the eastern Mediterranean into their empire, the Jews were no longer allies but just another ethnic group that was to be brought into the inchoate imperial system.

As the Romans were changing their mode of government, so were the Jews. Under the Persian and the Hellenistic monarchies, the Jews had been led by high priests who wielded political as well as religious power. However, during the initial period of Roman rule after Pompey's conquest of Jerusalem, the high priesthood lost virtually all its temporal powers and a new royal dynasty emerged that was not of priestly stock. Its opponents claimed that it was not even wholly Jewish! The Romans, for their part, were delighted to install a dynasty that owed its existence to Roman favor and therefore could be counted on to provide loyal support.

This new dynasty, usually called the Herodian after its most famous member, was founded by Herod's father, Antipater the Idumean. The Idumeans, who lived in the area south of Judah, had been incorporated into the Hasmonean empire and converted to Judaism by John Hyrcanus (Hyrcanus I). Antipater gradually insinuated himself into the circle of Hyrcanus II. When Julius Caesar came to Syria in 47 B.C.E., he conferred various benefits on the Jews. Hyrcanus II was appointed *ethnarch* (ruler of the nation), and Antipater the Idumean was appointed *procurator* (caretaker). A rival soon assassinated Antipater, and his mantle then fell to his son Herod.

Herod remained the undisputed leader of the Jews for more than thirty years (37–4 B.C.E.). Herod is an enigmatic figure. Tyrant, madman, murderer, builder of great cities and fortresses, wily politician, successful king, Jew, half-Jew, Gentile—Herod was all these and more. He is perhaps best known to posterity as the murderer of several of his wives, children, and other relations. The murders were prompted by Herod's suspicions (often justified) of all those who had an equal or better claim to the throne than he. In the first years of his reign, Herod executed the surviving members of the Hasmonean aristocracy. Since he was married to Mariamne, the daughter of the Hasmonean king Hyrcanus II, that meant that Herod murdered his wife's relations—her brother, her aunt, and her father. Finally, he murdered Mariamne too. At the end of his reign, he executed the two sons Mariamne had borne him.

Herod created a new aristocracy that owed its status and prestige to him alone. He raised to the high priesthood men from families that had never previously supplied high priests, including families from the Diaspora (the Jewish communities outside the Land of Israel).

Herod was also a great builder. Many of the most popular tourist sites in Israel today were Herod's projects—Masada, Herodium, Caesarea, and many of the most conspicuous remains of ancient Jerusalem, including the Tower of David, the Western Wall, and much of the Temple Mount. As a result of Herod's works, Jerusalem became "one of the most famous cities of the East," and its Temple, which he rebuilt, was widely admired. In the new city of Caesarea, Herod created a magnificent harbor, utilizing the latest technology in hydraulic cement and underwater construction. Herod also founded several other cities, notably Sebaste (on the site of ancient Samaria). He bestowed gifts and benefactions on cities and enterprises outside his own kingdom. Athens, Sparta, Rhodes, and the Olympic games all enjoyed Herod's largess.

Herod tried to win support and recognition from both the Jews and the pagans, within his kingdom and outside it. The support of his groups, however, would have meant nothing if Herod had not been supported by Rome. In 37 B.C.E., as we have seen, the Romans made Herod the leader of Judaea. In the struggle that developed soon thereafter between Mark Antony and Octavian, Herod supported Antony. That was perhaps because Antony was headquartered in the East. But at the Battle of Actium in 31 B.C.E., Octavian defeated Antony, and the entire Mediterranean, including Egypt, came to the hands of Octavian.

Herod had supported the losing side. He was obviously in deep trouble. But ever the survivor, Herod managed to convince Octavian that everyone's best interest would be served if he, Herod, were to remain king of Judaea. He had been loyal to Antony, Herod argued, and now would be loyal to Octavian. Octavian accepted Herod's argument and never had cause to regret his decision. Herod was true to his word, and during the course of his long reign was rewarded several times by the emperor (renamed Augustus) with grants of additional territory.

The *Antiquities of the Jews* by Josephus recounts two major complaints the Jews had against Herod, aside from their despising his violence and brutality. First was his violation of traditional Jewish laws. He built a theater and an amphitheater in Jerusalem (neither has yet been discovered by archaeologists), where he staged gladiatorial games and other forms of entertainment that were foreign to Judaism and inimical to many Jews. He built pagan cities and temples and seemed to favor the pagan and Samaritan elements in the population over the Jews. Many of his judicial and administrative enactments were not in accordance with Jewish law. Certain elements in the population were offended at his introduction of Roman trophies into the Temple and his erection of a golden eagle over its entrance.

The second reason for the general dislike of Herod was his oppressive taxation. Someone had to pay for Herod's munificent benefactions to the cities of the East, generous gifts to the Romans, and extravagant building projects at home. The Jewish citizens of Herod's kingdom had to foot the bill, and they objected.

Herod's death released the accumulated passions and frustration of the people who had been kept in check by his brutality. As Herod lay on his deathbed, two pious men and their followers removed the eagle that Herod had erected over the entrance to the Temple and hacked the statue to pieces. Immediately after Herod's death, riots and rebellions broke out in Jerusalem, Judaea, Galilee, and the Transjordan (Perea). The leaders of the riots had diverse goals. Some were simply venting their anger at a hated and feared regime; others were eager to profit from a period of chaos and disorder; still others dreamed of ridding themselves of Roman rule and proclaiming themselves king.

These riots illustrate the underside of Herodian rule. Herod's high taxes and extravagant spending caused, or at least accelerated, the impoverishment of a broad section of the population. A clear sign of social distress was the resurgence of brigandage—landless men marauded the countryside in groups and were either hailed by the peasants as heroes or hunted as villains. This phenomenon had surfaced earlier, in the decades after Pompey's conquest in 63 B.C.E. Although Pompey himself had respected the Temple and the property of the Jews, the governors he left behind (Gabinius and Crassus) did not. They engaged in robbery and pillage; Crassus even plundered the Temple. Perhaps as a result of these depredations, Galilee was almost overrun by brigands. In 47/6 B.C.E. Herod routed and suppressed the brigands. Several years later, they resurfaced and Herod again suppressed them. Brigandage reemerged in the years after Herod's death, especially, as we shall see, in the period from 44 C.E. to the outbreak of the Jewish rebellion against Rome in 66 C.E. The impoverishment of the country and its consequent social distress were an unfortunate legacy of Herod the Great.

Judaea was governed by Roman prefects from 6 C.E. on. Of the six or seven Roman prefects who were the governors, most are just names to us. The exception is the Roman prefect Pontius Pilate (ca. 26–36 C.E.). Pilate receives a negative assessment in the Gospels, in Philo, as well as in Josephus. According to the Christian Gospels, Pilate massacred a group of Galileans (Luke 13:1) and brutally suppressed a rebellion (Mark 15:7), quite aside from crucifying Jesus. According to Philo, Pilate introduced into Herod's former palace in Jerusalem some golden shields inscribed with the name of the emperor Tiberius. The Jews objected strenuously because they felt that any object associated with emperor worship, not to mention emperor worship itself, was idolatrous and an offense against the Jewish religion. Previous Roman governors had respected Jewish sensitivities in this matter, but Pilate did not. After being petitioned by the Jews, the emperor ordered Pilate to remove the shields from Jerusalem and to deposit them in the temple of Augustus in Caesarea, a mixed Jewish-pagan city. Josephus narrates a similar incident (or perhaps a different version of the same incident) involving the importation of military standards (which of course contained images) into Jerusalem. The people protested loudly, saying they would rather die than see the ancestral law violated. Pilate relented and ordered the images to be removed. Ultimately, Pilate was removed from office when Jews complained enough to his superiors.

The Romans realized that Judaism was unlike the numerous other native religions of the empire; the Jews refused to worship any god but their own, refused to acknowledge the emperor's right to divine honors, refused to tolerate images in public places and buildings, and refused to perform any sort of work every seventh day. Aware of these peculiarities, the Romans permitted Jewish citizens to refrain from participation in pagan ceremonies; allowed priests of the Jerusalem Temple to offer sacrifices on behalf of, rather than to, the emperor; minted coins in Judaea without images (even if many of the coins that circulated in the country were minted elsewhere and bore images); exempted the Jews from military service; and ensured that they would not be called to court on the Sabbath or lose any official benefits as a result of their Sabbath observances. In many of the cities of the East, the Romans authorized the Jews to create *politeumata*, autonomous ethnic communities, which afforded the Jews the opportunity for communal self-government.

The mad emperor Caligula and his legate in Egypt withdrew, or attempted to withdraw, these rights and privileges. Riots erupted first in Alexandria—the "Greeks" (that is, the Greek-speaking population of the city, most of whom were not "Greek" at all) against the Jews. Exactly who or what started the riots is not clear. The root cause of the conflict, however, was the ambiguous status of the city's Jews. On the one hand, the Alexandrians resented the Jewish *politeuma* and regarded it as a diminution of the prestige and autonomy of their own city. On the other hand, the Jews thought that membership in their own *politeuma* should confer on them the same rights and privileges the citizens of the city had. The result of these conflicting claims was bloodshed and destruction. Aided by the Roman governor of Egypt, the Greeks attacked the Jews, pillaged Jewish property, desecrated or destroyed Jewish synagogues, and herded the Jews into a "ghetto." The Jews were hardly passive during these events, resisting both militarily and diplomatically. The most distinguished Jew of the city, the philosopher Philo, led a delegation to the emperor to argue the Jewish cause.

The troubles in Alexandria were settled by Claudius, Caligula's successor, who ordered both the Jews and the Greeks to return to the status quo: The Jews were to maintain their *politeuma* but were not to ask for more rights than were their due.

Perhaps one of the most significant aspects of these events was the refusal of the Jews even to consider rebellion against the empire. In Alexandria, the Jews took up arms only in self-defense and only with reluctance—at least that is what Philo tells us. The Jews directed their fighting against their enemies, not against the emperor or the Roman Empire.

The years after Caligula's reign saw the growth of violent resistance to Roman rule. Caligula's madness seems to have driven home the point that the beneficence of Roman rule was not secure, and that the only way to ensure the safety and sanctity of the Temple was to expel the Romans from the country and to remove those Jews who actively supported them.

This process might have been prevented had Agrippa I been blessed with as long a reign as his grandfather Herod the Great. Instead, Agrippa I ruled for only three years (41–44 C.E.). Despite his short reign, he was a popular king; both Josephus and rabbinic literature have only nice things to say about him. In some respects he resembled his grandfather. He was a wily and able politician. He sponsored pagan games at Caesarea and bestowed magnificent gifts on Beirut, a pagan city. But unlike Herod, he was not criticized for these donations, for in other respects he was Herod's superior. He lacked Herod's brutality. Whereas Herod had refrained from flouting traditional Jewish laws in the Jewish areas of his domain, Agrippa was conspicuous for observing them. In the political sphere, he tried to attain a modest degree of independence from Rome. He even began the construction of a new wall on the northern side of Jerusalem; had it been completed, Josephus says, the city would have been impregnable during the Jewish revolt that erupted in 66 C.E.

Had Agrippa reigned a long time, perhaps the disaffected elements in Judaea would have been reconciled again to foreign dominion. On Agrippa's death in 44 C.E., however, Judaea once again became the domain of the Roman procurators. There was no longer a Jewish authority who, despite ultimate subservience to Rome, could satisfy Jewish nationalist aspirations. Moreover, the procurators after 44 C.E. were incompetent and insensitive at best, corrupt and wicked at worst.

In the fall of 66 C.E., after Gessius Florus (who would be the last of the procurators) had stolen money from the Temple treasury (for overdue taxes, he claimed), a particularly violent riot led to the massacre of the Roman garrison in Jerusalem. The governor of Syria intervened, but even he failed to restore the peace. He was forced to withdraw from Jerusalem, suffering a major defeat. The Jews of Judaea had rebelled against the Roman Empire.

The Great Revolt of 66–70 C.E. was in large part, especially in its early phases, a civil struggle among Jews—between the rich and the poor, between the upper classes and the lower, between the city dwellers and the country folk. Besides the brigandage that had increased significantly in the countryside after Agrippa I's death in 44 C.E., Jerusalem too was racked by social turmoil. Aristocrats in Jerusalem and throughout the country maintained bands of armed retainers to threaten their opponents and to work for their own interests. Within the priesthood there was strife and violence between the upper and the lower clergy. Peasants in Galilee in 66–67 C.E. wanted nothing more than to attack and loot Sepphoris, Tiberias, and Gabara, the three largest settlements of the district. After the Great Revolt began in 66 C.E., many peasants of both Galilee and Judaea fled to Jerusalem, where they turned on both the city aristocracy and the priestly elite. These tensions within Jewish society often surfaced violently during the Great Revolt. For many of the participants in the war, the primary enemies were not Roman but Jewish.

The revolutionaries may also have believed that they were living at the threshold of the end time. Josephus writes that "what more than all else incited them to the war was an ambiguous oracle . . . found in their sacred scriptures, to the effect that at that time one from their country would become ruler of the world." In the years immediately preceding the revolt, many "eschatological prophets" were active, predicting the imminent approach of the end time or attempting, by means of a symbolic action (for example, splitting the Jordan River), to hasten or implement its arrival.

The social tensions and eschatological expectations that drove Judaea to war with Rome were not uniquely Jewish. In fact the war of 66–70 C.E. follows a pattern evident in other native rebellions against the Roman Empire. Tensions between rich and poor and between city and country were endemic to ancient society and often contributed to such rebellions.

Like the uprising in Judaea, other native rebellions were often led by aristocrats, although peasants, day laborers, and landless poor formed the bulk of the revolutionary army. As so often happens in revolutions ancient and modern, in its initial phases the struggle is led by aristocratic (or bourgeois) elements, which, as the struggle continues, are ousted, usually with great violence, by more-extremist (or proletarian) groups. Like the Jews, other rebels in antiquity too dreamed of subjugating the universal Roman Empire. The revolt of the Gauls in 69 C.E. was prompted in part by a Druid prediction that Rome would be destroyed and that the rule of the empire would devolve on the tribes of Transalpine Gaul. The Jewish revolt was, therefore, hardly unique in the annals of Rome.

In the fall of 66 C.E., no one knew that a war between the Jews and the Romans was imminent. Some revolutionaries, perhaps, were dreaming of a final conflict, but even they had no way of knowing precisely when the conflict would erupt or what form it would take.

The spark was provided by the procurator Florus when he seized seventeen talents from the Temple treasury to compensate, he said, for uncollected back taxes. This act was not significantly worse than the depredations and misdeeds of previous procurators, and the riot it provoked was not significantly worse than the riots that had erupted during the tenures of previous procurators.

This riot, however, turned into the first act of a war because it came at the end of a period of almost twenty years of unrelieved tension and lawlessness. When Florus brutally suppressed the riot, the people responded with even greater intensity, with the result that Florus had to flee the city.

At this point various revolutionary factions stepped forward. It is difficult to determine the interrelationship of all these groups. Some scholars argue that all the anti-Roman forces formed in the aggregate a single "war party," which for purposes of convenience can be called Zealots, after its most distinctive constituent group. Others argue that no single "war party" ever existed and that each of the groups and figures had its own history. The diverse groups shared a common willingness to fight the Romans but differed from one another in many respects, which explains why they spent so much time fighting one another. The latter interpretation is much more plausible than the former.

At the outbreak of the war, an aristocratic priestly revolutionary party, led initially by Eleazar, son of the high priest Ananias, seems to have controlled the revolution. Eleazar suspended the sacrifice for the welfare of the emperor and the Roman Empire, which until then had been offered every day in the Temple. This act was tantamount to a declaration of war. As if to emphasize the point, after Florus retreated, Eleazar and his supporters turned on the Roman garrisons Florus had left in the city, and besieged them.

These priestly revolutionaries were soon eclipsed by another group, the Sicarii, led by one Menahem. In the fall of 66 C.E., the Sicarii entered Jerusalem. In addition to attacking the Roman forces that remained in the city, however, the Sicarii also attacked the Jewish aristocracy. They looted the homes of the well-to-do and massacred many of the nobility; the most prominent of their victims was Ananias the high priest, the father of Eleazar, who had led the priestly revolutionaries. The priestly group, headquartered in the Temple, fought back and killed the Sicarii leader, Menahem. Menahem's followers then fled to Masada, one of Herod's great fortresses, in the Judaean wilderness. There they remained for the rest of the war, doing nothing to help the struggle. Other bands of fighters, however, were already, or would soon become, active in Jerusalem.

Revolutionary ardor also spread outside Jerusalem. In Caesarea and in many other cities of Palestine and Syria, Jews and pagans attacked each other. The hostility toward pagans and paganism that motivated the revolutionaries in Jerusalem seems also to have motivated Jews throughout the country. The pagans, for their part, gave vent to the same animosities that had exploded in the anti-Jewish riots in Alexandria thirty years earlier.

The Roman governor of Syria went to Judaea to restore order, but after entering Jerusalem, he decided that he was not strong enough to take the Temple from the revolutionaries. In the course of his withdrawal, his troops were beset by the Jews and had to abandon much of their equipment.

After the defeat of the Roman governor-general of Syria, the revolutionaries, led by the priestly revolutionary party, assigned generals to each district in the country. Most of the commissioned generals were priests. Their task was to prepare the country for war, in anticipation of either negotiations or hostilities with the Romans.

With the appearance of the Roman army led by the Roman general Vespasian, in the summer of 67 C.E., the northern revolutionary army of Josephus all but disappeared, and the Romans had little difficulty in subduing Galilee. Only one location gave them trouble, the fortress of Jotapata. It held out for almost seven weeks before falling to the Roman assault. Galilee had been pacified.

The revolutionaries in the Golan congregated at Gamla, but after some fierce fighting, that fortress too was taken. The entire northern part of the country was once again brought under Roman rule.

After taking a winter break, Vespasian resumed operations in the spring of 68 C.E. and by early summer had pacified the entire countryside; Jerusalem alone (and some isolated fortresses, notably Masada) remained in the hands of the rebels. Everything seemed prepared for an immediate attack on Jerusalem, but during the summer of 68 Vespasian learned of the emperor Nero's assassination. The death of a reigning emperor meant that Vespasian's commission as general expired; accordingly, he discontinued his military activities. The cessation was extended because in the summer of 69, Vespasian had himself proclaimed emperor. He left Judaea to establish his own imperial power in Rome. By the end of the year 69 he was successful. In the spring of 70, Vespasian once again turned his attention to the situation in Judaea.

The two-year hiatus should have been a great boon to the revolutionaries in Jerusalem, allowing them time to organize their forces, fortify the city, lay away provisions, and so on. But the opposite was the case. As the refugees entered Jerusalem from the countryside, internecine strife intensified. The party of Zealots, consisting for the most part of Judaean peasants, emerged. They turned against the aristocratic priests, who until that point had been in charge of the war, and appointed a new high priest by lot.

Thus 68 C.E. was spent in fighting between the aristocratic (or "moderate") revolutionary groups and the more radical proletarian ones. The latter triumphed. In 69 the radical revolutionaries themselves fell to attacking one another. John of Gischala, supported by his contingent of Galileans, turned on his former allies, the Zealots, and ultimately succeeded in ousting their leader and bringing them under his control. But a new revolutionary faction then emerged, led by Simon ben Giora, a native of Gerasa (a city of the Transjordan). Like the Zealots, he had a radical social program and drew much of his support from freed slaves. The intense fighting among these various groups had disastrous consequences. Large stocks of grain and other provisions were destroyed. When the Roman siege began in earnest in 70 C.E., a famine soon followed.

Vespasian had by then securely established himself as emperor and wanted a resounding success to legitimate his new dynasty. In his propaganda, Vespasian had depicted himself as the savior of the empire, the man who, after a year and a half of political chaos, had restored order and stability. There was no better way to prove this point than to bring to a successful conclusion the protracted war in Judaea. In order to emphasize the dynastic implications of the victory, Vespasian appointed his son Titus to command the Roman army in its assault on the holy city of the Jews. In the spring of 70 C.E. the Romans, under Titus, besieged the city and cut off all supplies and all means of escape.

The fighting for the city and the Temple was intense. The major rallying point of the revolutionaries and, consequently, the major target of the Romans was the Temple. The Temple was a veritable fortress, but it still was a temple.

The Romans advanced methodically toward their goal. The Jews had been weakened by famine and internecine strife, and although Titus made some serious tactical errors in prosecuting the siege, the Roman victory was only a matter of time. Each of the city's three protective walls was breached in turn, and the Romans finally found themselves, by mid-summer 70 C.E., just outside the sacred precincts.

At this point, according to Josephus, Titus called a meeting of his general staff and asked for advice. What should he do with the Jewish Temple? Some of his adjutants argued that it should be destroyed because as long as it was left standing, it would serve as a focal point for anti-Roman agitation. According to the "rules of war" in antiquity, temples were not to be molested, but this Temple had become a fortress and therefore was a fair military target. No opprobrium would be attached to its destruction. Titus, however, argued that the Temple should be preserved as a monument to Roman magnanimity.

But Titus's plan was thwarted. On the day after the meeting, a soldier acting against orders tossed a firebrand into the sanctuary, and flames shot up, immediately out of control. On the tenth of the month of Av (in rabbinic chronology on the ninth), late August 70 C.E., the Temple was destroyed. Titus and his troops spent the next month subduing the rest of the city and collecting loot as the reward for their labors.

Upon his return to Rome in 71 C.E., Titus celebrated a joint triumph with his father, the emperor Vespasian. In the triumphal procession were the enemy leaders Simon ben Giora and John of Gischala and various objects from the Temple (notably the menorah, table, and trumpets). Simon was beheaded, John was probably enslaved, and the sacred objects were deposited in the Temple of Peace in Rome. Two triumphal arches were erected in Rome in the following years to celebrate the victory; one the Arch of Titus, with its famous depiction of the sacred objects from the Temple carried in the procession. The other arch, which is now destroyed, bore the following inscription:

> The senate and people of Rome [dedicate this arch] to the emperor Titus . . .
> because with the guidance and plans of his father, and under his auspices, he
> subdued the Jewish people and destroyed the city of Jerusalem, which all
> generals, kings and peoples before him had either attacked without success
> or left entirely unassailed.[1]

To punish the Jews for the war the Romans imposed the *fiscus Judaicus*, the "Jewish tax." The half-shekel tax, which Jews throughout the empire had formerly contributed to the Temple in Jerusalem, was now collected for the Temple of Jupiter Capitolinus in Rome. The imposition of this tax, collected throughout the empire until at least the middle of the second century C.E., shows that the Romans regarded all the Jews of the empire as partly responsible for the war.

The Romans did not, however, institute other harsh measures against the Jews. They confiscated much Jewish land in Judaea, distributing it to their soldiers and to Jewish collaborators, but that was a normal procedure after a war. They did not engage in religious persecution or strip the Jews of their rights.

The Jewish revolt was not a reaction to an unmistakable threat or provocation by the state. In the fall of 66, the Jews of Palestine went to war against the Roman Empire—as the result of the social tensions; impoverishment of large sections of the economy; religious speculations about the imminent arrival of the end time and the messianic redeemer; nationalist stirrings against foreign rule; and the incompetent and insensitive administration of the procurators. The war was characterized by internecine fighting. The fighting was not only between revolutionary groups but also between the revolutionaries and large segments of the populace. Many Jews had no desire to participate in the struggle. It was one thing to riot against the procurator, quite another to rebel against the Roman Empire. Wealthy and poor alike were afraid that war would mean the loss of everything they had, and since the Romans had not done anything intolerable, there was no compelling reason to go to war. This attitude was widespread. Aside from Jerusalem, only Gamla was the site of fierce fighting. Galilee Perea (the Transjordan), the coast, Idumea—all these saw some anti-Roman activity, but all were quickly and easily pacified immediately upon the arrival of the Roman forces. Jerusalem was the seat of the rebellion: where it began, where it ended, and the stronghold of the vast majority of the combatants.

The causes of the failure of the war are not hard to see. The war began with little advance planning, the revolutionaries were badly divided, and the timing was off. Had they rebelled a few years earlier, while the Romans were fighting the Parthians, the rebels might have been able to succeed at least to the point of exacting various concessions from the Romans in return for their surrender. Had they waited two years—after Nero's assassination in 68 C.E.—their odds would have been immeasurably better. At that time the empire was in chaos; the succession was vigorously disputed; Gaul had risen in revolt. That would have been a perfect moment for revolt, but for the Jews it came too late.

The destruction of the Temple did not mean the end of Judaism, however. The theological and religious crisis the destruction caused seems to have been much less severe than that experienced in the aftermath of the Babylonian destruction of the First Temple in 586 B.C.E., perhaps because during the Second Temple period new Jewish institutions and ideologies had been created that prepared Judaism for a time when the Temple and the sacrificial cult would no longer exist. By the time the Second Temple was destroyed, the Temple itself had been supplemented by synagogues, the priests had been supplemented by scholars, the sacrificial cult had been supplemented by prayer and the study of the Torah, and reliance on the intermediation of the Temple priesthood had been supplemented by a piety that emphasized the observance of the commandments of the Torah by every Jew.

In short, the path to the future was already clearly marked. The sufferings of this world would be compensated by rewards in the hereafter. The disgrace of Rome's triumph over the God of Israel and destruction of the Temple would be effaced by the glory of the new kingdom to be established by God for his people in the end time. The cessation of the sacrificial cult did not mean estrangement from God, since God could be worshiped through good deeds, prayer, the observance of the commandments, and the study of the Torah. Synagogues could take the place of the Temple, and rabbis could take the place of the priests. These were the responses of the Jews to the catastrophe of 70 C.E. and were greatly elaborated during the following centuries.

Notes

1. Translated in Naphtali Lewis and Meyer Reinhold, *Roman Civilization Sourcebook II: The Empire* (New York: Harper & Row, 1966), p. 92.

Suggested Readings

Cohen, S. J. D., *From the Maccabees to the Mishnah.* Philadelphia: Westminster Press, 1987.

Shanks, H., ed. *Ancient Israel.* Englewood Cliffs, N.J.: Prentice Hall, 1988.

Shanks, H., ed., *Christianity and Rabbinic Judaism* Washington, D.C.: Biblical Archaeology Society, 1992.

Smallwood, E. M., *The Jews Under Roman Rule.* Leiden: Brill, 1976.

4

The Literature
of the Rabbis

BURTON L. VISOTZKY

WHEN THE ROMAN LEGIONS LEFT the Jerusalem Temple in smoking ruins in 70 C.E., a new chapter began in Jewish history and literature. The daily and festival animal offerings had been the cornerstone of the priestly religion that most Jews observed. Before the destruction, thanksgiving, purification, atonement, and the calendar cycle were all achieved through the bringing of animal and grain gifts to God at the altar in Jerusalem. The central text of Jewish tradition (the Torah, or Five Books of Moses) was a document that attested to the centrality of the sacrificial cult in Jerusalem. The disastrous results of the Jewish rebellion against Rome brought an end to the centrality of the Temple altar as the prime locus for Jewish religious practice.

Even before the destruction of the Temple, there had been some movement within Judaism away from the Jerusalem center. Groups such as the community at Qumran and the nascent Christian community showed some opposition to the priesthood that ran the Temple cult. The founding of synagogues as places of prayer and study away from the Jerusalem sanctuary had already taken place while the Temple still stood. Nonpriestly leadership of charismatic, military, and intellectual groups was budding. The canonization of a Bible that included exilic books and works of prophets who fiercely denounced the potential emptiness of the priestly sacrificial cult had also begun in earnest.

The first century following the destruction of the Temple found these phenomena serving as the cornerstones of a new form of Judaism. While consistently claiming continuity with the sacrificial cult, Judaism continued to develop nonpriestly leadership of an intellectual and charismatic nature. This leadership cut across class and economic bonds to form a category of religious adepts who led more by received knowledge and teaching than by family lineage or priestly prerogative. The final canonization of Scripture gave these master teachers (rabbis) the opportunity to focus their traditions around and apart from the Bible. They passed on their traditions and exegeses of the Bible in disciple circles, which began to exert an increasingly prominent judicial role in the Palestinian Jewish community. Finally, the lack of a temple allowed the places of prayer and study to come to the fore as loci par excellence for the expression of Judaism.

The synagogue *(bet hakenesset)* became the place for Jewish worship—prayer and study. It appealed to a fairly large segment of the Jewish population, and there they gathered on Sabbaths, New Moons, and Jewish festivals for celebrations of Judaism that had previously taken place at the Jerusalem sanctuary. A second locus, more firmly under control of the rabbinic leadership, was the academy *(bet midrash)*. Whether taking place in homes and market stalls or in peripatetic master-disciple sessions, study of received tradition and biblical exegesis became the method for developing Jewish law, lore, and theology.

This formative period of Jewish history was buffeted by two military debacles subsequent to the disastrous rebellion of 66–70 C.E. that had brought about the destruction of the Jerusalem Temple. Widespread rioting in 115–117 C.E., often referred to as the War of the Diaspora, left thousands of dead in Jewish communities throughout the Roman world. The influence of those communities within their local Hellenic spheres was accordingly diminished for some time. Then, again in Palestine, a second revolt against Roman rule erupted in the years 132–135 C.E. This revolt, under the apparent military leadership of Simon ben Cosiba (Bar Kokhba), also ended in crushing defeat for the Jews.

The utter destruction of Jewish military pretensions further paved the way for the rabbis. Their regimen of religious observance, study, teaching, and judging on local levels gave them a firm (if not universal) foothold in the Jewish community. The Roman government's countenance of the Jewish patriarch of Palestine and the latter's good relations with the rabbinic community during the second and third centuries further strengthened the rabbinization of Judaism following the destruction of the Temple. One other phenomenon that merits mention was the shift in population following the two wars against Rome. The Jerusalem Temple had been the religious focus of a Judaean, agrarian people, but by the end of the second century, Judaism had become a largely Galilean, urban-centered, synagogue, and rabbinic movement.

Tannaitic Literature

In the two centuries following the destruction, the rabbis had an enormous task. They sought to preserve Judaism and keep its vital links with the Torah and the now-defunct Temple cult. At the same time, they were required to expand and refocus Jewish practice to encompass the growing trends toward scholasticism, synagogue, and rabbinic leadership. Without a Jerusalem Temple as the focal point for Jewish cultic practice, the rabbis shifted the loci to communities constituted around a canon (the Bible), which rabbinic (and not priestly) leadership interpreted to guarantee continuity with the very cult these communities had replaced. From the destruction of the Temple in 70 C.E., through the redaction of their own loose canon of rabbinic literature—the Oral Torah—by the mid–third century, the rabbis largely met that task.

One of the primary means the rabbis had of preserving continuity with the moribund priestly cult was commentary on the Torah, which first enshrined it and then preserved its memory. One of the results of this commentary, a constant meditation of the Torah as the revelatory word of God, was to keep the Temple cult alive to Jewish memory. But as with all acts of memory, the Temple in recollection differed from what it had been in practice. In looking backward, in constantly examining and reexamining every Torah rule about the cult, the rabbis made the Temple of memory more a rabbinic phenomenon than a priestly one. In a subtle yet persistent way, the rabbis' commentary on the cultic passages and their constant reference to the Temple usurped for themselves the very priesthood. In the eyes and ears of their listeners and disciples, the rabbis became the inheritors of the Temple cult and the natural, legitimate continuers of Jewish tradition.

At the same time, the rabbis were experimenting with their newfound authority in another fashion. Even as they based their power within Scripture, through their various interpretations and exegeses of matters practical (Halakhic) and theological (Aggadic), the rabbis gave voice to another form of their own authority. Although they claimed continuity and legitimacy by basing their teachings in the authority of biblical Scripture ("as it is written . . ."; "as it is said . . ."), they also found their own independent voice of authority ("Rabbi so-and-so says . . ."). One source of their authority was biblical exegesis, the adept interpretation of Scripture designed to prove through hermeneutic means that the rabbinic agenda was scripturally determined.

The other source of their authority was the "traditions of the fathers"— an unbroken chain of authoritative teaching that linked them with the Jewish community of the Second Temple, perhaps as far back as the latter prophets. The further back the rabbis could trace this intellectual (and nonscriptural) lineage, the better. Since the teachings were transmitted from master to disciple, they gave a very strong buttress to rabbinic claims of authority, one that was difficult to refute. Not surprisingly, rabbinic literature claims sources of tradition as far back as Moses at Sinai. This type of tradition was also well known in the philosophic schools of the Hellenistic world and gave the rabbis authority as teachers within the broader Greco-Roman world.

Each of these types of authoritative teachings found voice within the rabbinic literature of the early period. Both were claimed by the rabbinic community as Oral Torah, transmitted alongside and equal in authority to the written Torah, which detailed the priestly cult. The exegetic materials, in particular those on the latter four books of the Torah, came to redaction by the mid–third century in a form close to what we have today. These works are called the Tannaitic or Halakhic midrashim. They will be discussed in detail in this chapter but merit mention now, since their earliest oral formation precedes or is concomitant with the other type of rabbinic literature.

That other type, too, is Tannaitic and primarily Halakhic in nature. Before it is described in detail, a brief definition of some terms is in order. "Tannaitic" refers to the literature of the rabbis of the first two centuries C.E. A *tanna* (singular) is a rabbi and/or oral reciter of traditions who lived in the era circa 70–250. "Halakhic" refers to rabbinic literature concerned primarily with behavioral norms, or Halakhah (singular). The *tannaim* (plural) studied Halakhah by exegesis (midrash, singular) of Scripture, which yielded Halakhic or Tannaitic midrashim (plural). These collections of exegeses may have also included theological, nonbehavioral, folkloristic, and legendary materials called Aggadah. Aggadic midrash consists of scriptural exegesis that yields nonbehavioral results. To summarize, the rabbis of the early period *(tannaim)* studied Scripture (using midrash), which yielded behavioral (Halakhic) or other (Aggadic) teachings.

Yet these same rabbis often made pronouncements based on their own, rather than biblical, authority. This form was not midrash but took its own separate and independent organization. Often, the midrash and the separate materials quoted the same rabbis, even the same oral sources of these exegeses and traditions. Sometimes a rabbinic exegesis was recast as a rabbinic pronouncement. Sometimes, a tradition was justified by rabbinic exegesis. Inevitably, by the time the Tannaitic literature was edited and redacted in the early third century, it was very difficult to untangle the complicated relationships and the give-and-take between exegetic and traditional pronouncements. The Tannaitic midrashim often quote authoritative rabbinic pronouncements, whereas the edited works of those pronouncements quote exegeses or rabbinic statements found also in the Tannaitic midrashim.

Mishnah and Tosefta

The edited works of authoritative rabbinic pronouncements based on traditions and, to a much lesser extent, some of the earlier exegeses compose a set of rabbinic materials known today as Mishnah and Tosefta. The Mishnah was edited in its roughly final form around the year 200 C.E. by the patriarch of the Palestinian Jewish community, a scholar and Roman grandee named Judah. His esteem and authority in the rabbinic community are best exemplified by his designation in subsequent literature as simply "Rabbi." Rabbi Judah, also known in Hebrew as Yehudah HaNasi (Judah the Patriarch), was rabbi par excellence. Not only did he rule the Jewish community with the approval of Rome; he also led the rabbinic community and established the power of its second Torah, the Oral Torah, through the redaction and publication of the Mishnah.

The Mishnah was an independent document of rabbinic authority. It was not organized according to biblical passages but by six broad socioanthropological categories. Thus rabbinic pronouncements are summarized under the rubrics: Agriculture (Zeraim), Calendar (Moed), Women (Nashim), Torts (Nezikin), Taboos (Tohorot), and Sacred Things (Kodashim). Each of the broader orders (sedarim, the plural of seder) has subcategories. Calendar (Moed), for example, has the following subdivisions: Sabbath, Borders for Sabbath Movement (Eruvin), Passover, Sheqel (a temple coin) Offerings, Day of Atonement Ritual (Yoma), Festival of Booths (Sukkah), Lesser Holiday Rulings (Betza), New Year (Rosh HaShanah), Fast Days (Taanit), Purim (Megillah), Intermediate Days of Festivals (Moed Katan), and Festival Offerings (Hagigah).

Each order (seder) is broken down into various tractates (masechet, sing.) and each tractate into appropriate chapters. There are sixty-three tractates among the six orders of Mishnah.

It is said that Yehudah HaNasi's predecessors had already begun the process of organizing the oral traditions of the rabbinic community into earlier recensions of the Mishnah. Thus the second-century sage, Rabbi Aqiba, is reputed to have gathered and sorted traditions, much as one would gather and sort grain. Aqiba's disciple, Rabbi Meir, is said to have continued the process of winnowing and refinement. It was left to the third generation of editorial activity, under Yehudah HaNasi, to finalize and "publish" the work called Mishnah (Repetition or Second [Torah]).

The revolutionary nature of the Mishnah may be seen in part from its very organization into orders and tractates. No longer dependent upon Scripture, indeed only occasionally quoting it as a source of support, Rabbi's Mishnah served to strengthen the nascent rabbinic authority. Even as the Mishnah seemingly eschewed biblical domination, it embraced the Temple cult. The order of Sacred Things was all about the defunct Temple. The order of Taboos dealt with issues of ritual fitness, originally legislated by the Pentateuchal book of Leviticus for the priests in the sanctuary. Even the order on Calendar contained laws pertaining to the festival sacrifices, not offered since the Temple had been destroyed. Again and again the Mishnah makes the issues of the priesthood the issues of the rabbis. Again and again, one is left with the impression that the rabbis replace the priests as Israel's authentic leadership.

Other characteristics of the Mishnah deserve notice. It is very difficult to classify as a work of literature. Although it deals regularly with law (Halakhah), it is by no means a normative law code. On the contrary, it revels in contradictory rulings, recording minority opinions alongside the majority ones. Perhaps that practice merely recounts the value of case law in the Mishnaic worldview—each precedent needs to be on record, so that a subsequent jurist will have the right to rule other than according to the earlier majority opinion. This spirit of continuing change in Jewish law, an organic and fresh approach for each generation of jurists, is very much in keeping with the rabbinic view that the revelation that their Oral Torah embodied was an ongoing and not static process.

If it is difficult to classify the Mishnah in a category of ancient literature, it is equally difficult to guess at its intended function. In addition to recording disputes about case law, the Mishnah offers a schematized version of certain historic events—a kind of *Heilsgeschichte,* sacred history— rather than any modern notion of history. The Mishnah also contains moral and ethical maxims, scattered exegeses of biblical passages, and even *aggadot,* or legends about characters of the Bible. Stories about the rabbis and their practices (Halakhic and otherwise) may also be found in the corpus of Mishnah.

The Mishnah is terse, seemingly formulated for memorization, with the mnemonics still apparent in certain tractates. Yet the consistent reediting of Mishnah away from mnemonic organization and toward a topical one raises questions about the final document that Rabbi Yehudah HaNasi prepared for publication. Was the Mishnah published "orally" by recitation of the memory expert of the academy? Or might it have been a written document (despite its "Oral Torah" status) at its final recension? For many centuries the oral status of Mishnah has been unquestioned, supported by generations of rabbinic scholars who knew the text by memory. Recent studies, however, have questioned the absolute oral nature of the document. Since it is clear that within the rabbinic community of the second and third centuries there were rabbi-scholars who read and wrote and there were those who did not, it is imaginable that there were written and oral recensions of the Mishnah in circulation. In any case, the Mishnah became the core work of rabbinic literature for the next few centuries. Much of the literary production of the rabbis was bent to commentary, explication, and expansion of this crucial text.

The first of these works was a companion piece to the Mishnah called the Tosefta. It is generally assumed to have been edited in early- to mid- third-century Palestine. It, too, is organized into six orders and sixty-three tractates. The Tosefta often quotes Mishnah; therefore, it cannot be understood outside the context of the Mishnah. However, the Tosefta sometimes contradicts the rulings of the Mishnah. Furthermore, the Tosefta repeatedly expands the purview of the Mishnah's legal interests and, through such a shift, subtly alters the range of Halakhic opinions. Much of the material in the Tosefta consists of pronouncements of the rabbis that Yehudah HaNasi did not choose in his own editorial process. It is hard to determine whether the editors of the Tosefta preserved this material for the mere sake of preservation or to undermine the Mishnah's rulings. This determination is, however, essential in understanding just how authoritative the Mishnah was in rabbinic circles.

Although it is true that the Mishnah became the document of Oral Torah upon which all others seemingly commented, it is not clear what that indicates about the legal status of the Mishnah. If the Mishnah was consistently overturned by the Tosefta and later commentaries, it does not seem to have carried much absolute weight in the rabbinic world. However, where the Halakhic midrashim (to be discussed) indicate scriptural authority for the same rulings that the Mishnah offers on rabbinic authority, it would seem that these rulings are unimpeachable. The Tosefta offers some caution in the reification of the Mishnah and forces one to ask whether the Tannaitic midrashim perhaps were redacted to buttress the Mishnah's undermined authority. Did those midrashim provide scriptural support for Yehudah HaNasi's views, or did they redact the very sources that Rabbi Yehudah used for his rabbinic pronouncements?

Tannaitic Midrashim

The Tannaitic midrashim are arranged as commentaries on the Torah, covering the books of Exodus, Leviticus, Numbers, and Deuteronomy. It is generally assumed that there is no edited Tannaitic midrash on the book of Genesis because of the preponderance of narrative and the paucity of Halakhah in that first Book of Moses. This theory is also evidenced in the Tannaitic commentary to Exodus attributed to the School of Rabbi Ishmael, which begins at Exodus 12:1, that is, at the opening of the legal materials of Exodus. Thus, the Tannaitic midrashim (despite the significant proportion of Aggadic material) are also referred to as Halakhic midrashim.

With respect to the School of Rabbi Ishmael, it was a commonplace among nineteenth-century and early-twentieth-century historians to refer to two schools of Tannaitic interpretation of Scripture: the School of Rabbi Ishmael and the School of Rabbi Aqiba. Whether these groups constituted actual schools that produced discrete texts is currently under debate. Nevertheless, there are discernible differences between the hermeneutic technique of Rabbi Aqiba and that of Rabbi Ishmael, and these differences are noticeable in the various Tannaitic midrashim attributed to their schools. There are two sets of Tannaitic midrashim for Exodus, Numbers, and Deuteronomy, which are traditionally divided between the two "schools." However, each Tannaitic midrash contains sections that appear to favor the hermeneutic rules of the other school. Rather than enforce strained identifications of each Tannaitic midrash with each school, the works will be noted by name and their content briefly described.

On the biblical book of Exodus, the *Mekilta* [collection] *of Rabbi Ishmael* covers exegesis of a large number of verses from Exodus 12 on. Since the exegeses follow the pattern of the Bible and the book of Exodus mixes narrative with law, the *Mekilta of Rabbi Ishmael* has about one-half midrash Halakhah and the other half midrash Aggadah. The latter material is replicated in the second Tannaitic commentary on Exodus, the *Mekilta of Rabbi Shimeon ben Yohai.* This work actually begins earlier in the Exodus narrative and thus contains more Aggadah. The *Mekilta of Rabbi Ishmael* does follow the legal norms of that rabbi, whereas the *Mekilta of Rabbi Shimeon* follows the norms of his teacher, Aqiba. Current scholarship favors the theory that each redaction drew on a common stock of Aggadic (nonlegal) materials, since the differences between the rabbis were limited to legal hermeneutics. That would account for the shared (often identical) Aggadic materials.

There is only one extant Tannaitic midrash on the book of Leviticus, called *Sifra deBei Rav* or *Torat Kohanim.* This work opens with a preface: the thirteen hermeneutic norms of Rabbi Ishmael. What follows is a series of close readings on a small portion of Leviticus, mostly following the opinions and exegetical methods of Aqiba. The arcane nature of the priestly material in Leviticus combines with the very laconic style of the midrash to make this one of the most inaccessible texts of rabbinic tradition.

The book of Numbers has Tannaitic commentary in the form of *Sifre Bamidbar* and a second work, *Sifre Zuta.* These works cover much of the biblical book of Numbers and deal equally with the legal and narrative sections of the book. Finally, there is the *Sifre Deuteronomy,* on the last Book of Moses. This work also covers both legal and narrative materials, sometimes with extensive Aggadic sections. There is a work called *Midrash Tannaim* on Deuteronomy, reconstructed from quotations found in medieval commentaries. It rounds out the parity of commentaries from the two "schools."

A brief exposition of the hermeneutic theories of Rabbi Aqiba and Rabbi Ishmael will help put this discussion into perspective. Rabbi Aqiba (much like the Church Father Origen a century later) believed the Torah to be a divine code, in which no word or even letter could be superfluous. Aqiba is quoted inferring Halakhot from extraneous words in a verse, from doublets, and from solecisms. He is reported in much later rabbinic literature to infer Halakhah from the letter *"vav"* (a common conjunction), and in one *aggada* he is reputed to infer Halakhah from the calligraphic adornments on certain of the Torah's letters. This extreme hermeneutic afforded Aqiba the opportunity to find virtually the entire rabbinic agenda "within Scripture."

Aqiba's colleague Rabbi Ishmael (much like the Antiochene Church Fathers of the fourth and fifth centuries) demurred. "The Torah speaks in normal human discourse," he retorted to Aqiba in *Sifre Bamidbar*. Rabbi Ishmael insisted on reading the Torah with normative reading rules and making inferences that were well within the reading strategies of the Greco-Roman rhetorical system. His list of thirteen norms appears to flow each from a situation in the Torah text itself; that is, they appear to be commonsense rules. It is well advised to remember that common sense in the second century may not seem so in the twentieth, nor may it even have seemed so to a second-century colleague. Tastes differ, reading strategies differ, Halakhic communities differ. All of these differences are apparent within the literature that constitutes the Tannaitic midrashim.

As stated above, these midrashim often touch on the scriptural passages of Halakhah that are found in the Mishnah as based on rabbinic (not midrashic) tradition. Although it has recently been suggested that these midrashim were composed for the express purpose of grounding the Mishnah in scriptural authority, and that this was done in the face of Christian ascendance in the fourth century, the majority opinion remains in favor of an early dating for the Tannaitic midrashim. Though they may have been redacted in their current form in the early third century, immediately after the Mishnah, they contain material contemporary to or predating the Mishnaic corpus. The Dead Sea Scrolls, Philo, and Josephus certainly give evidence of close exegesis of Scripture in the first century. The style of the Hebrew of the Tannaitic midrashim also argues for a dating contemporary with the Mishnah. Thus it may be concluded that these Tannaitic midrashim contain authentic early rabbinic exegeses sometimes in common with the Mishnah, but more often in addition and separate from it.

The Tannaitic corpus consists, then, of Mishnah, Tosefta, and the texts of the Tannaitic midrashim. There is one additional extant source of Tannaitic materials: the traditions quoted in the two Talmuds. We turn now to these towering works of rabbinic literature.

Amoraic Literature

Talmud

During the period following the publication of the Mishnah, the activity of the rabbinic academies focused on close study of it. The Mishnah was compared to the Tosefta, to a lesser extent to the Tannaitic midrashim, and to Tannaitic statements otherwise not redacted. These latter texts are known as *baraitot* (plural of *baraita*), non-Mishnaic apocrypha. The *baraitot* were never edited in a systematic way but are preserved, scattered among the vast compilations of commentary and other texts amassed in the rabbinic study of Mishnah. These texts themselves, many of which appear to be records of the discussions about Mishnah that took place in the rabbinic academies, were redacted into commentary on the Mishnah known as Gemara. The combination of Mishnah and Gemara together make up Talmud.

There are actually two collections called Talmud. The earlier was compiled in the fifth century in Palestine and is accordingly referred to as the Palestinian or Jerusalem Talmud. The latter (which will be discussed in detail) was edited in the late sixth century in the Jewish community of Sassanian Babylonia. It is called the Babylonian Talmud (Bavli). Rabbis of the talmudic era, that is to say, the rabbis of the Land of Israel and of Babylonia, are called *amoraim*. The talmudic era is also referred to as the Amoraic era.

Yerushalmi

We turn now to the Palestinian Talmud (Yerushalmi) to examine its importance and characteristics. It is arranged ostensibly as commentary to the Mishnah. However, large portions of the Mishnah remain entirely without Yerushalmi commentary. For example, there is no Gemara to the order Kodashin (Sacred Things), and of the entire order of Tohorot (Taboos), only chapters 1–3 of tractate Niddah (Menstrual Impurities) have commentary. Moreover, in the order of Nezikin (Torts), there is no commentary on tractates Eduyot (Testimonies), Avot (Sayings of the Fathers), or to Makkot (Stripes) chapter 3. There is also Gemara lacking to the final four chapters of tractate Shabbat in the order of Moed (Calendar). All told, there is Talmud Yerushalmi to thirty-nine of the sixty-three tractates of the Mishnah. In addition to these structural matters, certain editorial principles of the Yerushalmi should be noted before turning to that Talmud's method and content.

Many sections of the Yerushalmi appear word-for-word in more than one place. Entire segments are found in various tractates, apparently inserted on the basis of a common topic of Jewish law or by means of a common mnemonic device that links the pericope, or unit of argument, to the broader subject matter under discussion. This duplication of segments is one of a number of signs of the style of composition of the Yerushalmi. Other signs of a relatively simple style include large segments of Aggadic materials dropped into tractates. In reading the Yerushalmi one must conclude that the editorial principles are radically different from modern redaction techniques. Earlier generations of scholars often referred to the Yerushalmi's crude or unfinished style of editing. It is, rather, far more associative in nature than current Western styles of editing.

Much of the Yerushalmi's dialectic is given to harmonization of the Mishnah with other Tannaitic sources. This harmonization, combined with the exercise of finding biblical authority for statements in the Mishnah, constitutes the bulk of the Mishnaic commentary. Added to that is a variety of Aggadic material. Some of it relates to biblical characters. Most, however, consists of anecdotes and *chriae* (Greco-Roman pronouncement stories) about the rabbinic sages. This material makes up a "lives of the saints" of rabbinic Judaism. It includes didactic narratives about their exemplary lives and occasionally stories of their reputed martyrdoms. There are also many stories of case law in which local rabbis offer opinions to litigants about issues directly raised or alluded to in the Mishnah. These seemingly historic incidents often stand in contrast to the legendary accounts found in the Yerushalmi about events of the rabbinic era (e.g., Bar Kokhba's rebellion).

Bavli

Over the centuries, the Yerushalmi was far less studied than the other Talmud, the Bavli. That was due to the political and social ascendancy of the Babylonian Jewish community from talmudic times through the Middle Ages. In part, the Christianization of the West prevented the growth of the Palestinian community. In part, the laws and customs of Sassanian Babylonia proved fertile ground for the growth of rabbinic Judaism there. In any case, the Fertile Crescent provided the economic security for the Jewish community of Babylonia to support a rich complex of rabbinic academies devoted to the study of the Mishnah and rabbinic Judaism. It was during the period from the third through the seventh centuries that this rich and powerful Jewish community produced the lasting monument of rabbinic Judaism: the Babylonian Talmud.

Like the Yerushalmi, the Babylonian Talmud (Bavli) does not, in fact, contain commentary to all of the Mishnah. All told, only thirty-six or thirty-seven of the sixty-three tractates have commentary. In the order of Agriculture (Zeraim), only the first tractate, Berakhot (Blessings), is treated. There is no Talmud for tractate Sheqalim (a Temple coin) of the order Moed (Calendar), no commentary on Avot (Sayings of the Fathers) or Eduyot (Testimonies) in the order Nezikin (Torts), two and a half tractates—Middot (Measures), Kinnim (Nests), and part of Tamid (Daily Offering)—are lacking from Sacred Things (Kodashim), and all of Taboos (Tohorot) is without commentary, save tractate Niddah (Menstrual Impurities).

Despite these omissions, the Bavli is a much larger work than the Yerushalmi. In its Mishnah commentary, the harmonization of Tannaitic sources and the presentation of biblical supports are carried out with a much more extensive dialectic. There are far more Aggadic sections in the Bavli than in the Yerushalmi. Not only do sage tales proliferate, but the Bavli also has numerous places where lengthy sections of Aggadah have been inserted. Excellent examples of this phenomenon are an entire dream book inserted into the ninth chapter of tractate Berakhot and a lengthy cycle of legends about the destruction of the Second Temple inserted into the fifth chapter of tractate Gittin (Divorce). Legendary materials, including stories of primeval monsters (in tractate Sanhedrin) long suppressed in biblical accounts of Creation, abound.

Although the Bavli teems with Aggadah, its nature differs in yet other ways from the Yerushalmi. Unlike the latter, the Bavli contains traditions from *two* countries. The Tannaitic and early Amoraic traditions of the Land of Israel are well reported in the Bavli. Added to those are not only the dialectics of Babylonian rabbis but also the stories of their lives and teachings. It is clear from these accounts that the Babylonian rabbis carried a fair degree of authority within the social and political structures of Sassanian Babylonia—at least far more than did their Palestinian colleagues.

Much of the Bavli reflects the studies of the various academies in Babylonia—notably those of Sura, Pumbedita, and Nehardea. Apparently the rabbinic arguments were collected by the fifth or sixth generation of rabbinic scholars, and the long process of redaction of the Bavli began. In addition to reporting actual disagreements of Babylonian masters, the successive editors of the Talmud took earlier traditions and presented them, too, as dialogue between rabbis. It seems that the later, anonymous, editors of the Bavli consistently provided this dialectical framework as a means for redacting the many and varied traditions of their predecessors. In its latest redactions, then, dialogue is the primary means of presentation of the rabbinic materials. Indeed, even stories of the rabbis and biblical legends are often presented with dialectical interruptions. Question and answer, give-and-take, and, above all, indeterminacy are the hallmarks of the Babylonian Talmud.

In some profound way, the Bavli is an authoritative commentary on the Mishnah. Just as the Mishnah revels in many opinions, so too does the Bavli. Just as the Mishnah remains open-ended, without clear resolution—glorying in possibilities rather than firm adjudication—so too does the Babylonian Talmud. As one modern talmudic scholar has put it, it is as though the Bavli makes it clear that God's ultimate will is unknowable. All that is left to humanity is the process of argumentation. Thus, what is law for one community may not be so for another. What is minority opinion in one place is normative in another. Argument, dialectic, and constant reconsideration are the ways in which God's revelation is manifested in the folios of the Babylonian Talmud.

Early Aggadic Midrashim

During the same period in which both the Yerushalmi and Bavli were being produced, the rabbis of Palestine were also busy composing Bible commentaries. These works, based on certain books of the Bible as they were read in the synagogue liturgical cycle, or lection, tend to be odd collections. Some cover virtually every verse of the biblical book on which they are focused. Others seem to consciously ignore the content of the biblical book while paying some scant attention to the lectionary cycle. Still others seem rigidly tied to this calendar of Torah readings in the synagogue and resemble synagogue homilies. The most that can be said about the overall editorial principles for these Amoraic Aggadic midrashim (as opposed to the rather uniform approach of the Tannaitic midrashim) is that they lack uniformity. Each editor, even when sharing material with other contemporary midrashim, seems to invent anew the structure of the midrash.

Foremost among the Amoraic Aggadic midrashim is *Genesis,* or *Bereshit, Rabbah.* To review, it is a work redacted in the Amoraic period, circa 200–600 C.E. Most likely, *Genesis Rabbah,* which concentrates on lore and legend and narrative rather than on law, dates from the middle to latter part of the period. It covers the biblical book of Genesis with startling thoroughness—virtually every verse in the work is commented upon in *Genesis Rabbah.* The style of midrash is atomistic, that is, it does not afford contextual integrity to the stories. Instead, each verse is broken into small parts from which specialized meaning is derived. This form of close reading, or exegesis, is also found in the Dead Sea Scrolls at Qumran, notably in the *Pesher* (exegetical solution) to Habbakuk. In *Genesis Rabbah* each verse of Genesis is patiently explained—sometimes grammatically, sometimes allegorically, sometimes philologically. The allegories in *Genesis Rabbah* tend to relate the fragments of scriptural verses under consideration to events of the rabbis' own days or to the messianic (and sometimes apocalyptic) future.

Genesis Rabbah parses each verse into small parts. Sometimes a phrase is considered, sometimes merely an individual word. In what earmarks rabbinic hermeneutics as unusual, sometimes even parts of words or single letters are considered by the exegete. It is, however, true that Alexandrian grammarians sometimes read Homer's works with similarly odd hermeneutics in order to explain away difficulties of grammar, logic, or ethics. The rabbis, too, read the Bible with every "modern" exegetical tool

at hand in an attempt to explain away contradictions, grammatical solecisms, or perceived moral lapses of biblical heroes. Thus Abraham, for example, is most often presented as a paragon of virtue, a moral exemplar,
and as father of the monotheistic faith—although a close modern reading
of Genesis in context may call these readings into question.

This constant atomization of the narratives of Genesis into much
smaller sense units breaks up the flow of the narrative, allowing a thoroughly rabbinic agenda to be imposed in the gaps rendered in the text.
This "rabbinic Genesis" is the essence of all midrash and particularly *Genesis Rabbah*. One might conjecture that the title of the work, literally, "the
Greater Genesis," refers to this rabbanization of the biblical text. Other
theories to account for the name of the work have been offered, but over
the years efforts to explain the title have foundered against manuscript
evidence.

Genesis Rabbah, as we have it in a variety of manuscript families, that is,
groups of manuscripts with common readings, varies in length from 99 to
104 chapters—in other words, a highly expanded reading of the biblical
work. It is not at all clear what principles were used by the editors or
scribes for dividing the work into chapters. Despite a theory offered in the
twentieth century, the division into chapters does not seem to be connected to the possible lectionary cycles of the Palestinian synagogues.

A word on the various Torah reading cycles is in order at this point. In
the Babylonian Jewish community, the Torah, or Pentateuch, was read in
the course of one year, in fifty-four annual Sabbath readings in the Jewish
lunar year. This annual cycle has persisted in synagogue customs to this
day. In the Palestinian synagogues, however, there was a vogue in this period to read shorter selections of the Torah each Sabbath. Thus it took
from three to three and one-half years for the entire Torah cycle to be completed. This varying length of time was complicated by the fact that there
was no fixed custom for the so-called triennial cycle of Torah reading.
One Palestinian synagogue could be at odds with another as to the
weekly scriptural reading. A given synagogue might be in Leviticus while
its neighbor was in Deuteronomy. Although this presented a challenge to
the itinerant preacher, it did not bother the villagers of a given synagogue, who were not wont to travel very often. They heard the Torah read
through in due course, studying whatever scriptural portion came before
them in any given week.

This broad variance of local custom has confounded scholars of the
nineteenth and twentieth centuries seeking to understand the principles
behind the redaction of the Aggadic midrashim. Assuming that the various interpretations of Scripture found in these works are, in fact, related
to what was preached in synagogues and academies, one would expect a
certain correspondence between the edited midrash and the apparent lec-

tionary cycle. With the notable exception of *Pesikta deRav Kahana* (to be discussed), that is emphatically not the case. Chapter divisions in *Genesis Rabbah* seem to have more to do with word count than with subject matter or with lectionary cycle.

Genesis Rabbah covers the entire range of the biblical book from Creation through the death of Joseph. In the early materials it touches on theories of cosmology, questions of gnosticism, and Jewish mysticism. In the family narratives of Genesis the commentaries impose rabbinic values into the dynamics of the narrative. Sometimes the text serves as pretext for rabbinic polemics against paganism, gnosticism, or Christianity. Overall, rabbinic religion, law, custom, and the rabbis' Hellenistic-stoic worldview are anachronistically read back into Genesis with the pretense that the characters of the Bible lived a rabbinic Jewish life. Again, this imposition of the rabbinic agenda is typical of all the Aggadic midrashim. Since *Genesis Rabbah* is among the earliest and longest, it is well to emphasize these characteristics of Aggadic exegesis here. *Genesis Rabbah* is also the Aggadic midrash that all subsequent midrashim depend upon; they borrow from it and often rework its material for their own redactive purposes. It stands as a key work of the rabbinic canon.

Leviticus Rabbah is roughly contemporary with *Genesis Rabbah*, its provenance and date being Palestine circa 425–550. Many of the rabbis mentioned by name in *Genesis Rabbah* are also found quoted in *Leviticus Rabbah*. Yet, the work differs profoundly in chapter structure and exegetical forms. *Leviticus Rabbah* does include some very close atomistic exegeses of verses in Leviticus, but by and large it ignores the legal details of the biblical priestly document in favor of pursuing a much more freewheeling and homiletical (rather than exegetical) rabbinic agenda.

Leviticus Rabbah is composed of thirty-seven chapters, each of which shares a similar overarching structure. Furthermore, each individual chapter seems to cohere with some sort of thematic unity. Often this unity is akin to the themes of Leviticus's biblical material, but *Leviticus Rabbah* pursues the relationship to Leviticus in a metaphysical rather than exegetical fashion. Thus, in the Levitical material dealing with the laws of leprosy, the midrash pursues the theme of the evils of gossip. The connection is the biblical punishment meted out to Miriam for her gossip about her brother Moses. Even more startling, the midrashic narrator bases the link between leprosy *(metzora')* and gossip on a play on words ("gossip" in Hebrew: *motzi ra'*). Thus it is clear that the editor of *Leviticus Rabbah* actually avoids the subjects of Leviticus in favor of his own rabbinic didactic and homiletic agenda.

Each chapter of *Leviticus Rabbah* opens with a number of very highly stylized proem forms, called *petihtaot* in rabbinic Hebrew. Each *petihta* (singular) opens with a verse from the Ketuvim, or Writings, section of the Bible. This verse is then expounded in an almost stream-of-consciousness form until the midrash comes to a close by quoting the verse of Leviticus under consideration. Many critics feel the Leviticus verse was the lectionary verse being expounded in the local Palestinian synagogue and that the *petihta* form of midrash represents an authentic synagogue homily. More recently, however, scholars have determined that these are literary forms imposed by the editor of *Leviticus Rabbah* on disparate materials and serve as introductory pieces to each chapter of the midrash. Again, as in *Genesis Rabbah,* the chapters (and, therefore, these *petihta* midrashim) do not correspond to any known lectionary cycle in the Palestinian synagogue.

It is more likely that the editorial principle of the redactor of *Leviticus Rabbah* was to anthologize around various loose themes conveniently attached to verses of Scripture. These expositions are presented in the order of scriptural verses in *Leviticus Rabbah* and leave the illusion of being synagogue homilies. It should be noted, however, that the sermons of *Leviticus Rabbah* are thematic, have a beginning, middle, and end, and thus may have genuine sermons as their source. As we have them in *Leviticus Rabbah,* the work is a highly polished, self-conscious literary document that ponders the themes of Leviticus without detailed commentary on the verse-by-verse content of the biblical book.

Many entertaining tales are recorded in *Leviticus Rabbah.* Some of them are legends of the sages. Some are stories of biblical characters that are patent rabbinic expansions of the biblical narrative. Some of the material in *Leviticus Rabbah* is folklore (including at least one of Aesop's fables). It is a thoroughly entertaining work that maintains the primary goal of advancing the rabbinic agenda in the (loose) guise of Bible exegesis.

The *Pesikta deRav Kahana* is a work contemporary with *Leviticus Rabbah* and closely aligned to it in that five chapters are shared virtually verbatim. Each of these chapters focuses on scriptural readings from the book of Leviticus. These five chapters, like the others in *Pesikta deRav Kahana,* are devoted to lectionary portions from the various special Sabbaths and holiday readings. In other words, the organizing principle of *Pesikta deRav Kahana* is the liturgical calendar—a principle sought but, in fact, lacking in *Genesis Rabbah* and *Leviticus Rabbah.*

The strict organization around the liturgical-synagogal readings leaves the reader with an impression that the homiletic materials found in this midrash indeed find their origins in oral sermons. Yet, here too, literary editing has left its mark. As is always the case in midrashic literature, the oral *Sitz im Leben* (life situation) that may be behind the midrash is overshadowed by the literary form in which the midrash is transmitted.

This midrash is also notable for its transmission history. It is cited by the medievals but was unknown throughout the early modern era. In

1832 Leopold Zunz, the great German midrash scholar, postulated the existence of the work. He theorized the content and order of the midrash. By the end of the century, manuscripts of *Pesikta deRav Kahana* had been discovered that proved Zunz's theories in every particular except chapter order. When a new, critical edition of the midrash was published in 1962, a new manuscript family also verified Zunz's prediction of chapter order. Thus, *Pesikta deRav Kahana* serves as a wonderful example of fifth- to sixth-century homiletic midrash based on the synagogue lectionary cycle as well as a testimony to midrash scholar Zunz's genius.

Midrash Shir HaShirim, or *Shir HaShirim Rabbah*, is also known by its opening phrase (citing Prov. 22:29) as *Midrash*, or *Aggadat*, *Hazitah*. It unevenly works its way through the verses of Song of Songs with proems *(petihtaot)*, homilies, and exegeses on various aspects of Song of Songs. There is much material in common with *Leviticus Rabbah*, *Pesikta deRav Kahana*, *Genesis Rabbah*, and the Talmud Yerushalmi. This common fund of text leads scholars to assume that *Midrash Shir HaShirim* is either contemporary with these other rabbinic works (fifth to sixth centuries C.E.) or that it borrows from them.

Shir HaShirim Rabbah consistently reads the Song of Songs as allegory referring to God and Israel. Either God is the beloved of Israel at the Exodus from Egypt (specifically, the crossing of the Red Sea) or God is the beloved of Israel at Mount Sinai. These readings are in keeping with Rabbi Aqiba's dictum that all poetry is holy and the Song of Songs is the Holy of Holies. Thus the Song of Songs is never taken by the rabbis literally as erotic poetry. It is always read as referring to God and Israel, much as in Christianity it is read as referring to Christ and the Church.

This constant allegorizing of the *pshat*, or contextual meaning, of the biblical Song of Songs leads some scholars to suggest that the *drash*, or communal reading of the rabbis, goes even beyond the allegory suggested above. To these scholars, the Song of Songs is the locus for early rabbinic mystical speculation on God's throne room, God's chariot, and even, God's body. However, *Shir HaShirim Rabbah* at most contains allusions to this mystical reading. The standard midrash of *Shir HaShirim Rabbah* is to read the biblical book against the deliverance at the Red Sea or the covenant at Sinai.

Others have suggested, in light of the Church's similar tendency to allegorize the biblical book, that *Song of Songs Rabbah* may carry a record of conversation or polemic between Church and Synagogue on the issue of "Verus Israel," or which religion was the authentic inheritor of biblical religion. Here, too, though each ecclesiastical body does read the work allegorically, there is insufficient evidence to suppose that the two sets of interpretation (e.g., *Shir HaShirim Rabbah* and the works of Origen or, later, Augustine) must be in dialogue. Each may have been composed in isola-

tion from the other, nevertheless using Hellenistic hermeneutics and allegory to solve the "problem" of the erotic nature of the biblical work.

Ecclesiastes Rabbah, known in Hebrew as *Qohellet Rabbah,* is a loosely
structured commentary on the biblical book by the same name. It is
unique among the early Aggadic midrashim in its organizational method.
Through the kind of associative thinking also found in the Talmuds, this
midrash collects materials on various topics. It is as though *Qohellet Rabbah* uses the verses of the Bible as topic headings for quasi-encyclopedic
entries on a given topic. Thus, for instance, on the verse "All things are
wearisome" (Eccl. 1:8), the midrashic editor comments: "Things related to
heresy are wearisome." Then follows a string of stories, many with parallels elsewhere in rabbinic literature, on the subject of heresy. This phenomenon of collection is repeated throughout the midrash, so that it remains a valuable compendium of rabbinic thought in the fifth to sixth
centuries.

Lamentations Rabbah, or *Eichah Rabbah,* is rabbinic midrash on the book
of Lamentations. The dirgelike quality of the biblical book is extended
from mourning over the loss of the First Temple to mourning and theodicy over the Second Temple and later wars as well. Stories of the destruction of the Second Temple abound here, too, with parallels elsewhere in
rabbinic literature. In addition to such stories, there are many other folk
legends and wisdom tales collected in this work. The rhetoric of *Lamentations Rabbah* is very much in keeping with that of the Hellenistic Second
Sophistic.

Lamentations Rabbah is unique in rabbinic literature for its array of
proems or *petihtaot.* As in *Genesis Rabbah* and, more particularly, *Leviticus
Rabbah* and *Pesikta deRav Kahana,* many literary *petihtaot* served as an organizational structure for the editor of this work. In the other works,
however, the *petihta* always came at the head of each chapter, leaving an
impression that the *petihta* might be associated with synagogal reading on
the lectionary cycle. In *Lamentations Rabbah,* however, all of the *petihta* material is found at the beginning of the midrash, without regard to its lectionary division. Since the biblical book of Lamentations is read at one sitting in the synagogue on the Ninth of Av (in commemoration of the
destruction of the First and Second Temples), this point may be moot.

The thirty-six *petihta* pieces found at the outset of *Lamentations Rabbah*
contain some original materials, some material also found in the remaining (less highly structured) segments of this midrash, and much material
paralleled elsewhere in the rabbinic corpus. One *petihta* (number 11) consists entirely of verses of Pentateuch contrasted with verses of Lamentations and presented in a reverse alphabetical acrostic, so that the *petihta*
ends on the opening verse of the book of Lamentations. This extreme enslavement to structure has given rise to many theories on the function of

the *petihta* in general and the function of the *petihta* section of *Lamentations Rabbah* in particular. Whatever resolution these debates about structure and function may have, all scholars agree that theodicy and consolation are the chief agenda of *Lamentations Rabbah.*

Later Aggadic Midrash

There are many other midrashim in the rabbinic corpus. Some of these works are linked to books of the Bible; others are structurally independent of Scripture and follow their own agenda. These midrashim generally were composed following the redaction of the Talmuds, in the Geonic (ca. 600–1000 C.E.) and later periods. This survey will touch upon representative works, but it should be noted that dozens of smaller (and some larger) Aggadic midrashim are not surveyed here, chiefly for lack of space. It is not the purpose of this chapter to be encyclopedic; the reader should consult the reference works at the end of this chapter for more information.

Midrashim are found to the biblical scrolls of Ruth and Esther. Each of these works is organized around the biblical book and, in the now-familiar stream-of-consciousness associative process, deals with the contents of the respective Scripture. Largely due to the content of Esther and the frivolity with which Purim (the holiday that marks the events recorded in the book) is celebrated, *Esther Rabbah* is lighthearted and often humorous. *Ruth Rabbah* shares a good deal of material with the early Aggadic midrashim. It either is contemporary with them or borrows from them. If the latter is the case, then both works most probably date from the early Geonic period.

Midrash Mishle dates from the mid–ninth century and was composed somewhere in the trading orbit of Babylonia on the east to the Land of Israel on the west. This work seems to be aware of customs of both Jewish communities. Moreover, it contains a clear anti-Karaite (a group that rejected rabbinic law and depended upon biblical strictures only) polemic, which helps date it as contemporaneous with the Karaite leader, Daniel al-Qumisi. *Midrash Mishle* generally comments on verses of the biblical book of Proverbs (Mishle), although some chapters are without commentary and the first half of the work is denser in commentary than the latter half. Occasionally the text breaks free of its terse commentarial style and spins Aggadic legends about biblical and rabbinic figures. *Midrash Mishle* is significant in the history of rabbinic literature, as it marks the beginnings of the transition from atomistic midrash to more context-based commentary.

Seder Eliahu Rabbah and Zuta, also known as *Tanna DeBei Eliahu Rabbah and Zuta,* is a work redacted roughly in the same time period as *Midrash Mishle* and shares a similar anti-Karaite polemic. It does, however, contain significant amounts of material recorded in the Babylonian Talmud as "The Greater (and Lesser) Teachings of Eliahu." The midrash holds a unique place in the rabbinic corpus, since it is narrated in first-person singular. Although we do not know the name of the author/redactor, the individual stamp of his style is as clear as the singular voice he employs. This midrash is not tied to any scriptural book but rather wanders from topic to topic, always with a clear ethical and didactic agenda.

Equally keen on its own agenda (and anti-Karaite polemic) is *Pirqe Rabbi Eliezer.* This work is tied to the Torah narrative by retelling it in medieval Hebrew, much as the Targum (as we will see) did so in Aramaic or as Philo and Josephus did so in Hellenizing Greek. The work as we have it is fragmentary, consisting of fifty-four chapters, which stop abruptly with the death of Miriam. Since the *Pirqe Rabbi Eliezer* opens at Creation and since there are structural elements left incomplete (ties to the eighteen benedictions of the rabbinic daily liturgy and to the rabbinic legend of the Ten Descents of God to Earth), it is likely that this was intended as (or once may have been) a much larger work.

The contents of *Pirqe Rabbi Eliezer* are highly idiosyncratic, humorous, and often linked to medieval (Geonic) customs. It also exhibits a thorough familiarity with Islam. For centuries this midrash was associated with the early Tannaitic teacher, Rabbi Eliezer ben Hyrcanus, whose name appears at the outset of the midrash. Citations of much later sages and contents, as well as the midrashim that the work cites (and others that subsequently cite it) firmly date the midrash in the first third of the ninth century.

Avot deRabbi Nathan also was redacted in this period. It contains at its core, however, a Tannaitic commentary on the Mishnah tractate Avot. Much like the Tosefta, this midrash comments upon and expands the Mishnah text. Since Avot itself is entirely Aggadic, *Avot deRabbi Nathan* also is thoroughly Aggadic in nature. The work abounds with legends of the rabbis and "lives," or hagiographic renderings of their "biographies," in an effort to teach the didactic points of the rabbinic curriculum.

The Hebrew language and the ideas often contained in the work seem to indicate that despite the early core work on Avot, the final editing came in the Geonic period. The current text of *Avot deRabbi Nathan* is in two recensions, apparently differing from the earliest eras. Perhaps oral transmission may account for these differing recensions; or perhaps historic development or even scribal laxity may account for the varying versions of this Aggadic work. Since it is primarily tied to an early version of Avot, it is organized around that tractate of Mishnah and remains untied to any biblical work. It does, however, contain occasional exegeses of scattered biblical verses.

Brief mention should be made here of *Pesikta Rabbati,* a late-Geonic work. This work should be distinguished from its predecessor, *Pesikta deRav Kahana*. Although the two works are organized on the same principle (special Sabbath and holiday lectionary cycle) the *Pesikta Rabbati* is distinguished by its apocalyptic contents. This work often slips into tours of heaven with angels abounding. It is not unrelated to the rabbinic mysticism of this period.

Mention should also be made of a remarkable work of the eighth century that is also organized according to the order of the Torah. The *Sheeltot* of R. Ahai Gaon were probably composed in Babylonia, although later rabbinic literature reports that the author immigrated to the Land of Israel late in his life. The work is 171 chapters, beginning at Genesis and working through a variety of selected texts to the end of Deuteronomy. In each chapter a rare combination of Aggadah and Halakhah provides Torah text exposition and Mishnah text teaching. Each chapter deals with a question of Jewish law that is homiletically connected to the Torah text.

The *Sheeltot* is unique for many reasons: It is the first rabbinic text published under the name of a known author, it mixes Halakhah and Aggadah freely, it appears to be Babylonian in provenance, and its Aramaic is largely Babylonian, although the frequency of travel between these locales tends to level both language and custom. Sections of this work are translated into Hebrew in *Sefer Vehizhir,* a rabbinic commentary on the Torah from, perhaps, two centuries later. This latter work also quotes freely, in Hebrew translation, from a legal codification called *Halakhot Gedolot.*

There is yet another Aggadic collection on the entire Torah that is similar to the *Sheeltot* in structure and format. The *Tanhuma-Yelamdenu* literature constitutes a library unto itself. Primarily written in Hebrew and probably stemming from Palestine in the centuries following the *Sheeltot,* the *Tanhuma-Yelamdenu* comments on each week's lectionary portion with midrashic-Aggadic materials mostly borrowed from earlier sources (such as *Genesis* and *Leviticus Rabbah*). *Tanhuma-Yelamdenu* is notable for its format question: "Yelamdenu Rabbenu" (Teach us, O Master). The opening formula follows with a question of Jewish law, which is answered by a Mishnah text. The latter text is dilated aggadically and linked to the Torah lection. As in the *Sheeltot,* Mishnah and midrash on Torah are linked together in the *Tanhuma-Yelamdenu* literature. There are many versions of midrashim in this format, so that the description of *Tanhuma-Yelamdenu* "literature" is more accurate than the designation of it as a specific midrashic work.

Among fragments discovered in the Cairo Geniza, the used-book depository of the synagogue in Fustat, Old Cairo, many rabbinic texts were found. In addition to hundreds of fragments and complete texts of midrashim, Halakhic and talmudic works, biblical texts, and wholly secular texts, fragments of Mishnah study lists have been found (T-S box 218, frag. 24a/b). These are arranged on a weekly basis, that is to say, there was a cycle of Mishnah texts linked to the annual Torah reading cycle. It is precisely such cycles that give further testimony to the linkage of Mishnah and Pentateuchal midrash, a linkage to which the *Sheeltot* and *Tanhuma-Yelamdenu* attest. It also demonstrates the attempt of preachers to teach Mishnah as part of the weekly synagogue lessons and relate their rabbinic teaching to Torah text. The latter served the purpose of promoting the rabbinic agenda among the broader Jewish populace and did so at a time when Karaism was perceived as a threat to rabbinic hegemony in the Jewish community.

Targum

Another popular approach to Torah text in this period was the retelling of the Torah in the vernacular, Aramaic. This open-ended translation, done live in synagogues and interspersed with public reading of the Pentateuchal text in Hebrew, is called Targum. Such translation of sacred Scripture into the local language has an ancient history in the Jewish world. It is already reported in the Bible that the scribe Ezra translated the Torah into Aramaic (or retold it) to the community that had returned from exile. In the third century B.C.E. the Torah had been translated into Greek for the Alexandrian Jewish community. The custom persisted throughout the Jewish world, and hundreds of Targum versions coexisted. Most shared a common fund of traditional materials, closely linked to Aggadic traditions. In the Islamic period, Aramaic Targum still persisted in Palestinian synagogues and these traditions were sometimes written down.

Many of these Aramaic texts from varying periods survive today; a brief survey of the major traditions follows. Targum Onkelos is the closest text we have to an "official" Targum. Revered by the Jewish community, especially the Yemenites, Targum Onkelos is attributed to a second-century proselyte. It is said that Onkelos (or Aquila) wrote his Targum under the auspices of the great *tanna*, Rabbi Aqiba. In any case, the Aramaic is a unique mix of Western (Palestinian) and Eastern (Babylonian) Aramaic with a fair touch of earlier imperial Aramaic. The translation is very close to the Torah text, but not slavishly literal.

Recent discoveries, particularly among Cairo Geniza fragments, have unearthed other works of Targum. These are mostly of the later period (sixth to ninth centuries) and occasionally betray post-Islamic content. They are grouped under the rubric of Palestinian Targum or Targum Yerushalmi. Though a misnomer, the most complete of this group of Targums is called Targum Yonathan (or Pseudo-Jonathan). Many fragments of like Targum texts are also extant. This entire group of texts tends to be much more expansive retellings of the Pentateuchal text, often waxing into lengthy narratives that are entirely extrabiblical. These narratives share a great deal of plot with the midrash *Pirqe Rabbi Eliezer*.

The Vatican Library contains a complete Targum, referred to by the name of its Vatican cataloguer, Neofiti. Discovered and published by the Spanish scholar Alejandro Diez Macho, this Targum has been the subject of much debate. Its content is not as expansive as Targum Yerushalmi traditions nor as rigid as Onkelos. In other words, it represents a Targum tradition that might be described as middle-of-the-road. The Aramaic seems to also date somewhere between the earlier language of Onkelos and the post-Islamic Aramaic of Yerushalmi Targums. Catholic scholars (Diez Macho among them) have claimed a very early dating for this text in an attempt to recover the first-century Aramaic of Jesus. It is doubtful if Targum Neofiti represents such an early tradition.

Recent translations and studies of the various Targum texts promise a rich harvest of scholarship in the coming decades. Targum study, still in its infancy, will teach a great deal about the intersection of rabbinic teaching and congregational thought. That is because most scholars agree that Targum is the best example of rabbinic literature explicitly directed at the masses of congregants. Although by definition Targum is limited to biblical topics, popular theology and practice may be well represented in the various surviving Targum texts.

Rabbinic Mysticism

If Targum represents the most public, or exoteric, face of rabbinic culture, rabbinic mystical texts are the most esoteric. As early as Tannaitic times, the Mishnah warns against public study of mystical texts. Such speculation is limited to initiates, studying together in very small groups. It is conjectured that the earliest forms of rabbinic mysticism centered on exegesis of Ezekiel's chariot vision (Ezek. 1) and, perhaps, mystical interpretation of the Song of Songs. Other likely biblical texts ripe for mystical speculation include Isaiah chapter 6 and Daniel chapter 7.

By Geonic times, rabbinic mysticism was well founded in the rabbinic community, though still reserved for the enlightened few. These texts were most often theurgic and included speculation on God's throne room (*heikhalot*), chariot (*merkaba*), and even God's body (*shiur qoma*). Permutations of God's name (the tetragrammaton) were the "mantras" by which the mystics achieved their various goals. Magical texts from this period include clearly rabbinic works rich in angelology such as *Sefer HaRazim*, which offers mystical formulas for success at the racetrack. A ninth-century *Shiur Qoma* text contains an incantation for warding off mosquitoes! Although this seems to be an absurd end for such esoteric mystical speculation, it is wise to remember that control over the forces of nature is a form of *imitatio dei* and thus an apposite goal for the mystic. If one can control the smallest of God's creatures (the mosquito), one may have begun learning the secrets of *Maasei Bereshit* (the Creation of the Universe).

Rabbinic mysticism has a good deal in common with early forms of Christian and perhaps pagan Gnosticism. Gershom Scholem was among the first scholars to write on this phenomenon and others in the study of rabbinic mysticism. It is he who gets credit for bringing this esoteric literature into the open light of modern scholarship. Many of his students and students' students are now publishing manuscripts and preparing critical editions and translations. The study of rabbinic mysticism is still in its infancy, and a great deal remains to be learned about the theology, practices, and thoughts of the various rabbinic mystical communities from the texts they produced.

Liturgy

A related aspect of rabbinic literature is prayer. Much of the "canonized" rabbinic liturgy has some textual roots in the earlier and contemporary mystical literature. The earliest rabbinic liturgical texts are found in the Mishnah, Tosefta, and, subsequently, in the two Talmuds. Synagogue and academy prayer practice has its origins in the wedding of biblical liturgies (particularly Psalms) and rabbinic texts (notably the Eighteen Benedictions). This interweaving of ancient biblical liturgies with more recent rabbinic prayers continues throughout all subsequent rabbinic liturgical texts.

From the earliest record, rabbinic prayer took place in two loci, the home and the synagogue. The former enveloped prayers related to bodily activities (awakening, dressing, eliminating, eating), whereas the latter was focused on the thrice-daily liturgies. As time went on, home prayer was formalized and even canonized into the synagogal service (e.g., the *Birkot Hashachar*). Thus, the central text for the study of Jewish liturgy became the prayer book, or Siddur.

The earliest recorded Siddur came to be as a result of a formal query asked of the Babylonian *gaon*, Rav Amram (mid–ninth century C.E.). In a responsum to a Halakhic question, Rav Amram put in writing the first rabbinic order of prayer (Siddur Rav Amram). It included not only the daily, Sabbath, holiday, and High Holiday orders of prayer, but even the earliest rabbinic liturgy, the Passover Haggadah. Rav Amram's commentary to all of this liturgy is also part of this valuable early work on Jewish prayer.

The Passover Haggadah is probably the oldest rabbinic liturgy. It contains the order (Seder = Siddur), or the home ritual for Passover eve. Modeled on the Hellenistic symposium banquet, the Passover Haggadah combines ritual recitations from the Torah and Second Temple with rabbinic midrash on the story of the Exodus from Egypt found in Deuteronomy 26. This combination of ritual reenactment with rabbinic study and exegesis marks the classic rabbinic attitude toward Jewish liturgy. Like all other prayer texts, the Passover Haggadah is laden with accretions from virtually every subsequent century.

Following the Passover ritual, Amram and subsequent rabbinic authorities (such as Saadia Gaon, Maimonides, Rashi, and the community of Vitry, France) outlined the daily liturgies. Holiday and High Holiday (Rosh HaShanah, or New Year, and Yom Kippur, or Day of Atonement) texts soon followed. The Jewish communities each shared a basic core liturgy, but the additions of later texts, particularly medieval liturgical poetry, make every community's Siddur unique to that community. Only the advent of printing forced anything at all like uniformity onto rabbinic liturgical texts. Particular distinctions may be drawn between Franco-German (Ashkenazic) and Iberian-Oriental (Sephardic) rites. Further distinctions may be drawn between Hasidic rites (which, though Ashkenazic, draw on Sephardic texts) and other premodern Siddur rites. In the modern era, some distinctions may be noticed between Israeli and Diaspora liturgical texts.

In summary, rabbinic liturgy is marked by a tension between modern expression and traditional text formula. Communal particularity is often at odds with ancient Jewish formulas linking Jewry worldwide. These tensions, including biblical versus rabbinic liturgical formulas, mark the creative spirit and conservative traditions of Jewish prayer.

Poetry

As already mentioned, Jewish prayer is richly expanded by each community's liturgical poetry. Synagogue poetry is abundant and not only marks a separate literature within the rabbinic library but also forms an intersection among various forms of rabbinic literature. The earliest Jewish poetry may be found in the Bible. But postbiblical poetry bursts forth in the late talmudic era and continues unabated throughout the more than millennium of rabbinic literary activity.

There is a vast and varied corpus of liturgical poetry. Poems were written to accompany various segments of the Sabbath and holiday synagogue services. In addition, the High Holiday liturgies encompassed some of the most poignant poetry throughout the Middle Ages. A further locus of this poetry was in the form of biblically inspired poetry, linking the holiday liturgy with the biblical lection for that day. All of this poetry (called in Hebrew *piyyut*) displays a remarkable creativity and a vast knowledge of rabbinic tradition.

Not only is *piyyut* tied to the synagogue liturgy, but some of the earliest *piyyut*, in Aramaic, is found as part of the Targum corpus. Since both liturgical and targumic *piyyut* draws on and alludes to the themes of Aggadic (and even Halakhic) midrash, this poetry is an important crossroad of rabbinic literary traditions. Modern scholars debate the exact relationship of *piyyut* (both Aramaic and Hebrew) to each of the three other rabbinic opera (the Midrash, Targum, and Siddur), but all agree that this poetry marks an important milestone in the comprehension of the literature as a whole.

Since the poetry is dense and allusive, study of *piyyut* stands as a scholarly field on its own merit, too. The intertextual nature of the *piyyut*, like other poetry, its allusions to biblical and earlier rabbinic texts, its adherence to strict formalistic requirements, all of these and more make the study of *piyyut* exacting and rewarding. Here, too, the discovery and publication of medieval texts combine with a growing interest in the field per se to promise a rich harvest of scholarship in the coming decades.

Halakhic Literature

Thus far the discussion has concentrated on Aggadic literature, liturgy, and poetry. It is necessary to recognize the towering role that Halakhic (legal) literature plays within the broad rabbinic corpus. Many have written about the intimate connection between Aggadic and Halakhic literature. These are, as it were, the soul and body, respectively, of rabbinic life. Thus, the Mishnah, Tosefta, Halakhic midrashim, and both Talmuds stress the importance of regulated behavior, Halakhah, in Jewish life. As with the other literature we have seen, Halakhic literature is rich and extensive throughout the rabbinic period.

The earliest post-talmudic works of Halakhah are commentaries to the Babylonian Talmud. *Geonim* of Babylonia wrote both shorter and longer works commenting on the Talmud with a particular interest in the legal aspects of the work. Geonic commentary seeks to codify principles for Halakhic interpretation of the often open-ended talmudic arguments. Since commentaries tend to cover the running text under consideration, there are also Aggadic commentaries from the *geonim* on those narrative sections of Talmud. By and large, it would not be wrong to characterize the main focus of Geonic commentary as Halakhic. This commentary is complemented by compilations of Geonic responsa, answering legal queries through extensive citation and discussion of the relevant talmudic passages on each question. In the modern era, these works have been collected in a *Thesaurus of Gaonica ('Otzer HaGaonim)* on the Talmud, divided into commentaries and responsa.

Other Geonic works are more focused on collecting, organizing, and, perhaps, codifying rabbinic Halakhah for the Palestinian or Babylonian Jewish community. In that way, rabbinic authority was extended further over the Jewish world. Works such as *Halakhot Gedolot* and *Halakhot Pesukot* are organized under the broad principle of talmudic commentary but show particular interest in grouping aspects of Jewish life under particular headings. These collections then offer a code of Jewish law that may be consulted by issue rather than by random appearance in the vast talmudic corpus. The push toward this type of topical codification (and movement away from commentary) persisted throughout the subsequent centuries.

The magnum opus of the eleventh-century North African rabbi Isaac ben Jacob al-Fasi also displays this tension between commentary and codification. In his work (called *Halakhot HaRIF* [Rabbi Isaac al-Fasi]), al-Fasi comments on the Babylonian Talmud but ignores all the Aggadic passages. By discussing Halakhic passages only and by supplementing his discussion with brief comments of post-talmudic sages, al-Fasi succeeds in creating a commentary that is primarily a Halakhic code. His work became (and remains) a standard talmudic commentary.

Rabbi Moses ben Maimon, or Maimonides, was a prolific twelfth-century Spanish and North African authority. He wrote on medicine, philosophy, and many aspects of Jewish law. A physician and community leader, Maimonides wrote epistles and responsa, commentaries (on the Mishnah), and an enduring work of Jewish law. His *Yad HaHazakah,* or *Mishnah Torah,* consists of fourteen books arranged topically on Halakhah. Borrowing an apparently Islamic systematization, Maimonides quotes from talmudic and post-talmudic authorities, mostly anonymously, offering what he expected to be the authoritative corpus of Jewish law. This work, written in Hebrew (unlike all his other works, which were in Arabic), became a pillar of Jewish legal literature. In the centuries after its publication, all subsequent Jewish scholars have quoted it, whether in support or disagreement. Maimonides, in typical genius fashion, completed the transformation from talmudic commentary to topical Halakhic codification.

In the following century, an unusual rabbinic authority wed the works of al-Fasi and Maimonides. Rabbi Asher ben Yehiel, born in western Germany, studied with the great Ashkenazic authority Rabbi Meir of Rothenburg. He was forced from Germany, first to southern France and ultimately to Toledo, Spain. There, Asher became rabbi of the Sephardic community. His major Halakhic work is a commentary to the Talmud that serves primarily as a commentary on the extracts that make up the earlier *Halakhot HaRIF.* Using al-Fasi's organizing principles, Rabbi Asher (RoSH) incorporates the legal findings of Maimonides and of Ashkenazic authorities (the *tosafot*). His work was widely accepted in both the Ashkenazic and Sephardic Jewish communities.

Rabbi Asher's son Jacob began his Halakhic work by publishing an extract of his father's great Halakhic commentary (called *Kitzur Piskei HaRoSh* [*Epitome of the Halakhic Decisions of Rabbi Asher*]). Jacob was not to be bound by the frame of commentary and, following Maimonides' lead, organized his next work according to subject area. He innovated and divided rabbinic law into four broad Pillars *(Turim):* Daily Life *(Orah Hayyim),* Forbidden and Permitted (especially relating to foods) *(Yoreh Deah),* Personal Life (including marriage and divorce) *(Even HaEzer),* and, finally, Civil Law, or Torts *(Hoshen HaMishpat).* The *ʾArbaʿah Turim* (the Four Pillars or the *Tur*) became the standard organizational framework for Jewish Halakhic literature through the twentieth century.

In part, the organizational power of the *Tur* was guaranteed by a commentary written on it by the sixteenth-century mystic and towering legal authority, Joseph Caro. Born in Sepharad (name given to Spain and Portugal) circa 1488, Caro emigrated when the Jews were expelled and traveled throughout Sephardic lands and cities (Turkey, Adrianople, Saloniki, and Constantinople) until settling in Safed, in Palestine. It was possibly there, in the legendary home of Jewish mystics, that Caro wrote his own mystical work, *Maggid Mishnah,* or *Maggid Mesharim* (a diary of Caro's conversations with the hypostasized Mishnah). Far more influential were his Halakhic works.

These Halakhic works began with his monumental commentary on the *ʾArbaʿah Turim* called the *Bet Yosef.* In this commentary Caro discusses the origins and development of each of Jacob ben Asher's legal decisions. Caro firmly offers decisions within the Sephardic tradition. He also comments on Maimonides and on the *Halakhot* of al-Fasi and of the RoSH, often basing his own decisions on a majority found among these three great teachers. In addition, Caro includes learned discussion and commentary of Geonic works, largely ignored by his predecessors.

In his later years (ca. 1550–1575) Caro condensed his vast commentary into a more accessible and less recondite work of Jewish law called the *Shulchan ʿAruch* (Set Table). There he simply offers the results of his lifework of commentary on the *Tur* and his own various studies and responsa. The *Shulchan ʿAruch* almost immediately became the preeminent Halakhic work of rabbinic literature and has remained so to this day. Ashkenazic authorities, particularly Caro's contemporary Moses Isserles, criticized the work. In an effort to keep Ashkenazic custom from being swept away by the power of Caro's *Shulchan ʿAruch,* Isserles composed glosses to the work indicating Franco-German custom. The *Shulchan ʿAruch* with the glosses of the RaMA (Rabbi Moses Isserles) remains the monumental code of Jewish law to this very day and an appropriate place to end this brief survey of Halakhic literature.

Medieval Midrashim

During this post-Geonic, medieval period, the production of Aggadic midrashim continued apace. Brief mention of significant works must suffice at this point. *Exodus Rabbah, Numbers Rabbah,* and *Deuteronomy Rabbah* were all composed between the tenth and thirteenth centuries. Each has a large portion of text that is part of the *Tanhuma-Yelamdenu* format, discussed above. Each of these three midrashim contain lengthy quotations of earlier material coupled with some medieval material. The redactor's hand and the linguistics of the Hebrew text confirm a later dating for these texts, which round out the *Midrash Rabbah* on the Pentateuch. As will be clear, this so-called *Midrash Rabbah* is a disparate collection of five differing midrashim composed in varying time periods. The unifying factor of the *Midrash Rabbah* is that each of the five constituent texts is on a book of the Pentateuch.

The midrash to Psalms, *Midrash Tehillim,* also called *Midrash Shocher Tov,* is possibly also from this late period (although some scholars date it earlier). It may have been composed in Italy (according to Zunz) or perhaps in the Middle East or the Fertile Crescent. It covers all of the 150 Psalms in the biblical collection by means of exegetical and occasional homiletical midrashim on selected verses of each psalm. The first half of the work covers Psalms 1–118 and is found in a variety of recensions in manuscripts. The latter half of the work (Psalms 119–150) is found only in printed editions and appears to be borrowed from *Yalkut Shimoni* (to be discussed).

Bereshit Rabbati is a medieval midrash on the book of Genesis. Composed by Rabbi Moshe HaDarshan (Moses the Preacher) in Narbonne, France, in the early eleventh century, it quotes earlier midrashim (such as *Genesis Rabbah*), and has original material from Moshe's school (he was a disciple of Rabbi Nathan ben Yehiel of Rome) and even certain Christian interpolations (e.g., to Genesis 30:41). The work is also notable for having been extensively quoted by the Christian monk Raymundo Martini (thirteenth century) in his disputation text, *Pugio Fidei.*

No survey of midrash (or rabbinics) would be complete without mention of Rabbi Solomon ben Isaac, Rashi, who flourished in Troyes, France, from 1040 to 1105 C.E. Rashi wrote commentary on the Babylonian Talmud that is so influential that every printed edition of the Talmud text has the Rashi commentary appended. Rashi's commentary on the Pentateuch is also a standard reference in rabbinic studies and is commended here as a rich epitome of earlier midrashic texts.

One final compilation of Aggadah merits mention in this survey. *Yalqut Shimoni,* attributed to Shimon HaDarshan, was probably composed in Spain in the thirteenth century. It is an anthology of rabbinic midrashim, quoting from more than fifty rabbinic works and commenting on every book of the Bible. This rich collection is in two parts: the first on the Pentateuch (with 963 sections) and the second on the Prophets and Writings (with 1,085 sections). The first edition of the *Yalqut Shimoni* has an appendix of Aggadic midrashic traditions from the Yerushalmi (256 sections) and the *Yelamdenu* midrashim (55 sections). The *Yalqut Shimoni* is valuable as a testimony to early texts and as a resource for rabbinic traditions on the entire Bible.

The Academic Study of Rabbinic Literature

As the preceding survey testifies, rabbinic literature covers a broad span of time, countries, and cultures. In the modern period the study of rabbinic texts has undergone a revolution, as modern academic methods have been brought to bear on this traditional, religious literature. Although traditional methods of study continue among pious Jews worldwide, in seminaries and universities the critical study of these texts has been under way for more than a century and a half. Like all religious texts, rabbinic literature presents certain problems for scholarly study. Some of these problems are found in the study of any traditional literature, some with any oral literature, some with any ancient literature, particularly with manuscript transmission to account for.

Without detailing the problems, I must mention certain issues unique to the study of rabbinic literature. Among these, this survey already points to the problem of periodization. More than most canons of Western literature, rabbinic literature is intertextual, that is, texts about earlier texts. Because of the constant citation and reworking of biblical and earlier rabbinic texts, it is difficult to fix securely the date of any rabbinic tradition within a text. It is also difficult for the same reason even to fix secure dates for the editing of many of these rabbinic volumes.

This problem is complicated by the general anonymity of rabbinic volumes. Not until the late Middle Ages do we actually know the names of authors and editors of rabbinic works. Furthermore, citations of rabbinic authorities within given texts are often unreliable. A tradition cited in the name of Rabbi X in one work may have a parallel in another work, but in the name of Rabbi Y. It is for this reason that many modern scholars prefer not to speak about individual traditions of individual rabbis but rather of the general trend of a given rabbinic work, its "documentary integrity." Although this may give some idea as to what the Mishnah or *Genesis Rabbah*, for example, says about a given subject, it limits research to broad generalizations only and to regarding anonymous works rather than individual opinions. This caution, although methodologically sound, leaves little to be said about specific eras or the rabbis in them.

Since earlier works on rabbinics have tended to take citations of individual rabbis at face value and presume them to be true, this caution is welcome but, nonetheless, extreme. Scholars are currently searching for a middle ground in the study of rabbinic literature. One means of finding this ground has been to treat rabbinic literature as literature rather than as a source for Jewish history. Although this treatment does violence to a major source of Jewish history in the period under discussion, it does enable scholars to discuss works of rabbinic literature using a known academic method.

This literary method also speaks to documentary integrity, since it treats entire works as literary products, much as one might treat *Crime and Punishment*. Interesting scholarship on literary intent, deconstructive readings, poetics, and the like is being pursued in the field of ancient rabbinic literature. Appropriately, these literary methods also serve for the writing of rabbinic theology. Caution must be raised, however, at the blanket application of the literary method to works not necessarily composed as literature per se. Other problems and considerations beyond method, that is to say, aside from the debate on historic and literary models, also must be noted here.

Significant segments of rabbinic literature deal with "the other." Unfortunately, it was the rabbinic tendency to suppress the other in blanket condemnation and obscure epithets rather than to cite and debate differing opinions, as the Church did. This attitude should be clarified, since rabbinic literature, as a whole, glories in debate and differing opinion. However, debate is promoted only so long as the partners are within the pale of the rabbinic community. Once they are outside, they are treated as sectarians, heretics, or total outsiders. When one reads rabbinic polemic, it is often difficult to discern exactly which sect the rabbis are engaged with. It is sometimes even hard to tell whether paganism or Christianity is the object of a rabbi's barbs. Although certain texts are clearly disputative, it is hard for the historian to determine who the precise disputant may be. This obscurity is occasionally overcome by careful scholarship and modest expectations, yet it remains vexing to the historian of rabbinic literature.

Although the scholar of religions may study rabbinic literature with the hope of learning more about Greco-Roman religions (paganism), Christianities of late antiquity, or formative Islam, the problems just alluded to often make that a difficult task. The very organismic nature of the literature precludes an ideal systematic presentation, exacerbating this difficulty. Clearly, knowledge of these "outside" religions is desirable and even necessary for the appreciation of rabbinic texts, but it is difficult to be precise in comparative study.

One last issue in the study of rabbinic literature is the theological primacy of the Land of Israel. The importance afforded the Land of Israel in all rabbinic literature often obscures the provenance of authorship of a given work. Hence, a work composed in Babylonia or Europe may appear to be the product of the Land of Israel. Moreover, the distinction between Israel and the Diaspora may contribute an obfuscating, rather than clarifying, lens for viewing the materials. Related to this matter is the problem of considering this Hebrew and Aramaic literature as wholly distinct from Hellenistic literature, rather than as an eastern variety of it. Each of these issues must be addressed in finding an appropriate method for the study of this important and vast literary monument. Despite the cautions raised here, the modern study of rabbinic literature has been rich and rewarding for the theologian, historian, and literary critic alike.

Suggested Readings

Holtz, Barry, ed. *Back to the Sources: Reading the Classic Jewish Texts*. New York: Summit Books, 1984. An elementary work written by Jews for a Jewish audience.

Mulder, M. J., ed. *Mikra: Text, Translation, Reading and Interpretation of the Hebrew Bible in Ancient Judaism and Early Christianity*. Compendia Rerum Iudaicarum ad Novum Testamentum [CRINT] 2:1. Assen/Maastricht and Philadelphia: Van Gorcum and Fortress Press, 1988. A scholarly work written for scholars by a mixture of Jews and Christians.

Safrai, S., ed. *The Literature of the Sages*. CRINT 2:3. Assen/Maastricht and Philadelphia: Van Gorcum and Fortress Press, 1987. A scholarly work written largely by Jews for scholars.

Strack, H. L., and G. Stemberger. *Introduction to the Talmud and Midrash*. Philadelphia: Fortress Press, 1992. This work is available in a variety of European languages. A scholarly handbook written by Christians for a scholarly audience.

Visotzky, B. *Reading the Book: Making the Bible a Timeless Text*, 2nd ed. New York: Schocken Press, 1996. A popular work on rabbinic interpretation of Scripture.

5

The History
of Medieval Jewry

ROBERT CHAZAN

URING THE MIDDLE AGES, Jews lived all across the western world.
The largest and oldest Jewish communities were found in the Mus-
lim-controlled Near East; important Jewish communities, under both Muslim and Christian rule, ringed the Mediterranean Sea; new but vibrant Jewish settlements were established from the tenth century on across Christian
northern Europe. As the balance of power in the western world swung
from the Muslims to the Christians, larger numbers of Jews found themselves living under Christian rule. Sometimes, as in Spain, the transition resulted from Christian conquest of territory previously held by Muslims;
elsewhere, as in northern Europe, Jews chose to move into Christian territories where promising developments made immigration enticing.

Both Christianity and Islam provided a framework for Jewish life that
was at one and the same time protective and restrictive. Both recognized
Judaism as a legitimate religion and assured Jews fundamental safety and
security. Jews were not to be persecuted for practicing their religion, nor
were they to be forcibly converted. At the same time, Jews were to comport themselves in ways that brought no harm to the ruling faith, whether
Christianity or Islam. Jews were forbidden, for example, to proselytize or
to vilify the ruling religion. The precise balance between protection and
limitation was often difficult to define and maintain. More important, the
particular social circumstances and spiritual environment of a given time
and place often swung the balance in one or the other direction, either toward careful protection or toward zealous limitation.

In both Christendom and the world of Islam, Jews tended to live
largely among themselves and to organize effective internal agencies for
supervising and enhancing Jewish life. The impetus for this segregation
and self-government came from both without and within. Majority society in the Christian and the Muslim spheres preferred to see minorities,

including the Jews, live among themselves and conduct their own affairs. The religious establishment of the ruling faith, ever concerned about minority impact upon members of the majority, reinforced the broad social inclination toward segregation. For their part, the temporal authorities derived considerable benefit from the self-governing arrangements of the minority communities. Effective self-government by the minorities meant that the temporal authorities could achieve maximal revenue at minimal cost. The self-governing apparatus of such minority groups as the Jews raised tax revenue for their rulers in a manner that was painless and to the rulers, cost-free.

To be sure, the Jews had their own reasons for desiring segregation and self-government. Jews were generally fearful and suspicious of their non-Jewish neighbors and thus wished to enjoy the security that living in a Jewish neighborhood under Jewish leadership afforded. At times of social tension, living in a Jewish quarter provided psychological security and often physical safety as well. Although paying taxes and accepting adverse court decisions are always distasteful, the discomfort felt by medieval Jews was certainly diminished by having fellow Jews serve as tax and court personnel. In addition, segregation and self-government insulated Jews from the blandishments of non-Jewish life, an objective dear to the hearts of the Jewish religious establishment. Relative isolation also meant the possibility of living Jewish life to the maximum. Jewish court procedures, for example, were those ordained by talmudic law. For all these reasons and others, Jews were as enthusiastic about segregation and self-government as were their non-Jewish neighbors and rulers.

Self-government meant the empowerment of a Jewish ruling class, usually in contact with and supported by the non-Jewish authorities. Not surprisingly, the wealthy tended to dominate the self-governing apparatus of the Jewish community. Wealth normally generated considerable influence within the community, and at the same time, well-to-do members of the community tended to be precisely those Jews who had most contact with the non-Jewish rulers. The other group that wielded power in the medieval Jewish community was the rabbinic elite. Given the Jewish commitment to observance of divine commandment, the rabbis, whose standing was grounded in their knowledge of Jewish law, obviously represented a potent force within the community. Generally, the elite of wealth and the elite of learning cooperated effectively with each other; in some instances friction and strife developed.

The level of sophistication of Jewish self-government varied. The smaller the community, the more informal the arrangements for conducting Jewish affairs could be; in larger Jewish communities, elaborate electoral and governance rules had to be developed. Self-governing power in the Jewish world was heavily concentrated in the local Jewish community. On occasion, particularly in the Muslim sphere, central institutions of Jewish self-government sought and achieved authority over Jewish communities spread across vast geographic areas.

The coalescing majority and minority desire for Jewish segregation and self-government should not conjure up a picture of radical isolation from society at large. Jews were in many ways bound up in the life of the larger environment in which they found themselves. The two most obvious avenues of Jewish involvement in the larger milieu were economic interaction and language. Rarely during the Middle Ages were Jews able to live and support themselves within their own circumscribed community. Instead, in almost all instances, Jews were intimately linked to the larger economy and interacted extensively with their neighbors. These interactions seem to have been by and large benign, with normal patterns of human trust and respect manifest. As we shall see, in some cases, particularly in the immigrant communities of northern Europe, Jews were shunted into limited and unpopular economic specializations, with negative impact on social relations between these Jews and their neighbors. Such instances represent, however, the exception and not the rule.

The other index of Jewish integration into the non-Jewish milieu was language. Although Hebrew dominated the Jewish classics and Jewish prayer, Jews in their daily activities generally communicated in the vernacular of the particular area of settlement. This linguistic integration was, in part, simply an extension of Jewish economic integration. Given that the Jewish minority had to carry on business with the majority, Jews had to be able to use the vernacular. Jewish utilization of the vernacular involved more than simply economic realities, however. Jews were, to a considerable degree, integrated in more general terms in their environment. In some of the older areas of Jewish settlement, Jews in fact felt themselves more deeply rooted than most of their neighbors, many of whom had come onto the scene relatively recently. Language was only the most obvious reflection of such rootedness.

Language integration led to and reflected broader cultural integration into the larger environment. Modern researchers have at times been misled by negative Jewish comments on the surrounding civilization. Jews were of course anxious to insist on the superiority of their community and its heritage. This inherent competitiveness notwithstanding, Jews could hardly maintain isolation from their milieu. Jewish cultural interests were shaped in considerable measure by the surrounding environment. In some instances, particularly in the medieval Muslim world, new cultural outlets such as science, philosophy, and secular poetry emerged from interaction with a vibrant intellectual context. In other cases, new forms of religiosity exerted influence on Jewish thinking and behavior, in the directions, for example, of self-sacrifice, asceticism, and mystical speculation.

Let us examine in more detail developments in three major arenas of medieval Jewish life—the largest and oldest medieval Jewry, that of the Muslim Near East; the vital Jewry of the Iberian peninsula; and the young immigrant communities of northern Europe. The focus will be on these three sets of Jewish settlements because of their importance on the medieval scene, because they illuminate broad developments in medieval Jewish life, and because of their significance for postmedieval Jewish history.

Medieval Jewry in the Muslim World

In late antiquity, the Near East and the Mediterranean basin were home to the vast majority of the world's Jews. During the centuries that preceded the emergence of Islam, the Jewish community of Mesopotamia came to dominate world Jewry numerically. The Jewish population of Palestine, although diminished, was still considerable, and Jewish communities ringed the Mediterranean, with the largest and oldest on the eastern shores of the sea and the newest and smallest further westward. All these Jewries had lengthy histories, were well rooted economically and socially, and were protected by safeguards that extended back to early antiquity.

Particularly important for Jewish circumstances in the Near East and around the Mediterranean basin (and subsequently elsewhere as well) was the evolution in Christianity of recognized status for the Jewish minority. Although the earliest writings of the Christian community included harsh condemnation of the Jews for their refusal to acknowledge Jesus of Nazareth, Christian leadership, as it moved to a position of power in the Roman world, worked out a modus vivendi with the Jewish minority in those areas under Christian control. In line with the Jewish status that had developed over the centuries under polytheistic rule, the Christian authorities acknowledged the Jewish right to physical security and to practice of the Jewish religion. Naturally, these minority rights were balanced by the needs of the Christian majority. Jews had to comport themselves in ways that would bring no harm to Christians and Christianity. Moreover, there was an element of the transitory in these arrangements, as it was anticipated that upon the full dawning of messianic redemption, Jews would be among the first of the non-Christians to acknowledge Jesus and the Christian faith.

During the early seventh century, an unsuspecting Near East and Mediterranean basin fell prey to remarkable conquest by the forces of Islam. The Muslim religious faith, as it developed on the Arabian peninsula, owed obvious debts to the prior western monotheisms, Judaism and Christianity. Both were acknowledged in the Quran directly and through citation. The stance of Islam was equivocal toward the prior monotheisms, acknowledging them as forerunners in appreciation of the one true God, while projecting itself as the final and full revelatory dispensation. With respect to Jews and Judaism specifically, both the Quran and authoritative reports about Muhammad indicate veneration mixed with antipathy.

Critical for the future status of the Jews under Muslim rule was the early development of treaties between conquered groups of Jews and their Muslim conquerors. These treaties involved a fairly simply quid pro quo: Jews would be entitled to protection by their new rulers and to freedom of religious expression, in return for which they would owe loyalty and taxation. With the acceleration and expansion of the Muslim conquests, this rudimentary arrangement came to approximate increasingly the balanced status developed for Jews in the Christian sphere.

During the seventh century the realities of prior Jewish demography and the remarkable extent of the Muslim conquests combined to bring the overwhelming majority of world Jewry under the control of Islam. The largest Jewish community, that of Mesopotamia, fell under the sway of the Muslims, as did the smaller communities of Palestine, the eastern shores of the Mediterranean, and all of North Africa. By and large, the Jews of the conquered areas were comfortable in accepting upon themselves the new overlords. For a variety of reasons, the Muslim conquerors were broadly congenial to the Jewish minority communities that became part of their realm. The Muslim conquerors had in fact good reason to treat the Jews positively. Constituting a considerable population element all across the conquered territories, the Jews had, prior to the Muslim conquest, lived as a subjugated minority; nowhere did they constitute a displaced ruling class. Whereas the Muslim armies had to be wary of displaced ruling elements such as the Zoroastrians in the eastern areas and the Christians in the western regions, Jews falling under Muslim domination were far more comfortable in their submission than much of the rest of the conquered population. With the passage of time, a high level of cooperation between Muslims and Jews became widely known and inclined Jews who lay along the path of the conquest to be increasingly well disposed to the impending change in circumstances. By the time the Muslim forces had reached the western end of the Mediterranean, the Jews of the Iberian peninsula seem to have been quite ready to cast their lot quickly and comfortably with the new rulers.

During the early centuries of Muslim rule, the circumstances of the Jewish communities ensconced in the orbit of Islam changed little. As Islamic political and theological theorizing matured, a tripartite view of human society developed. At the poles of this tripartite structure lay the world of Islam, perceived as the realm of truth, and the world of polytheism, perceived as the realm of error. Between these two poles lay the *dhimmi* peoples, those who might be viewed as precursors in the movement toward the full monotheistic truth embodied in Islam. Carefully defined status emerged for these subject peoples, not all that far removed from the status that Christianity in power had accorded to its Jewish minority community. The *dhimmi* peoples, Jews included, were accorded fundamental tolerance in the Muslim scheme of things, including physical security and the right to open practice of their religious traditions. Balancing this tolerance was a series of limitations, meant to assure that *dhimmi* peoples would bring no harm to the ruling Islamic faith and community and that the secondary standing of these *dhimmi* peoples would be fully obvious through the patterns of their behavior.

Although political theory is of great importance, theoretical status is always played out against a backdrop of societal realities. Buttressing Jewish political status all across the Muslim world were the realities of sizable Jewish population, age-old Jewish presence, and a diversified Jewish economy. Jews were well enough settled throughout the Muslim world to reinforce their theoretical protections with everyday acceptance. Unlike Christianity, Islam projected no fundamental anti-Jewish teaching as part of its essential mythology. As a result of the positive economic and social realities and the absence of anti-Jewish mythology, the circumstances of the Jews in the medieval Muslim world were relatively benign. Conspicuous by their absence were the afflictions of large-scale anti-Jewish violence and massive expulsion.

There seems to have been no radical shift in Jewish population from one sector of the Muslim world to another, although there was considerable movement in all directions. In the large Muslim world, with its far-flung network of transportation and communication, Jews traveled extensively and maintained considerable contact from community to community. The most important demographic change involved the movement off the land and into the centers of urban living. The Muslim tax structure discriminated harshly against non-Muslim agriculturalists, and during the early centuries of Muslim rule, the Jews seem to have shifted in a decisive way off the land and out of agriculture.

Beyond this one discrete change, there is no evidence of wide-ranging alteration of economic activity. Jews were active in all nonagricultural facets of the economy, continuing the diversification evident in antiquity. The extensive documentary evidence available from the Cairo Geniza shows Jews involved in hundreds of identifiable economic pursuits, from the most prestigious and lucrative down through the most menial and despised. This economic diversification reflected the profound social rootedness of the Jews in those sectors of the western world that became the realm of Islam. As noted, economic diversification in turn contributed to the relative stability of Jewish circumstances in the medieval Muslim world.

In all areas of the vast Muslim domain, Jews tended to live in their own neighborhoods and to organize their own effective web of self-governing agencies. As was generally the case all across the medieval world, groups tended to clump together demographically throughout the realm of Islam. In larger towns, sizable Jewish populations usually created more than one Jewish neighborhood. Within the Jewish neighborhood, a variety of social welfare, educational, and religious facilities were to be found. At times of stress, the Jewish neighborhood offered more than psychological security; on occasion, it offered physical security as well.

The multifaceted agencies of the local Jewish community reflect a high level of organizational need and expertise. Institutions for promoting Jewish social welfare, education, and religion abounded. To some extent, these were voluntary associations, dedicated to specific objectives. In other cases, the specialized agencies derived their funding and backing from the unified Jewish communal structure. Leadership in these institutions of Jewish social welfare, education, and religion involved both trained specialists and elected personnel. Beyond and above the specialized agencies stood a unified Jewish communal authority, with responsibility for the overall management of affairs within the local Jewish community. Leadership in this unified Jewish communal authority was generally vested in the elites of wealth and rabbinic prestige, who enjoyed the quiet but important backing of the non-Jewish powers as well.

In the medieval Muslim world, centralized organs of Jewish self-governance reached unusual levels of recognition and achievement. These central agencies received considerable support from the Muslim authorities, anxious to bolster their control over the Jewish minority. At the same time, many of the institutions of centralized Jewish self-governance had venerable roots within the Jewish world and commanded allegiance and compliance for reasons of both long-standing custom and religious obligation.

Perhaps the best known of these centralized agencies was the office of the *rosh-golah,* or exilarch. This office is attested during the period preceding the Muslim conquest, although its precise prerogatives are not altogether clear. Claiming authority by virtue of Davidic descent, the exilarch was, at least in the early centuries of Muslim rule, closely allied with the caliphate, deriving considerable backing and prestige from the Muslim rulers. The exilarch seems to have played a role of some importance in representing Jewish interests in the Muslim court, and Jews seem to have taken considerable pride in the standing of their exilarch in court circles. As the Muslim world became increasingly fragmented, it served the best interests of breakaway political rulers to encourage the independence of their Jewish subjects from the Baghdad-centered exilarchate.

Pre-Islamic Mesopotamian Jewry had developed, alongside the exilarchate, central institutions of rabbinic studies as well. Given the role of talmudic law in the judicial, social, and religious life of medieval Jews, knowledge of that law was of paramount importance, and proper training and certification of experts were critical. Many centuries prior to the emergence of Islam, Mesopotamian Jewry had founded outstanding academies devoted to the study of Jewish law, and it was out of these academies that the Babylonian Talmud evolved. Like the exilarchate, these central institutions of talmudic law survived into the era of Muslim rule and indeed emerged as yet stronger forces in Jewish life. The academies of Sura and Pumbedita and their leaders, the *geonim*, eventually relocated in the capital city, Baghdad. These two great centers of learning attracted outstanding students from a wide area and legal queries from communities spread across the length and breadth of the Jewish world. Once again, as the unity of the caliphate disintegrated, Jews and their more localized rulers increasingly sought to establish independent rabbinic authorities and to diminish reliance upon the academies located in the heartland of the caliphate. By the twelfth century, the Spanish Abraham Ibn Daud and the Spanish-Egyptian Moses ben Maimon were forcefully championing the independence of their own learning centers from the academies and *geonim* of Baghdad.

Indeed, the concentration of both political and religious authority in the exilarchate and the gaonate occasioned more than friction with rabbinic leadership in diverse geographic areas of the Jewish world. Not surprisingly, the centralization of Jewish power in the medieval Muslim world led to the creation of the most enduring schism in medieval Jewish history. The Karaite movement began in Baghdad, the very heartland of rabbinic authority; in fact, Anan, the dominant figure initially, was purportedly from the family of the exilarch himself. With the passage of time, Karaites spread widely through the Muslim world, creating especially important centers in Palestine and Byzantium. The loosely organized movement was rooted in opposition to the dominance of rabbinic prerogatives of leadership; it eventually absorbed other important elements as well, including a focus on the sanctity of the Holy Land and an emphasis on rationality in religious thought and life. Although always a fairly small minority on the medieval Jewish scene, the Karaites created a lively challenge in many Jewish communities and were strong enough to survive down to the present day.

Discussion of the academies, the gaonate, and the opposition they evoked serves as a useful bridge to the intellectual life of the Jewish communities in the medieval Muslim world. As noted, a measure of social segregation and effective internal communal organization should not be taken to imply rigid Jewish separatism and intellectual isolation. Nowhere in the medieval world were Jews more fully integrated into the fabric of general intellectual life than in the sphere of medieval Islam.

The key to intellectual involvement lay in language: Jews absorbed the language of their environment more fully in the Islamic context than elsewhere. They used Arabic as their spoken tongue and for most of their writing as well. In nearly every field of Jewish intellectual endeavor, including the traditional areas of biblical and talmudic study, Jewish authors were comfortable formulating and sharing their learning in Arabic. To be sure, the utilization of the Arabic language is but one significant index of the impact of the broad environment on Jewish intellectual creativity.

Since the Bible forms, from many points of view, the core of Jewish religious tradition, it seems appropriate to begin with biblical study. The Bible was extensively read and pondered by Jews living in the medieval Muslim world, as they sought to fathom the wellsprings of their tradition, to buttress their commitment to that tradition, and to meet the serious challenges mounted by the competing monotheisms and the skeptical philosophies that played an important role on the medieval scene. Biblical study began in childhood and continued throughout adult life. Many outstanding Jewish thinkers devoted a major portion of their intellectual energy and creativity to leading their followers to a deeper understanding of biblical truth. Translations of the Bible into Arabic were undertaken as a way of reaching Jews who lacked the requisite Hebrew to engage the text in its original. Biblical commentary was utilized to guide readers to a rigorous, linguistically accurate understanding of the text in its pristine sense; to introduce some of the key philosophic ideas and ideals common in the medieval Muslim world and to argue their compatibility with biblical teachings; to rebut biblically based argumentation of competitor faiths; and to plumb the deeper spiritual meanings of the biblical corpus. The biblical commentaries composed in the medieval Muslim world in fact provide a striking introduction to the diversified thrusts of Jewish intellectual endeavor in that environment.

Talmudic study was universal as well, since the Talmud and its related literature played so major a role in the everyday lives of Jewish communities and individual Jews. Again immersion began at an early age, and again opportunities for the development of expertise had to be provided. The Mesopotamian academies reigned supreme for a time, but eventually institutions of higher talmudic study were established all across the Muslim world. These academies occupied themselves, of course, with the text of the Talmud; at the same time, they addressed the concerns of the community, as formulated in carefully crafted queries. As the corpus of Jewish law expanded, efforts were launched from time to time to make this ever expanding corpus available in digest form. Although a number of major codes of Jewish law were created in the medieval Muslim sphere, perhaps the most remarkable was Maimonides' *Mishneh-Torah*, renowned for the learning of its author, for the audaciously rational organization of the sprawling domain of Jewish law, and for the formulation of that law into a remarkably pure Hebrew style.

Whereas biblical and talmudic study was traditional for Jewish life all through late antiquity and the Middle Ages, Jews in the Muslim sphere struck out in innovative directions as well. Islamic civilization preserved and absorbed the science and philosophy of the Greeks. Indeed, Greek thought underwent significant development in the Muslim world, enriched by the investigations and speculations of Muslims, Christians, and Jews. Jews, stimulated by the general environment, made considerable contributions to both science and philosophy.

To be sure, the Greek patterns of scientific and philosophic thinking posed a fundamental challenge to some of the key dogma and lines of thinking of the three monotheistic faiths. For some Muslims, Christians, and Jews, traditional beliefs were undone by scientific and philosophic thought; for others, the traditional patterns of Muslim, Christian, and Jewish thinking remained supreme and the scientific-philosophic challenge was dismissed out of hand. In many ways, the most interesting alternative involved the effort at accommodation, the attempt to find or create a synthesis between the traditional patterns and the new. In the Jewish sector of the Muslim world, some of the most creative minds were bent to this task. Once more, as in the realm of talmudic study, the figure of Maimonides dominates. The profundity of Maimonides' command of both traditional Jewish thought and the Greco-Roman legacy as mediated through its medieval Arabic formulations assured that his efforts at synthesis had an impact from his own days until the modern period. Of course, efforts like those of Maimonides at synthesis were not greeted with universal acclaim in the medieval Jewish world. Despite the widespread veneration for his talmudic knowledge, many medieval Jews ranged themselves in opposition to his philosophic writings, his acceptance of Greco-Roman ideas and ideals, and his perceived reformulation of traditional Jewish teachings. Creative periods are often highly contentious, and so it was in the medieval Muslim world.

By the twelfth century, unmistakable signs of a swing in the pendulum of power from the Muslim sector of the western world in the direction of Christendom had begun to emerge. The Muslim conquest of Jerusalem in 1099 was greeted by Christians as a sign of the new power balance; Muslims argued that the failure of the Christians to maintain their grasp on the Holy Land suggested the evanescence of purported Christian gains. However, Christians in fact began to dislodge Muslims permanently from their strongholds on the Italian peninsula and from their near control of the Iberian peninsula. The tide of power was indeed shifting. Jewish communities that had long lived under Muslim control, for example in Spain, found themselves passing into Christian hands. Areas of the Christian world that had historically been of little interest attracted Jewish immigrants, as these regions matured economically and culturally. By the end of the Middle Ages, the Jews of the western world were fairly well balanced between the worlds of Islam and Christendom, a radical change from the dominance of the Islamic sphere from the seventh through the twelfth centuries.

Medieval Iberian Jewry

The Iberian peninsula was neither the oldest nor the newest site of Jewish settlement during the Middle Ages. Poised at the western end of the Mediterranean Sea, the Iberian peninsula was, in all likelihood, the final settlement point for Jews filtering westward through the Mediterranean basin. Surely a much younger Jewry than that of the eastern Mediterranean or Mesopotamia, the Jewish communities of Spain prided themselves, not without reason, on the longevity of their sojourn there and their rootedness in the soil of Iberia.

The Jews of Spain had lived under pagan Rome, under the Christianized Roman Empire, and under the Christianized Germanic conquerors of Iberia by the time that the Muslim armies made their first appearance on the peninsula. For more than a century prior to the Muslim conquest, the Visigothic rulers of Spain had exerted considerable pressure on Iberian Jewry. As a result of anti-Visigothic sentiment and accelerating awareness of the comfortable Muslim-Jewish alliance farther east, the Jews of the peninsula seem to have been fully prepared to cooperate with the new rulers.

During the period of almost total Muslim control of Spain—stretching from the eighth century through the eleventh—the Jews played a useful and profitable role as allies of the authorities. In the tenth century, we encounter the fascinating figure of Ḥasdai Ibn Shaprut—diplomat in the service of the Muslim ruler, expert physician, serious scientist, and patron of Jewish culture in both its traditional and innovative forms. Iberian Jewry of the tenth and eleventh centuries is revealed as well established politically and socially, as increasingly well organized under the leadership of wealthy and powerful families, as rooting itself more profoundly in rabbinic tradition and learning, and as exploring new avenues of creativity along lines sketched out in the vibrant majority culture. Particularly striking at this juncture is the emergence of a new poetic style.

The vitalization of Christendom that began in the closing decades of the tenth century and accelerated thereafter was fated to have a decisive impact on the Iberian peninsula. Pressures began to mount from the north, as Christian armies of both Iberian and northern European warriors pushed southward. For the Jews, who had grown accustomed to the civilization of Muslim Spain, the successes of the Christian reconquest were frightening. To some extent, the discomfort was occasioned by the simple reality of disruption and change; moreover, the Christian forces represented two specific liabilities—a lower level of civilization and a more intrinsically negative stance toward Jews. Jewish fears were quickly augmented by a turn for the worse in those sectors of the peninsula still controlled by the Muslims. Waves of North African troops were introduced in order to stem the tide of the Christian advance. These troops brought with them less favorable attitudes and policies. Indeed, the Almohads of the early twelfth century introduced onto the peninsula a persecution of Jews that was highly unusual for the Muslim world.

The combination of seemingly hostile Christians streaming down from the north and overtly intolerant Muslims counterattacking from the south posed a dilemma for the Jews of twelfth-century Spain. In its most practical terms, the dilemma involved a choice of whom to support politically and economically; in more profound terms, the dilemma convinced some Spanish Jews that the end of the creative epoch in their history had arrived. The two most important proponents of that radical conclusion were the philosopher and historian Abraham Ibn Daud and the philosopher and poet Judah Halevi. Ibn Daud, in his highly influential *Sefer ha-Kabbalah*, advanced a number of historical theses, including the poignant argument that Iberian Jewry had enjoyed two centuries of creative endeavor and that this creative interlude was coming to a close. Perhaps better known is Judah Halevi's expression of his despondency in his decision to leave Iberia for the Holy Land and in some of the most stirring poetry ever composed in the Hebrew language.

These two highly creative figures, even in their despair, remind us that periods of pressure and tension need not be devoid of cultural creativity. In fact, twelfth-century Iberia was home to a galaxy of remarkable Jewish intellects whose talents were directed to the study of the Bible, to the analysis and expansion of talmudic law, to scientific inquiry, to philosophical speculation, and to creative belles lettres. The intellectual giant Maimonides was a native of Spain whose family was forced to flee the Almohad persecution. He continued to see himself as an Iberian Jew, and we are justified in perceiving him as a representative of the creativity of Spanish Jewry.

The intellectual and poetic brilliance of Abraham Ibn Daud and Judah Halevi does not mean that their radical conclusions were shared by all or even most of their Jewish contemporaries. Diverse views swirled about in the Jewish community. The most activist stance was that of the wealthy and powerful Jewish courtiers, who began to transfer their loyalty and skills to the Christian kingdoms. These courtiers made a fairly simple reckoning: The increasingly successful Christian monarchs were going to need considerable assistance—financial aid and expertise, bureaucratic know-how, urban skills—as they displaced more sophisticated ruling classes and civilizations. In the event, the pragmatic reckoning of the courtiers proved more accurate than the despair of the historian or the vision of the poet. In fact, Iberian Jewry, led by its courtiers, made a fairly smooth transition in allegiance and alliance from the Muslim authorities to the ascendant Christian monarchies. The Jews, as an established urban element on the peninsula, proved themselves invaluable to the Christian rulers, as the latter expanded their control of Spain.

Royal support was invaluable, but serious problems remained. Indeed, the alliance between the Jews and the Christian kings was not without its complications. Elements in the Christian populace that chafed under enhanced royal authority deeply resented the Jewish contribution to that enhanced authority. At the same time, urban Christians saw the Jews primarily as economic and political competitors. Equally significant was the stance of the Roman Catholic church. In the late twelfth and thirteenth centuries, the Church had improved its internal organization and its position within western Christendom. This more powerful Church was profoundly committed to clarification of required Christian behavior and thought and to aggressive lobbying for imposition of policies that would advance the cause of Christian living. The Jews were not the highest priority on the Church agenda; at the same time, however, they were not a negligible item. Particularly in Spain, where the Jews constituted a significant element on the urban scene and wielded considerable power in the royal courts, ecclesiastical demands for traditional limitations on Jewish power and Jewish fraternizing with Christian contemporaries were unremitting. With the passage of time, these demands were slowly met and took their toll on Jewish life.

Particularly striking in Spain was the ecclesiastical commitment to missionizing among Jews and Muslims. Representing the frontier between western Christendom and Islam, the Iberian peninsula gave birth to the most intense yearnings toward expanding the sphere of Christian belief. To some extent, these yearnings expressed themselves militarily, through the commitment to pushing back the frontiers of Muslim domination on the peninsula. At the same time, the Spanish Church led the way in winning over new adherents through the force of argumentation, rather than the force of arms. By the middle of the thirteenth century, Spain was the scene of a considerable effort to win over Jews. Key to this effort was the establishment of regular channels for dissemination of the Christian message into the Jewish community. The techniques of dissemination involved the forced sermon and the forced debate.

Churchmen led by converts from Judaism to Christianity immersed themselves in the writings and thinking of the Jews themselves, in an ef-

fort to identify new lines of argumentation that might promise some success with Jewish auditors. A leader in this movement was the former Jew
turned Dominican preacher, Friar Paul Christian. Friar Paul pioneered in
the effort to comb Jewish sources for effective missionizing materials.
With the backing of King James I of Aragon, he engaged one of the great
Jewish intellects of the Middle Ages, Rabbi Moses ben Nahman of
Gerona, in a public debate intended to prove Christian truth from talmudic sources, with the rabbi strictly limited to rebuttal of the Christian
thrusts from the Talmud and not to broad counterargumentation. The efforts of Friar Paul were subsequently taken up by Friar Raymond Martin
and a group of associates, who composed a mammoth missionizing compendium entitled the *Pugio Fidei*. Rooted in thousands of rabbinic citations, the *Pugio Fidei* was meant to guide Christian missionaries in mounting Talmud-based arguments for all major Christian doctrines. Although
evidence of real success in this campaign is not available from thirteenth-
century sources, the missionizing effort proved subsequently to be one element in a complex of factors that led to substantial Jewish conversion on
the peninsula.

By the fourteenth century, Iberian Jewry had achieved a position of centrality in the Jewish world, largely by default. The older Jewries of the Islamic sphere, although still numerically strong, were no longer associated
with the centers of power in the western world; the new Jewries of northern Europe had already grown and declined—by the early fourteenth century the Jews had been banished from the important kingdoms of England
and France. Nevertheless, Iberian Jewry had its own problems. The fourteenth century was beset with difficulties all across western Christendom,
and Spain was not immune. Spain's Jews were doubly affected by the economic and social dislocations of the period. On the one hand, they suffered along with all others; on the other hand, the growing pressures of
this difficult period moved majority Christians toward less tolerance with
respect to minority Jews. Resentments that were easy to swallow in times
of growth and expansion deepened considerably in an era of decline and
retrenchment. The voices of discontent were those noted earlier—the nobility, the burghers, the Church. The calls for increased limitations on the
Jews were, however, delivered in far more strident and threatening tones
than previously. Iberian Jewry negotiated this difficult period, but signs of
both external and internal problems abounded.

The crisis erupted in 1391, with the explosion all across the peninsula of
wide-ranging assaults on the Jewish minority. Underlying these assaults
were simmering discontents, socioeconomic grievances, and traditional
religious hatreds. Thousands of Jews lost their lives, and scores of Jewish
communities disappeared, never to be reconstituted. The efforts of the
royal courts to stem the tide of violence were largely unavailing, and even

when order was reestablished on the peninsula, there was little effective punishment of malefactors. Particularly noteworthy in the 1391 assaults was the high percentage of Jews who chose to avoid death by accepting the traditional alternative of conversion. To be sure, many of these converts saw their acceptance of Christianity as a temporary expedient, which would be quickly undone when life returned to normal. By the end of the fourteenth century, however, the decision to convert had proved impossible to reverse, which had been common in prior centuries. Thus, the assaults of 1391 left in their wake devastation, the inevitable despair that follows such a catastrophe, and a new and problematic group of converts. These New Christians were destined, over the ensuing century, to create considerable problems for Spanish society, for the Church, and for the Jewish community of Spain as it sought to rebuild itself.

Although the attention of scholars has focused heavily on the important, distressing, and moving story of the New Christians, the efforts of the Jews of the peninsula are noteworthy in their own right. One thrust of the reconstruction effort lay in the economic and political spheres, as Jews sought to reestablish themselves, to reconstitute their links to the authorities, and to recoup their influence over their prior protectors. At the same time, the internal problems of the community had to be addressed and were. In particular, organizational and educational deficiencies had to be redressed, posttrauma despair had to be combated, and the vexing problems associated with the New Christians had to be dealt with. In considerable measure, the rebuilding was successful, although Iberian Jewry never regained its pre-1391 strength.

Throughout these rebuilding efforts, the problem of the New Christians hovered over the Jewish community. In its most direct form, the New Christians challenged their former fellow Jews in both practical and spiritual terms. Practically, the issue was how to behave toward relatives and friends who had converted. In Jewish eyes, converts out of the faith were ultimately to be treated as Jews, with every effort expended to bring them back into the fold. However, such a policy was impossible. To make any overture toward reintegration of the converts would entail transgression of one of the basic rules governing the Jewish place in Christian society. Jews were rigorously forbidden from attracting Christians into Judaism. From the Christian perspective, the converts were by no means Jews gone astray; they were simply Christians and as such off-limits for any religious persuasion. The practical problems were exacerbated by larger spiritual issues: Jews had to ask themselves about the viability of a faith that so many relatives and neighbors had abandoned.

The New Christians impinged on Iberian Jewry in a less direct but ultimately more costly way. The New Christians constituted a serious problem for the Church, concerned about their integration into the Christian fold. Whereas small sets of converts had historically been integrated in relatively smooth fashion, the large numbers of fifteenth-century New Christians posed vexing problems. The Christian majority was inevitably reluctant to extend easy social acceptance. Given the size of the New Christian community, its members could in effect create their own social grouping. Even though the emergence of a New Christian social grouping is perfectly understandable, this arrangement threatened the process of religious integration. Increasingly, the New Christians were perceived as socially recalcitrant and religiously backsliding. Their social recalcitrance is difficult to measure, since they were to a considerable extent rejected by the "Old" Christians. The question of religious backsliding is equally problematic and has been much debated by historians recently. For some, religious backsliding was real; for others, the allegations were nothing more than a pretext masking social animosities and economic cupidity. Whatever the truth of the matter might be, the Church began to agitate for measures to combat real or alleged religious relapse in New Christian ranks.

By the fifteenth century, the Christian world was familiar with the problem of heresy and had adumbrated a number of approaches to it. A liberal approach argued that heretics—a category into which backsliding New Christians technically fit—should be treated with respect and warmth and should be won over to full espousal of proper Christianity through a combination of intellectual suasion and loving acceptance. An alternative approach was to see heretics as criminals and to expose them to the full severity of the law. It was the latter approach that won out in fifteenth-century Iberia, with the establishment of an Inquisition to ferret out heretics among the New Christians, to convince such heretics to accept Christian truth fully, and to punish those unwilling to do so. Persuaded that the Jews of the peninsula played a significant role in the purportedly widespread heresy, the supporters of a punitive program for the backsliders urged, along with the establishment of an inquisitorial network, the expulsion of the Jews. The Inquisition was established and began its work, an effort that would stretch through a number of centuries. The call to expulsion was eventually heeded as well. Although the motivations for the expulsion of 1492 were complex, the justification for banishment of the Jews was rooted in the notion that Jews were prohibited from bringing harm on Christian society and that alleged support of New Christian backsliding constituted ongoing and unacceptably harmful Jewish behavior.

The expulsion of 1492 from the kingdoms of Aragon and Castile and the subsequent expulsion of the Jews from the kingdom of Portugal constituted the last of the great medieval banishments of Jews. By the end of the fifteenth century, Jews had been removed from all the kingdoms of western Europe, those areas that stood indisputably at the forefront of the western world. The history of Iberian Jewry did not, of course, come to a close with removal from the peninsula. The Jews of Aragon, Castile, and Portugal made their way eastward, largely into the Islamic principalities of North Africa and the rapidly developing Turkish Empire, which controlled the eastern Mediterranean basin. Many of the New Christians who remained on the peninsula subsequently played an important role in opening up areas of western Europe to Jewish resettlement. Moving to western France, the Low Countries, and England as Christians, some of these descendants of Jews returned to their ancestral faith, thereby creating a new Jewish presence on western European soil. All across the western world, the Iberian heritage was reestablished in new settings.

Medieval Northern European Jewry

The focus thus far has been on the well-established Jewries of the Near East and the Iberian peninsula. Ashkenazic Jewry presents innovative patterns of Jewish existence, introducing us to a new and rapidly developing sector of the western world and to immigrant Jews struggling to find a place for themselves in an exciting, promising, and problematic majority environment.

Northern Europe lay outside the range of Jewish settlement in antiquity and the early Middle Ages. Although Jews traveled across northern Europe, the backward state of life in the region made it unappealing for permanent settlement. Incentives for Jewish immigration to northern Europe developed only in the tenth century, as a result of the general vitalization destined to turn this backward area into the center of western civilization. Once the process of vitalization began, Jews were increasingly attracted to the area. In fact, in many instances they were actively recruited by the most farsighted rulers of northern Europe. Jewish settlement in northern Europe began in the core areas of northern France and Germany, eventually extending westward to England and eastward into Poland.

Jewish settlement in northern Europe was fueled by Jewish perceptions of economic vibrancy in that heretofore backward area and by a sense on the part of many barons that Jewish immigrants might broadly contribute to the general well-being of their domains and might, at the same time, directly enrich baronial coffers. Unfortunately, no memoirs in which Jews identified their motivations for moving northward are extant. In an interesting document in which he invited Jews to settle in Speyer in 1084, Bishop Rudiger, as temporal lord of the town, suggests that the immigration of Jews would enhance the glory of his town a thousandfold. What the bishop seems to be alluding to is the economic advantage that would accrue from Jewish settlement.

The early Jewish settlers seem to have been involved primarily in the burgeoning trade of northern Europe. Documents both Jewish and non-Jewish show these Jews buying and selling a wide range of goods, interacting with a variety of Christian neighbors, setting up shop in town in some cases, traveling considerable distances to carry on their business in other instances. Involvement in trade spilled over inevitably in a number of related directions. Exchange of coinage was a major economic need in this rapidly developing area, and Jews seem to have been active in this arena. Extension of credit constituted yet another business-related enterprise, and Jews seem to have done that as well, although only in the most rudimentary ways. There is little evidence of genuine Jewish economic diversification. The Jewish immigrants came as businesspeople and seem to have remained businesspeople. The process of settling in did not include movement into crafts or agriculture. The essentially business orientation of the early Ashkenazic Jews was appreciated by many in majority society; nevertheless, it was clearly resented by others, particularly those for whom the burgeoning business of this rapidly developing area was both new and threatening.

The major obstacle to Jewish settlement in northern Europe was the general insecurity and instability of the area. The maturation of northern Europe was predicated on the capacity of the ruling class to govern more effectively and to establish better conditions of safety and security. For the Jewish immigrants, improved governance held the key to successful Jewish immigration. To be sure, the occasional anti-Jewish violence notable in the sources for tenth- and eleventh-century northern Europe often reflects animosity and cupidity directed against Jews as businesspeople, rather than against Jews as Jews. In many cases, Jews suffered simply as traders traversing the unsafe roadways of the region.

In some instances Jews were, however, assaulted specifically as Jews. The Jewish immigrants were not enthusiastically welcomed by the bulk of majority society for a number of reasons. Throughout the world, immigrants tend to be unpopular, viewed as newcomers and usurpers. Moreover, the Jews immigrating northward represented the only non-Christians in a region unified by Christian identity. The business orientation of the Jewish immigrants reinforced resentments felt toward Jews as newcomers and dissidents. Anti-Jewish business sentiment, on the one hand, enflamed those who were suspicious of the new business climate of northern Europe. On the other hand, Christian burghers, who were themselves part of the new business environment, saw the Jewish immigrants as unwelcome competitors. Although Bishop Rudiger of Speyer imagined Jewish immigrants as a boon to the town, many of the Christian businesspeople surely felt otherwise.

Overshadowing all these realistic elements in Jewish life that aroused antipathy—Jewish newness, Jewish dissidence, and Jewish business orientation—was the traditional Christian sense of the Jew as more than simply a nonbeliever. From the earliest stages in its history, Christianity had perceived and portrayed Jews as ranged in hurtful opposition to Christianity—opposition to its central divine-human figure, to the members of the community founded by Jesus, and to the Christian religious vision. The most compelling symbol of this purported Jewish antipathy was the alleged role of the Jews in pressing for the crucifixion of the divine-human figure that Christians saw in Jesus of Nazareth. To be sure, the sense of the Jews as hate-filled enemies varied over the ages, depending on general conditions and the specific circumstances of Jewish life in Christian society. In the early stages of Ashkenazic Jewish history, perceptions of the immigrating Jews as historic enemies do not seem to have been too intense. Such perceptions, however, were omnipresent and ever threatening.

Since potentially negative anti-Jewish stereotypes were widespread, the key to successful Jewish immigration lay with the authorities of both Church and state. To the extent that the ecclesiastical leadership could maintain the normative Church doctrine of the right of Jews to safety and security, and—more important—to the extent that the secular authorities could in actuality protect those Jews whose presence they were interested in sponsoring, Jewish settlement could proceed smoothly. The sense of accelerating Jewish immigration all through the eleventh century suggests that the protection of the authorities was effective in limiting anti-Jewish violence and encouraging Jewish movement northward.

The early Ashkenazic Jews fashioned for themselves rudimentary but effective structures of self-government. The Jewish community constituted a town within a town, with Jews raising their own revenues, adjudicating their own disputes, caring for their own needy, and providing for their own religious and educational needs. Especially striking is the rapid intellectual and spiritual maturation of early Ashkenazic Jewry. Migrants are normally the least well rooted and least conservative members of Jewish (or any other) society. Most new Jewries take centuries to create viable cultural institutions and to exhibit significant intellectual and spiritual creativity. Although the earliest Ashkenazic Jews were surely of the adventurous type, within an unusually short time their descendants began to erect the necessary institutional framework for cultural activity and to produce indigenous intellectual and spiritual leadership. Within the first century and a half of its founding, early Ashkenazic Jewry spawned a number of major figures, culminating in Rabbi Solomon ben Isaac of Troyes (Rashi). Rashi's massive commentaries on the Bible and the Talmud are among the most widely copied, printed, and read books in Jewish history. For such important works to emerge so early in the development of a young Jewry is exceptional, a reflection of the vigor of these new Jewish settlements and—not to be overlooked—of the vitality of the larger environment as well.

The first major crisis encountered by early Ashkenazic Jewry came in 1096, as a result of the call to the First Crusade. Pope Urban II, who exhorted the warriors of western Christendom to fight against the Muslim forces holding the Holy Land, surely made no reference to Jews, and the organized crusading armies that responded to his exhortation and eventually conquered Jerusalem in 1099 inflicted no harm on European Jewry as they made their way eastward. The papal call, however, aroused a wide variety of knights, preachers, and common folk. In many instances, the popular militias that were formed saw the crusading venture in highly idiosyncratic ways. Particularly extreme in both their thinking and behavior were the popular German crusading bands. For some of these bands, the call to take up arms against the Muslims in the Holy Land was generalized into a slogan of hatred toward and revenge upon all enemies of the Christian faith. This radical generalization led the German crusaders to ask themselves why they were journeying long distances to engage the Muslim enemy in the Near East, while a profounder enemy—the Jews of Germany—was living nearby. The animosity toward Jews that developed in some crusader circles out of the traditional Christian motif of Jewish guilt for the crucifixion of Jesus resonated among some of the burghers of the Rhineland cities as well. A potent coalition of crusaders and burghers assaulted the major Rhineland Jewish communities of Worms, Mainz, and Cologne, wiping out these three great centers of early Ashkenazic Jewish life. Although the attacks of 1096 were localized and the bulk of early Ashkenazic Jewry survived unscathed, the ferocity of the assaults, the devastation that they wrought in those three Rhineland cities, and the remarkable Jewish responses combined to make the events of 1096 both disquieting and memorable.

The leadership of the Church, the barons and kings of northern Europe, and the Jews themselves learned well the lessons of 1096. None of these three groupings would subsequently be oblivious to the dangers associated with renewed crusading. Although the call to a new crusade always aroused anti-Jewish passions and sporadic attacks on Jews did occasionally take place, the level of violence manifest in 1096 was never repeated. Ecclesiastical leaders warned against anti-Jewish assaults, the secular authorities made arrangements to forestall them, and the Jews of northern Europe took intelligent steps to protect themselves.

Jewish life flourished across northern Europe through most of the twelfth century. The general growth and development of the area were reflected among its Jews as well. Jewish business affairs prospered; the Jewish alliance with the secular authorities deepened; Jews founded new settlements for themselves in the burgeoning towns; Jewish cultural activities proliferated. Exciting new developments took place in the realms of talmudic study, biblical exegesis, historical narrative, and mystical speculation. In all this, the Jews were once again exhibiting their own dynamism against the backdrop of a highly creative majority ambiance.

However, a number of disquieting developments were manifest as well. The first was the increasing Jewish specialization in moneylending, indeed, in a particular kind of moneylending. The rapid development of northern European society occasioned the need for augmented sums of capital to finance ever larger armies, building programs, and business ventures. At the same time, the Church was engaged in a strenuous effort to prohibit Christians from engaging in usury. The combination of financial need and ecclesiastical restriction opened up fertile business ground for the Jews, who were not included by the Church in its attack on usury. Once again, farsighted rulers recognized that support of Jewish moneylending—like their earlier support of Jewish immigration and trade—could prove generally useful to their domains and specifically profitable to their treasuries. Some of the most powerful rulers of northern Europe became, in a sense, business partners of the Jews. They backed Jewish loans and promised to enforce obligations made to Jews, in return for tax revenues, which might well be seen as a percentage of the Jewish profits. The result was considerable Jewish business success, with a number of highly visible Jewish financial magnates emerging both in England and across northern France. This business success came at a high price, however.

As already noted, the Jews of northern Europe had, from the outset, been unpopular as a result of the realistic contours of their existence as newcomers, dissidents, and businesspeople and as a result of the traditional legacy of Christian anti-Jewish imagery. To the prior anti-Jewish thinking, two new motifs were added: the intense animosity that moneylending generally produces and the anger normally directed at those perceived as lackeys of the ruling class. Jewish moneylending across northern Europe was highly useful to that rapidly developing society. Certainly, many Christians benefited enormously from the capital that Jews put at their disposal. Many other Christians, however, felt themselves severely disadvantaged by Jewish lenders. In a more general way, Jewish lenders became symbolic of the kind of change that many were coming to resent. The intensified alliance between Jews and the temporal authorities, particularly the most successful temporal authorities, can similarly be seen as a significant contribution to the maturation of northern Europe; however, many felt themselves harmed by the development of royal power in areas such as England and France. When a minority group such as the Jews is perceived as allied to the temporal authorities, it is far easier to vent anger at the minority partner than at the potent rulers.

On both these scores, the already questionable Jewish image in northern Europe was further damaged by the new specialization in moneylending.

During the middle decades of the twelfth century, a new sense of the Jews and their alleged hostility to Christian society and Christians emerged. The prior perception of the Jews as historic enemies, responsible for the crucifixion, expanded to a sense of the Jews as here-and-now foes, ever ready to do economic and physical harm to their neighbors. The most striking form of this new sensibility was the allegation that Jews took every opportunity available to them to murder Christian neighbors, particularly youngsters. Thus, when corpses were discovered in suspicious circumstances, as frequently happened, many Christians immediately fastened responsibility for the crime upon the Jews. By and large, the temporal authorities, increasingly more powerful and effective, were able to protect their Jews in the face of these dangerous allegations. The long-term impact, however, was considerable. Indeed, the anti-Jewish sentiment of the middle decades of the twelfth century must be seen against the broader context of growing anti-outsider anxiety and animosity. Northern European society felt itself increasingly threatened by such groups as Jews, heretics, homosexuals, lepers, and witches. All these groups began to suffer enhanced hostility and increasing persecution.

The Church, it will be recalled, had always called for a balance between protection of the Jews and Judaism and requisite restriction. To the extent that churchmen came to share the sense of Jews as malevolent and harmful, they began to highlight the importance of limiting Jewish behaviors and to expand the range of behaviors to be limited. Increasing pressure was brought to bear on Jewish social contacts with Christians, culminating in the early-thirteenth-century demand that Jews wear apparel that would distinguish them from their Christian neighbors. Intended largely to promote more effective social segregation of the Jews, this distinguishing garb—which often took the form of either a patch on the Jews' outer garments or a special Jewish hat—came to have demeaning overtones.

Another area of traditional ecclesiastical concern was Jewish blasphemy. In this regard, it was suggested by a number of thirteenth-century converts from Judaism to Christianity that Jewish liturgy and the Talmud were replete with negative references to Christianity and Christians and should be censored or banned. Talmudic literature was carefully examined in a number of locales. In some places it was prohibited, and in others it was regularly censored to remove allegedly injurious material. The most innovative Church efforts were aimed at Jewish business activities. Sensing that their own assault on Christian usury had opened the way for Jewish specialization in moneylending, churchmen began to press for limitations on Jewish lending, aimed at protecting Christians—particularly the poorer classes—from the negative impact of Jewish moneylending. The effect of all these ecclesiastical efforts was to shift the balanced Church program far in the direction of limitation of the Jewish minority in northern Europe and to set in motion protracted efforts to win the backing of the temporal authorities for these new restrictions.

From the beginning of their sojourn in northern Europe, the early Ashkenazic Jews had leaned heavily on the support of the temporal authorities. By the end of the twelfth century, the alliance between the Jews and their royal and baronial sponsors had begun to fray. In part, the problem lay with the increasing strength of the temporal authorities and the augmented Jewish dependence upon them. As the kings and barons came to involve themselves more fully in lucrative Jewish moneylending, they inevitably came to be better informed about Jewish transactions and wealth. Pressing fiscal needs led many of the strongest rulers to exploit their Jews increasingly, even to the point of destroying Jewish business. At the same time, the Church campaign for limitation of Jewish behaviors slowly took its own toll, with the temporal authorities acceding to ecclesiastical demands for implementation of the new Church regulations. Finally, some of the rulers of northern Europe came to absorb personally the negative image of Jews that had developed. It is clear, for example, that the great king of France, Louis IX, recognized subsequently as Saint Louis for his piety, felt intense visceral animosity for the Jews of his ever expanding domain. Loss of the support of their royal and baronial protectors was the most grievous of the blows suffered by thirteenth-century northern European Jewry. By the end of that century, the king of England had expelled his Jews, and the turn of French Jewry came shortly thereafter. With the removal of royal and baronial support, the position of northern Europe's Jews was untenable.

To be sure, not all rulers in northern Europe expelled their Jews. In a general way, the Jews were banished from the better-developed westerly areas of northern Europe, those areas that had matured sufficiently to dispense with the Jewish contribution. In central and eastern Europe, the areas of Germany and Poland, need for the Jews remained, and so did the Jews. By the end of the Middle Ages, the great centers of Ashkenazic Jewish life lay in Germany and Poland. In the northern sectors of western Christendom, as in the south, the pendulum of Jewish settlement had swung eastward.

In the sixteenth century, the two largest centers of Jewish population were to be found in the Turkish Empire, where the earlier Arabic-speaking Jews had maintained their continuity and the immigrating Spanish Jews had found their refuge, and in the kingdom of Poland, where the vigorous new Ashkenazic Jewry had implanted itself. Few Jews could have, at the time, sensed that another swing of the historic pendulum would bring Jews back into the countries of western Europe from which they had been removed. Resettlement in these more westerly areas is one of the defining developments of the modern Jewish experience.

Suggested Readings

Primary documents are extremely useful for studying history. For the Jews in the medieval Muslim world, a valuable collection of such documents is provided in Norman A. Stillman, *The Jews of Arab Lands* (Philadelphia: Jewish Publication Society, 1979); for the Jews of western Christendom, see Robert Chazan, *Church, State, and Jew in the Middle Ages* (New York: Behrman House, 1980). Overviews of the Jewish fate in the medieval Muslim world are provided by S. D. Goitein, *Jews and Arabs: Their Contacts Through the Ages* (New York: Schocken Books, 1955), and Bernard Lewis, *The Jews of Islam* (Princeton: Princeton University Press, 1984). For medieval Jewish life on the Iberian peninsula, see Eliyahu Ashtor, *The Jews of Moslem Spain*, trans. Aaron Klein and Jenny Machlowitz Klein, 3 vols. (Philadelphia: Jewish Publication Society, 1973–1984), and Yitzhak Baer, *A History of the Jews in Christian Spain*, trans. Louis Schoffman et al., 2 vols. (Philadelphia: Jewish Publication Society, 1961–1966). For the Jews of northern France, see Robert Chazan, *Medieval Jewry in Northern France* (Baltimore: Johns Hopkins University Press, 1973), and William Chester Jordan, *The French Monarchy and the Jews* (Philadelphia: University of Pennsylvania Press, 1989); for the Jews of medieval England, see the opening chapters of Cecil Roth, *A History of the Jews in England*, 3rd ed. (Oxford: Clarendon Press, 1964); unfortunately, there is no handy overview of the Jews in medieval Germany; for the nascent Jewish community in Poland, see the opening chapters of Bernard D. Weinryb, *The Jews of Poland* (Philadelphia: Jewish Publication Society, 1973).

6

Medieval Jewish Literature

RAYMOND P. SCHEINDLIN

Byzantine Palestine

The sages of Byzantine Palestine (fourth to mid–seventh centuries) produced, besides the Palestinian Talmud and midrashim, a great mass of
liturgical poetry, called *piyyut*. Much of this poetry is anonymous, like the
Talmud and Midrash themselves, though much was also written by poets
whose names are known. The Byzantine *piyyut* belongs to the same cultural and religious matrix as the Talmud and the midrashim and has
points of contact with the Midrash both as to its themes and literary techniques. It would therefore be logical to treat the *piyyut* together with the
Talmud and Midrash as a third literary product of rabbinic Judaism of the
Byzantine Age. Yet, for reasons having more to do with the history of
scholarship than with the subject itself, it is customary to treat the Talmud
and Midrash as the end point of Jewish antiquity and the *piyyut* as the
starting point of the Jewish Middle Ages. The student should be aware
that all three bodies of literature look both backward and forward in approximately the same degree.

A huge mass of liturgical poetry from Byzantine Palestine has been preserved, but like the traditions embedded in the Talmud and Midrash, this
material is hard to date. Although some progress has been made in establishing a relative chronology based on the development of the poetic
forms, there has been little success in fixing absolute chronology. The earliest poet known to us by name was Yose ben Yose, but his dates are unknown and he must have been preceded by a long tradition of poetic activity. Two later poets, Yannai and Eleazar Kallir (Qilliri), are said to have
been master and disciple, and Kallir is thought to have been active no
later than the beginning of the seventh century, before the Muslim conquests. A few other poets are known to have been active in the same pe-

riod. It is best to think of Yannai and Kallir as representing the classical period of Byzantine Hebrew *piyyut* and of Yose ben Yose, along with many anonymous authors, as their forerunners.

The emergence of *piyyut* is closely connected with the early development of the liturgy, and both processes are obscure. Scholars no longer believe that liturgical poetry came into being after the prose liturgy was fixed in approximately its present form. Today it is thought that at the stage of the liturgy represented by the Mishnah, worshipers, especially in Palestine, had the freedom to improvise the text of the prayers, as long as they adhered to rabbinic rules regulating the forms and the sequence of themes. In the course of the Amoraic period, certain formulas came to be adopted that satisfied these requirements, and these eventually emerged as the fixed liturgy that would eventually be canonized by the *geonim*. But given the freedom that existed before the Geonic canonization of the liturgy (late ninth century), many different textual realizations of the rules governing prayer were in existence, and some communities preferred prayer texts in verse form. The earliest liturgical poetry is therefore not to be considered a supplement to the liturgy or even a replacement for it, but rather an acceptable variant of it.

The process of canonization turned the *piyyut* into an optional supplement to the standard text. Liturgical poetry retained its freedom well past the point of the Geonic canonization of the liturgy; new *piyyutim* (poems) were constantly being written, so that the prayer service in each community was constantly being varied and renewed within a traditional and statutory framework. But gradually, the different communities adopted particular sets of liturgical poems, and these in turn became fixed, as had the prose prayers before them. Even after this process was completed, some genres of liturgical poetry retained their freedom well into the Middle Ages.

Most Jewish liturgy takes the form of series of benedictions *(berakhot)*, statements of praise built on the formula "Blessed are You, Lord." Sometimes the prayer begins with this formula and continues with a relative clause describing some action of God's that is the subject of the praise. In this case, the prayer will end with a second "Blessed are You, Lord," followed by a two- or three-word summary of the theme. In such prayers, the concluding formula, for example, "Blessed are You, Lord, who makes evening fall," is fixed, but the material between the two recitations of the formula may be in prose or in verse, and many versions of both types have survived in manuscript fragments.

Many benedictions take a simpler form, in which the opening benediction-formula is absent. The prayer begins with a statement praising God in the second person and ends with the same kind of concluding formula described above, for example, "Blessed are You, Lord, who loves His people Israel." In this case, too, the concluding formula is fixed, but the opening text may be in prose or verse, and many versions of both types have survived.

The service in ancient Palestinian synagogues was mostly performed by the precentor, who would recite the benedictions; the congregation would participate mostly by responding "amen" after each benediction. Most congregations were probably satisfied with familiar and simple versions of the prayers that were recited day in and day out, but in others, the precentor was expected to vary the service by reciting different versions of the prayers, and these versions were often in verse. If verse was chosen, the precentor would versify not just a single benediction but the entire series required for the service.

Two main groups of poetic benedictions became standard, based on the two main groups of benedictions composing the morning and evening services. These are the Shema, which consists of a passage from the Torah accompanied by three or four benedictions, and the Tefila, a series of benedictions that fluctuates from seven to nineteen, depending on the occasion. Series of poetic benedictions based on the former are called *yoṣerot*, and series based on the latter are called *qerovot*. The individual poems that together constitute the series take their names from the benedictions that they represent. In the earlier Byzantine period, the poems within each series were usually identical to one another in form (with one exception of outstanding importance, the *qedushta*, to be discussed), but later, specific verse patterns became associated with each benediction.

The earliest Hebrew liturgical poetry was unrhymed and was based on a loose meter of eight stresses to a line with a strong caesura in the middle; its language was close to biblical Hebrew. In the course of the Byzantine period, these simple poems evolved into complex forms with distinctive diction and style. These reached their fullest development in the work of Yannai and Kallir, the two poets whose work, together with that of poets sharing their style, is regarded as constituting the classical *piyyut*. Their huge production consists almost entirely of rhymed, strophic poetry. The rhyme frequently imposes the difficult requirement of two identical root consonants, dictating a very forced use of the language. Meter continues to be based on stress, with a great variety of stanza types based on three- or four-stress lines. Acrostics are nearly always present, usually alphabetical or reverse alphabetical, often with an acrostic of the poet's name in addition to or instead of the alphabetical acrostic.

The most notable formal feature of the classical *piyyut* is its distinctive language, which is partly present in Yannai and full-fledged in Kallir, a register of Hebrew that was never adopted for any other purpose. Its distinctive features are the nonstandard morphological treatment of common roots; the use of the vocabulary of rabbinic Hebrew and words of Aramaic and Greek origin; the replacement of most nouns by epithets drawn from biblical texts associated with them; and an allusive manner of referring to talmudic and midrashic motifs. These features bestow on the liturgical poetry an opaqueness that would render much of it nearly incomprehensible if it were not for several mitigating features: The morphology, though nonstandard, is quite regular and thus constitutes a grammar that can be learned; the epithets, although freely composed, tend to become standardized and based on biblical phrases associated with the person or thing intended; and the subject matter is fairly circumscribed by tradition. Despite these mitigating features, the language can be quite difficult. The poets probably did not expect to be understood in detail except by small numbers of auditors possessing extensive rabbinic education. The reasons for the creation of this distinctive poetic register are still being debated, and no consensus has yet emerged to explain it. Today all would agree that it does not reflect ignorance of Hebrew on the part of the writers or a desire to conceal the contents of the poetry from non-Jewish political authorities, though both theories were current in earlier stages of research and are still encountered in the secondary literature.

The vast majority of *piyyutim* are variations on a rabbinic theme, whether belonging to a holiday, an event in Israel's mythic history, a legal institution, or simply a passage of Scripture as interpreted by the rabbis. Thus, with the important exception of one category of *piyyut*, the subject matter is not religious experience per se, nor is it philosophy, theology, or nature; revelation itself is the predominant theme. *Piyyut* rehearses the text of the Bible in infinite permutations and combinations, based on homiletical and legalistic interpretations such as those of the rabbis of the Talmud and Midrash; in fact, *piyyut* may well have been one of the arenas in which homiletical interpretations were devised, as it is not an uncommon occurrence to find a *piyyut* embodying a midrash not found in any known source.

The exception referred to above, *qedushta,* is the complex of *piyyutim* relating to the Qedusha. Although many of these poems focus on homiletical exposition of biblical passages involving visions of the divine world, the majority are ecstatic hymns, often in litany form. Such poems are far less rich in intellectual content than ordinary *piyyutim,* but seem to be designed rather to imitate or even induce the visionary's state of mind.

The main subject of a particular *piyyut* is partly determined by the benedictions whose text the *piyyut* was intended to supply, replace, or supplement. In the cycle of benedictions surrounding the Shema, the themes are creation, Torah, God's love for Israel, and redemption. In the cycle constituting the Tefila, the themes are God's covenant with the ancestors, resurrection, God as sacred king (benedictions 1–3); the Temple service, gratitude, and peace (benedictions 5–7 on Sabbath and most festivals; benedictions 16–18 or 17–19 on weekdays); and the sacred character of the occasion of the service (benediction 4 on Sabbaths and festivals). But the poets often expand their treatment of the subject of the benediction by introducing other subjects, especially homiletical materials associated with the reading of the Torah. Poets exercised much ingenuity in linking the theme of the benediction to passages from the Torah reading of the day, which is often quoted verbatim in the text of the poem; they often elaborate midrashically at length on the Torah reading, sometimes seeming to lose sight of the theme of the benediction, then artfully reintroducing it just before the concluding benediction formula. The pattern of such *piyyutim* is thus very similar to that of the contemporaneous prose homiletic midrashim, in which the author begins with a verse from the Bible that appears to be remote from the one he wishes to expound and then artfully leads the discussion in such a way that a link between the two is discovered. In liturgical poetry, the passages from the Torah play the role of the seemingly irrelevant biblical verse that is artfully shown to have reference to the benediction at hand.

Yannai is the first known author of cycles of *qerovot* containing a set of *piyyutim* corresponding to each week's reading in the cycle of Torah readings. In the practice of Palestinian synagogues of the time, there were approximately 150 such readings, spread over a period of three and a half years. Yannai's *qerovot* are mostly of the type called *qedushta;* in this type, the first two benedictions of the Tefila are represented by poems of identical form, as in the normal *qerova* (singular). But the third benediction is preceded by a large number of poems of varying forms, all designed as an introduction to the recitation of the verse: "Holy, holy, holy is the Lord of Hosts; the whole earth is full of His glory" (Isa. 6:3) and certain other biblical passages, which, together with the poems that link them, are known as the Qedusha. In the communities that used poems of this type, this ritual must have been the climax of the service, for *qedushtaot* do not include poems for the remainder of the Tefila as in the normal *qerova;* presumably, after the Qedusha, the precentor would recite the standard prose benedictions for the remainder of the Tefila. Like other liturgical poets, Yannai composed similar cycles for festivals and other notable occasions.

Many communities incorporated the Qedusha not into the Tefila but into the first benediction of the Shema, known as *yoṣer;* accordingly, the cycles of *yoṣerot* composed by Kallir and later poets contain additional poems elaborating the Qedusha of *yoṣer,* though these poems are not as elaborate as those of the *qedushta.* The prominence of the Qedusha in the Palestinian rite is probably related to the prominence of *merkaba* (relating to God's chariot, particularly as described in Ezekiel, chapter 1) mysticism throughout the period, though the extent of this relationship is a matter of debate.

Among the many genres of liturgical poetry, some are defined as much by theme as by function. In addition to the types already mentioned, a few must be briefly described here:

1. *Seliḥot* are poems that were originally designed as an expansion of the benediction in the Tefila dealing with the forgiveness of sins. They were recited on fast days, expressing the contrition of the entire community for sins, especially with reference to the idea that the persecution and exile of the Jews are punishment for these sins. Although this type of poetry was to have its greatest efflorescence in the period of the Crusades, it played an important part as early as the Byzantine period, when even Jews living in the national homeland suffered systematic persecution. Lament for national suffering, anger at the oppressor, and hope for national redemption, themes that suffuse Hebrew liturgical poetry of all types and at all periods, were prominent already in the Byzantine period and concentrated in the *seliḥot*. Eventually the *seliḥot* were detached from the Tefila and recited in special prayer sessions held before dawn, especially during the week before and after Rosh HaShanah.

2. *ʿAvodot* are poems that describe the ritual of the Temple in Jerusalem on Yom Kippur and were designed for insertion in the fourth benediction of the Yom Kippur Tefila, the benediction dealing with the sanctity of the day. Nearly all *ʿavodot* begin with a sketch of the creation of the world, the election of Israel, and the election of Aaron and his descendants to serve as Israel's intercessors; they then quote Leviticus 16:30 to mark the thematic transition and go on to describe the ritual. The account focuses on the role of the high priest and concludes with poems of lament for the collapse of the sacrificial system with its expiatory rites.

3. *Hoshaʿnot* are litanies designed to accompany the processions of the Sukkot festival, a ceremony that was adopted by the synagogue from the Temple service. They are quite different in origin and function from the bulk of liturgical poetry, since they did not come into being as variant forms of rabbinic prayers. Nor are they poetically so rich; they consist mostly of lists of epithets for God, the Temple, or the Land of Israel, which the leader would recite in alphabetical order, and to which the congregation would respond, "Save us." But this ancient form was carried on by prominent liturgical poets, and new *hoshaʿnot* were composed through the Middle Ages.

Piyyut is, on the whole, a ritualistic kind of poetry, as befits its function as a public liturgy and as a vehicle of official doctrines and points of view. Its arcane language, its rigid strophic structures, its typological treatment of events, and its multitude of conventions make it more conducive to technical artistry than to self-expression; for the author of *piyyut*, creativity was more a matter of reinventing the language than of imitating nature or baring his soul. Thus, although it has been possible to chart the development of poetic forms for the *piyyut*, it has not been possible to sketch the literary personality of any of its creators, nor has it been possible to relate the vast majority of the thousands of extant *piyyutim* from the Byzantine period to specific historical events. Even those poets whose names are known can be characterized only by the ways in which they managed the conventions rather than by their particular religious outlooks or psychological profiles. Nevertheless, despite its remoteness from the more individual kind of poetic expression characteristic of romantic literature, its obsession with language, and its hermetic manner of expression, *piyyut* sometimes seems surprisingly congenial to the modernist temperament.

Iraq in the Early Geonic Period

With the Muslim conquest of the main centers of Jewish population in the seventh century and the establishment of Baghdad as the capital of the Abbasid Empire in the eighth, the center of Jewish cultural life shifted from Palestine to Iraq (which the Jews continued to call Babylonia). During the heyday of the Abbasid Empire (until the tenth century), Jewish literary production was dominated by the talmudic academies of Sura and Pumbedita, the heads of which were known as *geonim*. As the most prestigious figures in the intellectual life of the Rabbanite community in Iraq, these authorities lent their name to the entire period until the demise of the academies in the eleventh century; but the changes that occurred in the tenth century make it appropriate to treat the latter two centuries of the academies' existence separately.

The literary work of the *geonim* consisted mostly of Halakhic writing in Aramaic. The first important Geonic work, the *Sheeltot*, by R. (Rabbi) Ahai of Shavha (first half of the eighth century), is a homiletical work with a strong Halakhic component. Around the same time appeared the *Halkhot Pesuqot* of R. Yehudai Gaon, a primitive legal code. In the ninth century appeared the *Halakhot Gedolot*, another code of law, by Simeon Qayyara of Basra. Also typical of the Geonic period are responsa, written answers to Halakhic questions submitted for adjudication by rabbis from various parts of the world to the *geonim* as the final authorities.

In the field of Aggada, new midrash collections such as *Tanna Devei Eliyahu* and *Pirqe Rabbi Eliezer* appeared. Both works are rather different in structure from the midrashim of the Amoraic period; the former clearly reflect the Islamic milieu and attest to more developed interest in narrative than is evident in earlier midrashim.

The synagogue poets of the Geonic period continued to produce liturgical poetry in patterns largely inherited from the earlier period. But liturgical poetry came increasingly into conflict with the religious program of the *geonim*. The *geonim* strove to consolidate their control over Jewish law and ritual throughout the territories of their influence, which during the height of the Abbasid Empire included, at least theoretically, nearly all the territories reached by the Arab conquests. In addition to propagating the Babylonian Talmud as the sole authoritative base of religious law, the chief subject of rabbinic education, and the most prestigious Jewish book after the Bible, the *geonim* also attempted to unify synagogue ritual. The result was the nearly complete suppression of the Palestinian liturgical tradition in favor of the Babylonian and the emergence of a more or less canonical text of the prayers intended for use in all communities. Although minor local differences never disappeared, the *geonim* were quite successful in imposing a uniform text. But this program of unification could not tolerate prayer services dominated by constantly changing poetic texts that varied from week to week and from place to place; the *geonim* therefore discouraged the use of liturgical poetry, sometimes prohibiting it outright.

Despite their success in imposing a canonical liturgy, the *geonim* failed to banish poetry from the synagogue. By this time, many specific poems had become so familiar and widely used that they were incorporated into the canonical text itself. Some communities had cycles of liturgical poems that were so well established that they would not give them up. And in many communities, the desire for liturgical variation remained strong enough that they refused to give up the practice of commissioning new poetry. The compromise that was eventually reached and that is still the practice in those traditional communities in which liturgical poetry has survived is to recite the canonical service in accordance with the Geonic regulations but also to insert the liturgical poetry in suitable places—not always the ones for which the poems were originally designed—as a supplement to the fixed liturgy. In this way, the prayer ritual came to be seen as consisting of a fixed, statutory text mostly in prose and fairly uniform throughout the Jewish world and a body of poetry regarded theoretically as optional and varying from community to community.

In the course of the Middle Ages, most communities gave up commissioning new poetry and adopted a set of poems for the entire year, creating local rites authoritative for large areas (like the French rite, the Italian rite, and the Western Ashkenazic rite) or for particular towns or groups of towns (like the rites of Frankfurt am Main; of Aleppo; or of Asti, Montcalvo, and Fossano). To this day, the deviations in the canonical prayer text worldwide remain nugatory; the local rites are mainly distinguished by their different selections of poetry. Though the Hebrew poets of early Geonic Iraq continued to experiment with the forms of liturgical poetry, they did not innovate much with regard to the liturgical functions of the poetry, its language, or contents. There were also some rites, such as that of Yemen, from which liturgical poetry largely disappeared, though there is none from which it is wholly absent.

The popularity and prestige of liturgical poetry throughout the Jewish world are widely attested by several facts: It continued to be composed throughout the Middle Ages; most important rabbis made some attempt to compose liturgical poetry; and it was the subject of learned commentaries, like other religious texts. Its popularity is also attested by descriptions of Jewish liturgy by medieval observers. Of those, one of the most memorable is a satire by Judah al-Ḥarizi (d. 1225) implying that ordinary people—absurdly, from the point of view of religious law—attended the synagogue more for the sake of the poetry than for the canonical prayers. Al-Ḥarizi's satire presupposes that this preference was widespread.

Local liturgical practices were not the only centrifugal force with which the *geonim* had to contend in consolidating their control. A number of opposition movements arose during the early Geonic period, of which two were literarily productive. In a remote corner of Iran, a Jewish heretic named Ḥivi of Balkh wrote a treatise attacking the Bible for its apparent internal contradictions and irrational statements. Saadia Gaon wrote a treatise in Hebrew verse refuting Ḥivi's objections. In the Geonic heartland of Iraq arose the Karaite movement, which proved very influential in the later development of Jewish literature. Beginning in the eighth century, this movement broke with Geonic authority, denying the authenticity of the rabbinic tradition and attempting to restore the Bible as the sole authoritative guide to religious life.

Karaism developed into an important force in the ninth and tenth centuries, growing in numbers and influence, so that in many countries two distinct Jewish communities existed side by side. From a literary point of view, Karaism was a stimulus to intensified study of the Bible, which the rabbis had tended to neglect in favor of the study of rabbinic tradition. Karaite scholars were the first to develop two important areas of Jewish studies that came to appear to be characteristic of Jewish scholarship: the writing of commentaries on the books of the Bible and the systematic study of the Hebrew language. The Rabbanites responded to the Karaite challenge by themselves taking up these activities. Thus, it is theorized that the Masoretes, who developed the vowel and cantillation marks attached to the words of the Hebrew Bible, created authoritative biblical codices, and were the first to explore Hebrew grammar, were Karaites and that they were led to these studies by the centrality of the Bible in their religious outlook. So responsibly was their work performed that it was accepted as authoritative even by the circles of the *geonim*, their arch-enemies. To this day, the standard editions of the Bible are based on the Masoretic text.

Another feature of Karaite writing that was groundbreaking for later Jewish literature was the fact that much of their writing on religious subjects was in Arabic. We shall see that in their concern with the Bible, their interest in Hebrew language and grammar, and their use of Arabic for writing on religious subjects, they were followed by one of the greatest rabbinic authorities of the Middle Ages, Saadia Gaon, through whose prestige these subjects would become important for rabbinic Judaism as well.

The Later Geonic Period

It was precisely during the decline of the Abbasid Empire that a figure arose in Iraq whose career heralded a radical shift in the nature of Jewish literature, paving the way for the scarcely paralleled achievements of the next two centuries. Saadia ben Joseph, a rabbi of Egyptian origin who rose to the position of *gaon* of Sura in 928, had a forceful personality, a driving ambition, a broad education, and a fluent pen. He is the first medieval Jewish figure whose biography is known in some detail. Some aspects of Saadia's career had antecedents among his predecessors in the gaonate, but he was the first to unite a number of particular interests, skills, and character traits, and to generate from them a substantial literary production that became a landmark in the history of Jewish literature.

We start by considering language. By the tenth century, Aramaic and Greek, the languages spoken in the Jewish heartlands (Palestine, Iraq, and Egypt), had been replaced by Arabic. The Jews spoke, on the whole, the same Arabic as that spoken by Muslims and Christians. When writing, Jews preferred to use the Hebrew alphabet, just as Christians in Iraq often preferred to continue using the Syriac alphabet. Today, the language of Jewish writings in Arabic using the Hebrew alphabet is called Judeo-Arabic, but except for Hebrew technical terms used by Jews to refer to ritual matters when speaking or writing Arabic, this language was completely intelligible to non-Jews and hardly at all different from the Arabic generally spoken. It was only after the Middle Ages, with the increasing segregation of Middle Eastern Jews from the Muslim populace, that Judeo-Arabic would diverge significantly from Muslim Arabic. For most of the Middle Ages, it is simpler and more accurate to speak of the Arabic writings of the Jews as being in Arabic.

The early *geonim* were slow to adopt Arabic as a written language, and even when they did so, they did not attempt to use it for major literary works. Saadia was the first of the *geonim* to use Arabic as a matter of course as the language of his books. He lent Arabic quasi-liturgical status by translating the Bible into it; he also composed a lengthy commentary on the Torah and commentaries on many other biblical books in Arabic.

But commentaries were a traditional form of Jewish literary production. Saadia went further, adopting not only the language of the Arabs but also their literary genres and breaking with the genre categories of the Jewish tradition: He was the first known postbiblical Jewish writer to compose treatises devoted to a single topic and organized by logical principles not deriving from earlier Jewish works. Saadia, in effect, introduced to Jewish literature the modern idea of the book. Each of his books has an introduction in which the motives for writing it are described, the thesis succinctly stated, and the contents outlined. This procedure, so natural and obvious to modern readers, was entirely new to the Jews and may be regarded as an important legacy of Arabic, and ultimately of Hellenic, literature.

Saadia's books were not all written in Arabic. He wrote some works in Hebrew and also devoted significant efforts to promoting the use of Hebrew. Most notable in this regard is his dictionary, the *Agron,* organized to facilitate the efforts of Hebrew poets to find appropriate acrostics and rhymes and prefaced with an introduction in Hebrew amounting to a manifesto for a program to revive the use and study of Hebrew, perhaps even as a spoken language. From this introduction, it is clear that Saadia was responding to the challenge of the Arabic idea of *ʿarabiyya,* the notion of the unsurpassable perfection of the Arabic language, an idea that was reinforced for Muslims by theological doctrine of *iʿjaz al-qurʾān,* the miraculous character of the Arabic style of the Quran. Saadia attempted to counter this challenge by promoting the talmudic idea that Hebrew was the original and most perfect language of mankind. The cause of its decline and apparent imperfection vis-à-vis the other languages, especially Arabic, was the Jewish exile, which was responsible not merely for the loss of territory and sovereignty but also for the debasement of the Hebrew language, with the result that the superiority of Hebrew had been temporarily obscured; it was a religious duty to cultivate and attempt to restore the language to its original splendor.

Saadia saw the writing of poetry in Hebrew as an important part of this linguistic agenda, given the tremendous prestige of classical Arabic poetry throughout the Muslim world. He wrote Hebrew liturgical poetry extensively, much of it in an extremely difficult style that he seems to have devised in a conscious attempt to re-create the Hebrew poetic idiom along lines related to his polemical linguistic agenda. He seems to have viewed Hebrew liturgical poetry as the Jewish literary heritage corresponding to classical Arabic poetry for Muslims and saw its cultivation as a part of the attempt to establish Hebrew language and literature within the Jewish community as a cultural force of corresponding weight and prestige. In this regard, he seems to have been in disagreement with the other *geonim,* though in liturgical practice he may have come around to the more conservative view. By experimenting with poetry, by using it outside the sphere of liturgy, and by writing a dictionary for poets, he laid the intellectual foundations for the flowering of Hebrew poetry in Spain, as we shall see.

A large part of Saadia's career was devoted to polemics, and several of these resulted in innovative literary works. His book on the calendar played a central part in the notorious controversy between the *geonim* and the Palestinian rabbi Ben Meir. His *Book of the Festivals,* a commemoration of the controversy, was written in two versions, one in Arabic and one in Hebrew. The Hebrew version was in a ceremonious, quasi-biblical style and provided with vowel and accent markings, like a biblical codex. Saadia followed this procedure also with the Hebrew introduction to his dictionary for poets, and with his *Open Book,* a defense of his gaonate, written during the period of his exile, when he had been temporarily deposed. Other polemical works by Saadia include his Hebrew poem refuting the critique of the Bible by the Jewish heretic Ḥivi of Balkh; his poem against the Masorete Ben Asher; and, especially, works directed against the Karaites.

Saadia is best known today for his Arabic theological treatise, *The Book of Beliefs and Opinions.* This book again shows Saadia as an innovator, for it is the first known Jewish book of systematic theology. It is also early evidence of a cultural fact of great importance for the development of Jewish literature. The adoption of Arabic as the chief language of Jewish intellectual life from the time of Saadia was not merely a linguistic development but signaled the writers' intellectual Arabization as well. It reflects the tendency of the Jewish intelligentsia to acquire an Arabic education, in addition to their Jewish education, and to join in the intellectual activities that were cultivated by contemporary Muslim intellectuals, especially in the fields of poetry, Arabic grammar, science, philosophy, and theology. Their Arabic education gave them access not only to traditional Arabic lore but also to the literary tradition of late antiquity in the form of works of Greek science and philosophy that had been translated into Arabic during the eighth and ninth centuries.

The Jewish intellectuals' Arabization made it possible for at least some of them to share in the activities of the *faylasufs,* Arabic-speaking intellectuals of varied religious commitments, who cultivated the learning of antiquity and who would meet for discussion of topics of common interest. Improbable as it may seem in a world dominated by religious absolutism, the climate in the late Abbasid and Buwayhid periods was favorable to interconfessional intellectual life. There were intellectual gatherings attended by Muslims, Christians, Jews, Zoroastrians, atheists, and members of all manner of sects, where serious discussion was made possible by the common language, Arabic, and the common intellectual guidelines of formal logic. Although it is not known whether Saadia personally participated in such gatherings, his work reflects the interpenetration of attitudes, methods, and ideas characteristic of the highest intellectual life of the times. His desire to put the Jewish tradition on the basis of pure reason emerges out of the spirit of the time and established the problematics of Jewish philosophy for the duration of the Middle Ages.

As if all these innovations were not enough, Saadia left Jewish literature another important legacy in the form of a literary personality. Rabbinic literature had always been communal literature. In the thousands of Hebrew poems written in the period preceding Saadia, not one personality is in evidence, even where the poets' names are known. In the Talmud, traditions are attached to the names of authorities, but no personality is attached to most of these names, which, from a literary point of view, are virtually interchangeable. Most stories of the famous rabbis of the Talmud and midrashim tend toward the exemplary and the typological, and autobiographical statements are disconnected and rare. By contrast, in the introductions to his works and especially in his *Open Book*, Saadia, writing in the first person, describes his own experiences, his own motivations, his own attitudes. It does not matter whether these statements are literally true or are a literary device. Saadia is the first rabbinic writer to use the word "I" to create a convincing literary persona. The only known postbiblical precedents in Jewish writing—and they cannot have been known to Saadia—are Josephus and Philo, in the Hellenistic period.

From the time of Saadia, Jewish writing in the Islamic world acquired a character wholly distinct from Jewish writing in Christian Europe. Writers in the Christian territories continued to be limited in language to Hebrew; in literary forms, to those established by the ancient rabbis, such as commentaries, codes, and liturgical poetry based mostly on midrash (though they also employed sporadically some new prose forms); in content, to religion, especially religious law; and in intellectual background, to the Jewish tradition (including, of course, whatever foreign ideas had been haphazardly incorporated into the rabbinic tradition). Writers in the Islamic world had three languages at their disposal (Hebrew, Arabic, and Aramaic) for their books and a wide range of new subjects. Religion remained at the center of their concern, but secular themes increasingly took root among Jewish writers, both in Arabic and in Hebrew. Even their writing on religious subjects was strongly marked by contact with Arabic writing, as can be seen in the influence both of Islamic terminology and ideas on Jewish religious writers and, especially, in the influence on them of Greek philosophical and scientific ideas. Above all, their intellectual interests were as broad as those of Arabic-speaking, non-Jewish intellectuals.

These differences can be accounted for by three factors. The Islamic world inhabited by the Jews embodied a strong, complex, and advanced culture, which was actually the dominant culture of the Western world and the Middle East for many centuries, whereas intellectual life in Christian Europe during this period was relatively stagnant. Furthermore, the Jews of Islamdom enjoyed both the wealth and the knowledge of Arabic necessary to afford them access to the prevailing high culture, whereas the Jews of Christiandom were blocked even from the much narrower intellectual life available there because it was controlled mostly by monasteries and because its official language was Latin rather than the vernacular. Finally, Islamic society, in its periods of domination, was sufficiently secure to permit easy interaction between Muslims and non-Muslims.

The differences between the intellectual state of Christendom and Islamdom and the Jews' position within them account for the fact that until the decline of Islam after the Crusades, the center of Jewish intellectual activity and literary production would be the Islamic countries. Jewish Christiandom, for all its attainments in the field of religious law and liturgical poetry, would never be so vibrant.

The cosmopolitan character of Judaism in the Islamic world of the tenth century is reflected in a work that has only recently come to attention. The author, Sa'id b. Babshad, is otherwise unknown. His book, known simply as *The Proverbs of Sa'id b. Babshad*, is a collection of versified proverbs in rhymed, metrical couplets. It defines the goal of religion as knowing God and asserts that this knowledge is achieved through intellectual activity, a position quite natural to the *faylasufs* of the age; the Torah and the Jewish covenant with God are scarcely mentioned. In the following century, such attitudes would become commonplace among the Jewish intellectuals of Spain. Other, anonymous works reflect a pattern of literary interchange between Jews and environment on the level of the folktale. *The Alphabet of Ben Sira*, a collection of cynical, parodic stories and proverbs attributed to the infant Ben Sira, unfolds in a generally prurient atmosphere. The purpose of this unusual book has not yet been explained; oddly, it was carried to Italy and Ashkenaz, where it was taken seriously by the Ashkenazic Pietists (*Haside ashkenaz*). *The Tale of the Jerusalemite* is an elaborate story based on the widespread folklore motif of a man who marries a female demon. This story too was carried to Ashkenaz, and was even attributed to the Ashkenazic Pietists. Also possibly from this period is *The Tales of Sendebar*, the Hebrew version of a piece of international lore that originated in India or Persia and exists in many languages. Like the *Thousand and One Nights* and other collections of folktales and fables of the age, it consists of a collection of stories within a framework story. In the framework story, a king accuses his wife of attempting to seduce his son, but the son is barred from defending himself by the warnings of astrologers that he will die if he speaks for a certain period. The wife tells a series of stories intended to prove that sons are disloyal to fathers, and the king's counselors tell stories that are intended to prove that women are deceitful to their husbands. The work is frankly misogynistic. It too was disseminated throughout the Jewish world.

Byzantium and Ashkenaz

Although the *geonim* held sway in most of the Islamic territories, Palestinian liturgical traditions were carried on in Palestine itself and, to some extent, in adjacent Egypt, but especially in the Byzantine Empire. In the eastern part of the empire, the liturgy of the Greek-speaking Jews came to be known as the Romaniot rite. There it persisted until the sixteenth century, when the collapse of the Byzantine Empire and the arrival of large numbers of refugees from Iberia brought about the Sephardization of the region.

Byzantine Italy also had important centers of rabbinic scholarship that remained in close contact with Palestine, and many rabbis of this community wrote liturgical poetry. Of these, the most notable were Silano (Venosa, early ninth century), Amittai ben Shefatia (Oria, late ninth–early tenth century), and Solomon b. Judah of Rome, usually called Solomon the Babylonian (second half of the tenth century).

Silano's few remaining poems are *selihot* lamenting the exile and sufferings of the Jews. One of them still forms part of the *Ne'ila* service in the Ashkenazic rite. Amittai also wrote a number of *selihot*, some of which were inspired by the persecution of the Jews of Byzantine Italy by the Emperor Basil I, some of which remain in the Ashkenazic liturgy. In consonance with the religious spirit of his time and place, Amittai's poetry is much concerned with angels; it describes the kind of religious experience and employs the kind of religious language associated with the *hekhalot* (throne mysticism) literature. Particularly noteworthy in this regard is a poem describing Moses' ascent through the ranks of the angels to receive the Torah. Amittai's language is not as opaque as that of most liturgical poetry, and the small part of his production that is extant is of high quality.

This preoccupation of Amittai and the other poets of this period with mysticism is reflected in a major prose work of the tenth century, the extensive commentary by Shabetai Donnolo on *Sefer Yeṣirah*. The work is prefaced with a long poem with an acrostic of Donnolo's name, written in order to guarantee that his name would be forever attached to the work.

The third of the great Italian liturgical poets of the period was Solomon the Babylonian, whose work strongly influenced the Ashkenazic rite. He is known for his *selihot*, which are sometimes called *shalmoniyot*, after his name; they are powerful laments for the sufferings of Israel in exile and petitions for divine retribution against the enemy. He is especially famed for his monumental *yoṣer* for Passover, one of the most impressive components of the Ashkenazic liturgy and also one of the most difficult. The many individual parts of which it is composed are strung together on the literary thread of the Song of Songs, with each successive stanza concluding with a quotation from the successive verses of that biblical book, one of the cornerstones of the homiletic traditions of Passover. Later Italian and Ashkenazic poets were to compose imitations of this great work.

The tenth century also saw the rise of a group of poets in the northern Italian city of Lucca. There, most of the poetic activity sprang from members of a single family, known as the Kalonymides. Of them, the most important were Moses ben Kalonymos, author of the *qedushta* for the last day of Passover in the Ashkenazic rite; Kalonymos b. Moses the Elder, author of a series of poems for Yom Kippur in the Ashkenazic rite; and, especially, Meshullam ben Kalonymos, author of one of the *qedushtaot* for Yom Kippur in the Ashkenazic rite and especially famous for his ʿ*avoda*, which is still recited even in congregations that have drastically reduced the amount of liturgical poetry in their services. As we shall see, several poets of this family moved to the Rhineland in the tenth century; they thus serve as a bridge between the Palestinian-Italian poetic tradition and the new Ashkenazic rite.

Several important prose works have come down to us from the early Italian Jewish community; they are of such high quality that they must reflect more extensive literary activity in the area than can be reconstructed today. In 953, a Hebrew historical work called *Yosifon* appeared, recounting the history of the Jews from the creation through the Second Commonwealth. Attributed to an otherwise unknown Yosef ben Gurion, the work is an abridgment and adaptation of the historical work in Greek by the first-century Jewish writer Josephus, whose name is reflected in the title. *Yosifon* is written in excellent biblical Hebrew in a narrative style so vivid that it has remained extremely popular throughout the course of Jewish history. Since the twelfth century, manuscripts of *Yosifon* have incorporated the Alexander Romance, a cycle of stories about Alexander the Great deriving from the Hellenistic memoirs of Alexander the Great, known as Pseudo-Callisthenes, and widely disseminated throughout medieval Christian Europe. This is a cycle of literary lore that the Jews shared with their Christian neighbors. In Hebrew there are no fewer than six works on the subject; they are not simply translations of an original text but, like the versions in other European languages, develop the story freely, sometimes drawing on legends of Alexander from the Talmud that are independent of the Hellenistic source. The earliest Hebrew version probably appeared in the eleventh century.

Finally, Aḥimaʿaz b. Paltiel, a scion of a notable family of rabbis and mystics that included Silano and Amittai, told of the activities and adventures of his ancestors in a charming chronicle, *The Scroll of Ahimaaz*, written in Capua in 1054. This unusual work is one of the outstanding Hebrew literary productions of the Middle Ages. Replete with folklore, fantastic stories, and factual information, it is written from beginning to end in rhymed prose. This is a technique that was used in Hebrew liturgical poetry at least since the time of Yannai, but that was first applied to narrative by Hebrew writers of al-Andalus in imitation of the Arabic *maqāma,* a genre that will be defined later in this chapter. If Aḥimaʿaz adopted this technique in imitation of Iberian Hebrew writers, it would be the earliest known case of Arabic influence on Hebrew literature in Italy in this period. In any case, he handled the technique with great mastery.

In the tenth century, the center of creativity in the field of liturgical poetry shifted from Italy to the Rhineland, as in the concrete case of the Kalonymides, who actually relocated there. The founding fathers of the great religious academies of the Rhineland, R. Gershom, "the Light of the Exile," and Simeon b. Isaac, known as "Simeon the Great," were both important liturgical poets. Simeon is the central figure of the famous legend of the rabbi whose son, abducted by a maid, was baptized and rose through the ranks of the Church until he eventually became pope. This legend was attached to his poem in the Ashkenazic rite for the second day of Rosh HaShanah because of its acrostic "Simeon b. Isaac . . . Elhanan my son."

Most of the poetry of the writers named so far in this section continue the forms and liturgical functions of the Palestinian school of liturgical poets. The tenth to the twelfth centuries saw the consolidation of the Ashkenazic liturgical tradition, including fixed cycles of *yoṣerot* and *qerovot* for the liturgical occasions of the year; this tradition was canonized in the *Maḥzor Vitry* (ca. 1100). With the consolidation of the liturgical tradition, new poems in many genres of liturgical poetry were no longer in demand; accordingly, the composition of new *yoṣerot* and *qerovot* ceased; new composition came to be limited mostly to *seliḥot,* a genre in which greater liturgical freedom prevailed, though a few new types of liturgical poetry were also devised.

The *seliḥa* became the most distinctive area of Ashkenazic poetic creativity. *Seliḥot,* originally intended for fast days, were also recited on days that were established for the annual commemoration of local persecutions. Such commemorative days multiplied as a result of the persecutions connected with the Crusades and, later, with the Black Plague, and so did the number of *seliḥot.* The *seliḥot* of the period of the Crusades have features that distinguish them from those of Byzantine Palestine and Italy. They often deal explicitly with the mass murders and with the mass suicides that were a distinctive expression of Ashkenazic piety under Christian attack. Accordingly, they are far more intense and anguished than most of the earlier *seliḥot.* Furthermore, unlike most Hebrew liturgical poetry, which almost never reflects actual events, they often mention and sometimes even describe specific incidents, naming particular Jewish communities that were destroyed and individuals who were killed or who committed suicide. There are cases of *seliḥot* describing the experience of an individual with an explicitness ordinarily associated more with the Hebrew poetry of

Spain—for example, Rabbi Eliezer b. Judah's poignantly detailed poem on the death of his wife and daughters in the First Crusade.

But most of the poetry, like Hebrew liturgical poetry in general, continued to operate on the basis of typology. The theme of the near-killing of Isaac by Abraham became a characteristic subject of *selihot*, for this story came to be associated in the minds of the congregations with the slaughter of children by fathers who wished to prevent them from falling into the hands of the mobs; *selihot* on this theme are called ʿ*aqedot*. The stories of the ten rabbinic martyrs of the Hadrianic persecutions and of Hannah and her seven sons from the Maccabean age were also worked up into stirring poems. Even the biblical account of the suicide of King Saul and his son Jonathan was, quite appropriately, brought into the poetry.

The greatest Ashkenazic *seliha* poets were Ephraim of Bonn (not only because of his famous ʿ*aqeda*), his brother Hillel, Eliezer b. Natan, and Meir of Rothenburg (who made a remarkable attempt to write a long poem in the style of Judah Halevi's ode to Zion, using the Arabic quantitative meters, which were mostly unknown to Ashkenazic writers).

The Crusades were also responsible for the creation of a prose literary genre in Ashkenaz, the crusade chronicle. The authors of the surviving works on the First Crusade were Solomon b. Samson, Eliezer b. Natan, and an anonymous writer; and on the Second Crusade, Ephraim of Bonn.

The circles of the Ashkenazic Pietists produced a major prose work, *The Book of the Pious*, by Rabbi Judah the Pious (beginning of the thirteenth century). This work, which became a religious classic, consists of some 400 exempla (moral instructions in the form of stories and anecdotes). Remarkably, its form and content recall in many ways those of Christian exempla works, a genre that reached full flower in this very period. But unlike the Christian exempla works, the stories in *The Book of the Pious*, rather than merely retellings of ancient stories, are mostly new stories, many of them probably inventions of Rabbi Judah the Pious himself. The masters of the Ashkenazic Pietist school themselves became the subjects of legends, which eventually found their way into postmedieval collections like the *Maase Buch*, in both its Hebrew and Yiddish versions.

The Ashkenazic Pietists also wrote poetry, which, though intended for recitation in the synagogue, did not belong to any already existing genre, a most unusual phenomenon in Jewish liturgical history. These poems, known as the "Hymns of Unity" and "Hymns of Glory," were meditations on mystical theological doctrines, and some of them are still in use.

Medieval Jewry produced a variety of Hebrew prose works of a literary nature. The midrashic tradition of Byzantine Palestine had an afterlife in the Middle Ages, producing encyclopedic compilations of mostly older material, such as *Genesis Rabbati*, by the disciples of Moses the Preacher (Narbonne, eleventh century); *Lekah Tov*, by Tobias b. Eliezer (Balkans, eleventh century); *Yalqut Shim'oni*, attributed to Simon the Preacher (Frankfort, thirteenth century); and many others. Besides these late midrashim, there are many prose stories that elaborate on biblical and talmudic stories. There are also longer works consisting of reworkings of stories that originated in the Muslim world in the late Geonic period, as already described, and belonging to the international folklore tradition shared by the Arabic-speaking Middle East and the Latin West. It is generally not possible to determine exactly the dates and provenance of these works in the form in which they have come down to us, as their transmission history is often so complex that it cannot be untangled. Some exist in several versions, none of which is definitive; they were constantly being reworked, embellished, and abridged, and some continued to grow and develop after the Middle Ages. They form a continuum between folklore and formal literature. Of this type is the *Alexander Romance*, mentioned in connection with *Yosifon*; and *The History of Jesus*, a parodic biography of Jesus that exists in many versions. This work contains elements that are found already in the Talmud and in Geonic literature, but it also reflects the influence of the *History of Ben Sira*. Beyond that, its history is obscure.

Rather more formally a literary work, *The Fox Fables*, by Berekhya Hanaqdan (twelfth–thirteenth centuries), is written in rhymed prose. This collection of animal fables is heavily dependent on the European fable tradition going back to Aesop via Marie de France. The author was a Jew of Normandy or Norman England.

The fourteenth century marked the emergence of Yiddish as a literary language, beginning with the adaptation in rhyme of biblical tales. Stories of Abraham, Moses, Esther, and of the binding of Isaac are known; a poem of Moses dates from 1382. Important biblical epics in Yiddish are the *Shmuel Buch* and the *Melokhim Buch*, presumably written in the fifteenth century.

Islamic Spain

The Jewish community of Islamic Spain, like that of the rest of the Muslim world, was part of the cultural sphere of Iraq and the *geonim*. In the tenth century, when Islamic Spain broke openly with the Abbasid caliphate and became an independent caliphate, the Jewish community, formerly quite obscure, suddenly burst into world prominence and produced a distinctive and brilliant Jewish culture, often referred to as the Golden Age of Hebrew literature. This culture reflected the easy interaction between Jewish and Muslim intellectuals that we have already seen in tenth-century Iraq; it was also the culmination of the Arabizing Jewish culture propagated by Saadia Gaon.

We know little of Spanish Jewry until the time of Ḥasdai Ibn Shaprut (915–970), except that by the tenth century it was sufficiently prosperous and cultured to have produced a man of his accomplishments and stature. Though he was not known to have been a writer himself, he was learned enough in medicine to have a position in the court at Cordoba and to have been involved, on the Andalusian caliph's behalf, in a translation project involving a Greek pharmacological text. In Jewish writings, he is referred to as *hanasi* (the chief); we do not know exactly whether the title was merely an honorific or whether it designated a particular office within the Jewish community. But he does seem to have controlled the life of the community and thus may be regarded as the first of the "courtier-rabbis" who were to be characteristic of Muslim Spain and influential in the development of Hebrew letters there.

A twelfth-century Hispano-Jewish writer said, "In the days of Ḥasdai the Chief, they began to chirp, and in the days of Samuel the Nagid, they lifted their voices." This maxim expresses the awareness of Andalusian Jews themselves that their time was a Golden Age of Hebrew literature, that their writers had achieved something completely new in Jewish history, something outstanding, something of permanent value. From today's perspective, it appears that the achievement of Andalusian Jewry from the tenth to the twelfth centuries was not to be surpassed until our own time, when Hebrew Reborn has produced a new flowering that finally has outshone the Andalusian one. Social historians no longer look upon the experience of the contemporary Jewish community as a Golden Age; but for the literary history, the term is as apt today as when it was first applied to the Hebrew literature of Andalusia.

Ḥasdai is generally regarded as the immediate founder of the Hebrew Golden Age partly because of the two poets who were his protégés. These poets addressed poetry to him, dedicated books to him, and produced poetry for his use as the chief spokesman for Andalusian Jewry.

Menaḥem ben Saruq must have served Ḥasdai as a kind of Hebrew secretary, for he composed a letter in Hebrew that Ḥasdai sent via Jewish merchant-travelers to the king of the Khazars in an attempt to make contact with that community. The letter is written in simple, dignified Hebrew, modeled on the Hebrew of the Bible. It is prefaced with a Hebrew panegyric poem, the language of which is also close to biblical Hebrew but with some influence of the language of liturgical poetry. This poem may probably be regarded as the first manifestation of the new Hebrew poetry in Spain. It is a secular poem, in the sense that it was written for a nonliturgical purpose; it praises a human being in elaborate—perhaps to us, extravagant—language, in the style of Arabic panegyrics (*madīḥ*) of the time; it uses the typically Arabic technique of monorhyme. Except for the absence of a consistent meter, it closely resembles Arabic political poetry;

and in writing it, Menaḥem was playing the role of a Muslim court secretary within the Jewish community. In light of this achievement, Menaḥem's activity as a lexicographer seems less innovative, though his Hebrew-Hebrew dictionary was to achieve no little fame and would eventually become known to Ashkenazi scholars.

Menaḥem did not begin his career as a Hebrew poet under Ḥasdai; we know that he had already served Ḥasdai's father as a poet as well, though we do not know what Ḥasdai's father's position was. Menaḥem also wrote formal mourning poems on the death of Ḥasdai's parents, and such poems (marāthī) are also part of the Arabic literary tradition. Finally, when, as would often happen to courtiers, Menaḥem fell out of favor with Ḥasdai and was treated brutally, Menaḥem wrote a formal epistle, complaining of how he had been abused and demanding justice; the epistle is a long work of sustained power and dignity in nearly perfect biblical Hebrew. Even without considering that Menaḥem appears at the very beginning of the Golden Age, his Hebrew poems and the epistle show great refinement and literary mastery.

Ḥasdai's other protégé was Dunash ben Labrat, author of religious poems, a few of which are still in liturgical use today. Dunash had been a student of Saadia's in Iraq. He arrived in Spain with a literary invention that provided the one element missing in Menaḥem's system of imitating Arabic literary style: quantitative metrics. The system of writing poetry in a metrical pattern based on the alternation of long and short syllables, as in Latin and Greek, was standard in Arabic but had seemed impossible to duplicate in Hebrew. Dunash solved the problem somewhat artificially by considering the Hebrew reduced vowel called שׁוא נע and its variants as equivalent to the Arabic short vowel; all other vowels, he considered long (except the prefix ו, which is also short). In this way, he was able to imitate the myriad permitted combinations of long and short vowels that make up the Arabic system. Such poems are monorhymed, whether consisting of two lines or of one hundred. (For a thorough discussion of Golden Age metrics, see the *Encyclopaedia Judaica*, s.v. "Hebrew Prosody.") Dunash's innovation aroused a violent debate; he was attacked by Menaḥem's disciples because of the grammatical distortions that his system inevitably caused when it was applied to Hebrew. But these attacks did not prevent the new system from becoming popular immediately. From the time of Dunash on, all secular Hebrew poetry—and some liturgical poetry as well—written in Spain and in the communities influenced by Jewish Spain is in Arabic quantitative metrics.

The adoption of literary models from Arabic was only one part of a larger pattern, for the Jewish grandees of Muslim Spain adopted the manners of the Muslims in many other ways, imitating in their social lives the patterns of the Muslim upper classes. Their Hebrew poetry reflects a Jewish world that resembled the Muslim world in every respect but religion, a world of luxury, fine manners, sophisticated entertainment consisting of music, dance, wine drinking, and flirtation. To what extent the poetry reflected real life is hard to determine; but it seems reasonable to assume that at least some of the Jewish grandees were leading the life of pleasure and refinement described in their Hebrew poetry. Dunash wrote a poem describing a drinking party held by Ḥasdai; the poet described enthusiastically the varied sensual pleasures offered by the banquet, and he balanced against these worldly delights the sober thought that such pleasures were inappropriate for a people undergoing punishment by God for exile.

The poetry of the Golden Age would embrace many genres adopted from Arabic literature. Among these are short poems on themes of pleasure: poems describing wine and the pleasures of drinking wine with friends; love poems describing beautiful women or beautiful boys, often expressing the poet's frustration at their coquettish refusal to be drawn into a love relationship; poems lamenting the brevity of such a delightful life. There are also short poems of worldly and religious wisdom.

There are also several genres of longer poems. Many of these are in the *qaṣīda* form characteristic of Arabic poetry of all periods; these poems are constructed of two parts: The first deals with a general theme, often love or nature description, and the second part deals with the poem's actual purpose. The two parts are linked by a transition. Part of the poet's skill consists in making this transition a convincing one. *Qaṣīdas* are formal poems, often having a public function. Typical themes are the praise of a patron or friend; praise of a person who has died (in which case the *qaṣīda* serves as a formal eulogy of the kind that Menaḥem must have composed for Ḥasdai's parents); and complaint or reproach. All the poetry is dominated by conventions borrowed from Arabic. The same features of the wine, of the girls, of the gardens, of the patron, or of the friend are described again and again; and the same imagery is used and reused in comparisons. The situation of lovers is always the same. Yet poets exercised great ingenuity in exploiting the conventions to design lovely artifacts. And the fact that they were heirs to a stylized tradition did not prevent them from striking out on their own. Each of the great poets found ways to exploit the rigid conventions of Arabic poetry in order to make a personal statement. As a result, they have left us not only a mass of lovely conventional poetry but also a set of precious documents of human imagination and aspiration.

Besides imitating Arabic prosody and themes, the poets made extensive use of another technique adopted from Arabic: rhetorical devices and figures of speech. Although present to some extent in all poetry, these had come into vogue in Arabic in the ninth century, and the Arabic poets of Spain who provided the Hebrew poets with their immediate models made heavy use of them. Hebrew poetry makes extensive use of simile, metaphor, antithesis, parallelism, puns, and wordplays of all kinds. Another literary device known to Arabic poetry but central to the literary technique of the Hebrew poets is quotation: Hebrew poets made artful use of biblical quotations, often creating interesting effects by distorting the meaning. This device was common in Hebrew poetry long before the Jews came into contact with Arabic literature, and the Golden Age poets developed it into one of the mainstays of their art. That was possible because the basis of a Hebrew literary education was the memorization of the Bible; a Hebrew poet could count on his audience being able to recognize any quotation from it and to respond to his manipulation of the quotation.

Besides composing poems in classical Arabic verse patterns, the Hebrew poets used an Arabic verse pattern that was invented around the time when Ḥasdai's protégés were inventing the new Hebrew poetry. This new form, which Arabic literary theorists never considered completely respectable, but which, nevertheless, was extremely popular in Spain, is called *muwashshaḥ* in Arabic. It differs from the classical Arabic poem in being strophic, not monorhymed. It normally has five stanzas. Each stanza consists of two parts: The first, consisting of three to five lines, has a rhyme peculiar to that stanza; and the second, consisting of two lines, has a rhyme shared with the last two lines of all the stanzas. The last two lines of the final stanza are called the *kharja*, or exit. In Arabic *muwashshaḥat*, the *kharja* is not in classical Arabic but in vernacular Arabic or Romance, the vernacular descended from Latin that was commonly spoken alongside Arabic in Muslim Spain. It is theorized that these lines are a quotation from popular songs around which the Arabic poet built his poem. Hebrew did not have a colloquial register, as it was not a spoken language; therefore, Hebrew *muwashshaḥat* ordinarily have their *kharja* in Romance, colloquial Arabic, or even in a mixture, though sometimes they simply end in Hebrew. *Muwashshaḥat* originally were poems on the light themes of love, gardens, and wine drinking, but they soon came to deal with most of the themes of secular poetry: friendship, panegyric, and even religious themes. The *muwashshaḥ* form was soon adopted by liturgical poets as well, without, of course, the colloquial *kharja*.

It does not seem that many Hebrew poets could have earned a full-time living as poets writing for patrons, but there must have been some who did. The first known by name is Isaac Ibn Khalfun (late tenth century). He wrote formal panegyrics and also witty poems to friends complaining about his personal troubles. Among his patrons was a man who was himself a poet of first rank, the first truly great Golden Age poet: Samuel the Nagid (993–1056), also known as Ismāʿil Ibn Naghrālla.

Samuel was a courtier in the service of the ruler of Granada, an independent kingdom during most of the eleventh century. The power he amassed in this position makes him outstanding among Jewish courtiers of the Middle Ages. But he was also a scholar, learned and productive both in the rabbinic tradition and in the new literary fields. He is said also to have composed poetry in Arabic, but none has come down to us.

His poetry has survived in three big collections, named after books of the Bible. *Ben Tehilim* contains his long poems on a large number of topics. Some describe the battles he attended in his capacity as a courtier (some say as a general). These poems also speak of his personal ambitions, his doubts about the propriety of his public role, his hopes for his son Yehosef, and his anxiety about old age and death. These poems were probably written with an eye to enhance his own position vis-à-vis the Jewish community of Granada; they thus serve the same function as panegyrics, but they are written by the subject himself. Arabic poetry includes a genre of poems in which the poet describes his own prowess, and some of the Nagid's boasting tone derives from this type of poetry. But he keeps the poems close to the Jewish tradition by constant reference to biblical models for his own career, such as the courtier Mordechai, and especially King David. He seems to base his claim for religious legitimacy on the parallel between his own career and that of David, who was also a statesman, a warrior, and a poet (for according to tradition, King David was the author of the Psalms). This typology is probably what suggested to the Nagid the idea of calling one of his collections of poetry *Ben Tehilim,* "The Little Book of Psalms."

His other two collections of poetry, both named after biblical books traditionally by King Solomon, are actually collections of poetic epigrams. *Ben Mishle* is a book of advice dealing with courtly life. It belongs to the genre, widespread in the Middle East, of a courtier's advice to his son. *Ben Kohelet* deals with thoughts of life and death. Like the book of Ecclesiastes, for which it is named, it is somber in tone and secular in attitude. Solomon Ibn Gabirol (1021 or 1022–1058), a younger contemporary of Samuel the Nagid's, was the first of the great Golden Age poets who was extremely productive both in secular and liturgical poetry.

In dealing with religious poetry, it is important to make a distinction between two types. The old tradition of liturgical poetry had not died out with the coming of the Golden Age; rather, the eastern tradition of *piyyut* was carried on in the late tenth century by such major figures as Joseph Ibn Avitur and Isaac Ibn Mar Saul, whose work reflects almost no influence of the exciting new developments. This tradition was carried on by the great poets of the Golden Age. But with the exceptions to be mentioned, the bulk of their liturgical poetry follows the old patterns and themes. Its diction is somewhat simplified; but its forms and functions derive from the old tradition, and its language, while simpler than that of the old *piyyut,* is not in the neobiblical style of the secular poetry.

Alongside this older tradition, a new type of liturgical poetry came into being in the Golden Age. The first known example is a penitential poem by Isaac Ibn Mar Saul still widely in use; though intended for the liturgy, it is very personal in tone, with the speaker addressing God directly, as if in private conversation. The poem uses Arabic-style rhyme and meter. This innovation was followed up intensively by Ibn Gabirol, and the poems he wrote in this style are among the most characteristic parts of his work. They are mostly either *reshuyot*, short poems intended to be inserted in the morning service at one of several points between the private and public parts of the service; or *ge'ulot*, short poems intended to be inserted in the benediction on the redemption of Israel. The *reshuyot* are very intimate in tone and give much attention to the nature of prayer itself; some of them are little philosophical poems in which the nature of the human soul is the theme, not didactically, but based on the assumption—derived from contemporary philosophical ideas—that the soul of man is actually derived from God and longs to be united with Him, prayer being a verbal manifestation of this yearning on the part of the soul. Ibn Gabirol developed this neoplatonic theme in a work written on a much bigger scale, his monumental penitential meditation, *The Royal Crown*. This is one of the greatest pieces of medieval Hebrew writing, and it is still recited by Jews throughout the non-Ashkenazic world on Yom Kippur. Besides its metaphysical concerns, the prayer is notable for its extensive citation of astronomical data and its depiction of the spheres of heaven in terms then thought of as scientific.

Ibn Gabirol also composed much secular poetry. Some of it is addressed to patrons; in his youth, he was apparently supported by a Jewish courtier in Saragossa named Yequtiel Ibn Ḥassān. Ibn Gabirol dedicated panegyrics to him and, upon his death, a massive lament as well as a four-line epigram that will keep Yequtiel's name alive as long as Hebrew is still known. He also wrote panegyrics to Samuel the Nagid. But Ibn Gabirol also wrote an impressive quantity of personal poetry, sometimes in the form of independent poems dealing with his own life and complaints, and sometimes in the first part of his *qaṣīdas* addressed to others. In both kinds of poems, he presents a complex persona. He is sickly, orphaned, lonely, and destitute; he is a philosopher, so obsessed with death and with his philosophical speculations that he neglects worldly concerns, caring nothing for the false honors that this world can bestow. At the same time, he complains bitterly that his philosophical attainments have not gained him recognition from his fellow men; he expresses determination to force the world to grant him fame and glory. Ibn Gabirol's philosophical work, *The Source of Life*, was soon forgotten by the Jews, though its Latin translation survived.

Isaac Ibn Ghiyath (sometimes spelled Ibn Ghayyath, 1038–1089) was the one major poet of the period whose poetry (as far as is known) was exclusively liturgical; very few of his liturgical poems are in the new, intimate style of the *reshuyot* and *ge'ulot*. In a way, therefore, he might be thought of as a traditionalist. Such a characterization would seem in conformity with his career, for he was the only one of the great Golden Age poets who made a career as a rabbi, serving as the head of the famous academy of Lucena. Yet even Ibn Ghiyath's liturgical poetry reflects the peculiar character of Andalusian Jewry, for some of the hymns included in his great cycle of poems for Yom Kippur deal with cosmological and scientific data, far removed from the traditional themes of liturgical poetry, but subjects of intense study among Andalusian Jewish intellectuals.

Moses Ibn Ezra (ca. 1055–ca. 1135) held public office in Granada, where he spent the first part of his life; later, for reasons not well understood, he was compelled to wander in the Christian territories in the north of Spain. Much of his secular poetry consists of poems on the life of pleasure and poems of praise to friends. His *muwashshahat* contain particularly audacious recommendations of the life of pleasure. Yet he wrote a great deal of religious poetry as well, especially *selihot*, which are as sober and as somber as is customary for the genre. Much of his secular poetry follows the models of formal Arabic courtly poetry even more exactly than that of the other Golden Age poetry; he is the only one among the poets, for example, to make use of the desert encampment theme in the opening part of his *qasidas*. In his later years in exile, he wrote many long poems of personal complaint, in which he bewails his isolation in a land of lesser cultural sophistication, where he missed the material pleasures of Andalusian courtier life and the sophisticated audience for his poetry that that world afforded. He composed a book of poetic epigrams on such topics as gardens, love, wine drinking, asceticism, and friendship; the little poems all share the device of having homonyms for their rhyme words. Given the fascination of both Arabic and Arabizing Hebrew poets with rhetorical devices, this book was greatly appreciated and was imitated by later poets. Ibn Ezra also wrote several prose works in Arabic, including *The Book of Discussion and Debate*, a treatise on Hebrew poetry, which is one of our main sources of information about the literary theory common to the poets of the age. Another Arabic treatise, *The Book of the Garden: On Figurative and Metaphorical Language*, is a study of figurative language in the Bible and in Hebrew poetry.

Judah Halevi (ca. 1075–1141) was the most prolific of the Golden Age poets. His secular poetry, including the usual light verse on the pleasures of life and *qasidas* to friends and associates, reflects a witty, outgoing, sensuous personality, a man who took much pleasure in social life. His religious poetry is dominated by an attitude of pious awe and tranquillity, a willingness to let God take over all initiative. But the most distinctive feature of his work is his series of poems connected with his late-life decision to abandon Spain, go on pilgrimage to the Land of Israel, and spend his last years there. That was a shocking, even irrational-seeming plan, for it meant abandoning his family and a comfortable life (Halevi was a physician and a businessman) for a dangerous journey and an old age of hardship in a war zone (these were the years just prior to the Second Crusade) with only a small and poor Jewish community.

In several long poems, Halevi lays out his reasoning and his view of his religious mission, giving the impression that he felt the need to justify his behavior to others and to himself. He also composed several fine poems celebrating Jerusalem and the Holy Land and mourning their desolation (one of these poems, "Zion, Will You Not Greet Your Captives?" not only became part of the liturgy for the Ninth of Av but also inspired many imitations). Finally, he wrote a series of poems describing the ocean voyage itself. Some of these poems may have been products of pure imagination, written in advance of the journey, but others may have been written during his stay in Alexandria during the winter of 1140–1141, when he had already experienced the sea, or even on the deck of the ship itself. Not belonging to any existing genre, these poems are a major achievement of individual expression in an age in which most poetic form was dictated by convention.

Halevi laid out the theoretical basis of his decision and provided a statement of the nature and meaning of Judaism in a theological treatise written in Arabic. The book is generally known as *The Kuzari*, but its Arabic title was *The Book of Proof and Demonstration in Defense of the Despised People*. The book's form reflects Halevi's literary propensities, for he chose to present his religious thought as an imaginary dialogue between a rabbi and the king of the Khazars, a dialogue occasioned by the king's interest in converting from paganism to a more satisfactory religious system. In the process of winning the king's attention, convincing him of the rightness of Judaism, and continuing the king's education after his conversion, the rabbi expounds Halevi's views and concludes by announcing his intention to leave for the Holy Land.

Abraham Ibn Ezra (ca. 1092–1167) was a younger contemporary of Halevi, as well as his close associate. Ibn Ezra's secular poetry includes some clever epigrams describing his impoverished condition and some good *muwashshaḥat*, but it is as a religious poet that he was strongest and most prolific. His religious verse has a strongly neoplatonic bent, even occasionally inclining toward pantheism. He also wrote a rhymed prose treatise containing a fantasy of a journey through the cosmos, entitled *Alive, the Son of Awake*, based on a similar work in Arabic by the famous Islamic philosopher Avicenna. Abraham Ibn Ezra would achieve lasting fame as a Jewish writer for his commentaries on the Bible.

With Judah Halevi and Abraham Ibn Ezra, the most intense part of the
Golden Age comes to an end. This occurred because of an extraliterary
circumstance. Muslim Spain, having already lost much territory to Christian invaders from the north, was conquered in the 1140s by a fanatical
Berber dynasty from North Africa. These invaders, known as the Almo-
hads, outlawed the practice of Judaism and Christianity in their territories, putting an abrupt halt to all Jewish intellectual life in Muslim Spain.
Many of the elite families left: Maimon, the Cordoban judge, took his
family, including his young son Moses (later known as Maimonides), to
Morocco, Palestine, and eventually, Egypt; Joseph Kimhi and Samuel Ibn
Tibbon took their families to Provence; Abraham ben David went to
Christian Spain. These migrations had a stimulating effect on Jewish liter-
ature in the countries to which the refugees went, as we shall see.

When Abraham Ibn Ezra left Spain, he embarked on a life of wandering
throughout western Europe, living in Italy, Provence, France, and England.
In Europe, he became a prolific writer of biblical commentaries, and it
was these works that first introduced the Italian and Ashkenazic Jews
lacking in philosophical and scientific training to the linguistic and philosophical outlook of the Andalusian community. Those were the first biblical commentaries in Hebrew to incorporate the new learning. Abraham
Ibn Ezra also wrote books in Hebrew on mathematics and science. He introduced the Italian and French Jews to the Andalusian techniques of
prosody. R. Jacob Tam, a famous talmudist, tried his hand at writing short
secular poems in Arabic metrics, even though the system was but partially understood. He addressed these poems to Ibn Ezra, to the latter's
amusement. As we have seen, Rabbi Meir of Rothenberg wrote a poem in
imitation of one by Ibn Ezra's friend Judah Halevi. There is evidence that
Ibn Ezra's religious ideas were of great interest to the Ashkenazic Pietist
movement.

The main influence of Andalusian Hebrew poetry, however, was in the
Arabic-speaking world. Although few poets of stature arose outside of
Spain, Andalusian poetry, especially liturgical poetry, was admired and
imitated everywhere. When Halevi arrived in Egypt, he found many admirers who appreciated his poetry and circulated it. Isaac, the son of
Abraham Ibn Ezra, who accompanied Halevi to the East, found a patron
for his poems in Syria. Maimonides, who arrived in Egypt a generation
later and spent the rest of his life there, was unusual for an Andalusian
Jewish scholar in not writing poetry. Egypt did not produce any major
poets until the late thirteenth century, when Joseph ben Tanhum
Yerushalmi and Moses Dar'i, the latter a Karaite, were active. Iraq also
produced few poets except for Eleazer b. Jacob (1195–1250), but the Spanish Hebrew poet Judah al-Harizi managed to find patrons there for his
maqāmāt.

Christian Spain

In Spain, Jewish literature did not come to an end. Jews were welcome in the burgeoning Christian kingdoms, and after a period of adjustment, a new generation of Hebrew writers came forth in Castile and Catalonia. It is important to remember that in the twelfth century, contrary to all previous experience, the Jews of Spain saw the Christians as their saviors and the Muslims as their enemies. At the very time that Jewish life was drying up in the once-glorious al-Andalus, it was reconstituting itself in the Christian kingdoms.

Hebrew literature fell silent for about a generation, but toward the end of the twelfth century, new poets and literary figures began to emerge. Nor did the influence of Arabic literature on Hebrew suddenly end. At the time of these dislocations, a new genre of Hebrew writing appeared, the *maqāma*, narratives in rhymed prose studded with short poems. The pattern is derived from an Arabic genre of the same name. In the Arabic *maqāma*, the narratives follow a fairly regular pattern and are mostly designed to provide an opportunity for an elaborate display of rhetoric. The Hebrew *maqāmāt* (the plural), while retaining a strong rhetorical element, tend to have more elaborate narratives. A good example is the first known Hebrew *maqāma*, Solomon b. Saqbel's love story *Asher ben Judah*. This story, the only extant one of a group of stories now lost, appeared just before the Almohad cataclysm, at about the time that the Arabic *maqāmāt* of al-Ḥariri reached al-Andalus, where they were destined to become enormously popular.

The Hebrew rhymed prose narrative, for all its roots in the Arabic-speaking world, bloomed in Christian Spain, as if Hebrew writers were still connected with Arabic literary life. But for all their rhetorical similarity to the *maqāmāt* of the Arab East, most of the Hebrew fictions in rhymed prose are different from the Arabic models in ways that seem to link them to the nascent Romance literatures. One of the outstanding Hebrew fictions is *The Book of Delight*, by Joseph Ibn Zabara of Barcelona (born ca. 1140), which resembles the *maqāma* in its use of rhymed prose interspersed with poems, but whose narrative technique and stress on character recall the romance. Like the *maqāma*, the book describes the travels and adventures of a narrator, who plays the straight man, with a rogue, who beguiles the narrator into taking the journey. But in the *maqāma*, the successive brief episodes are not related to one another, and though the characters may appear in many guises, they never grow or change. In *The Book of Delight*, the characters, and therefore the relationship between them, change in the course of an extended narrative, so that by the end, the narrator dominates the trickster and resolves to return home.

Other Hebrew narratives in rhymed prose interspersed with poems also diverge to one degree or another from the pure *maqāma* genre. *The Offering of Judah: The Misogynist*, by Judah Ibn Sabbetai, is the story of a youth who foolishly wants to escape matrimony and devote his life instead to scholarship but who is duped into an outrageous marriage by an angry community of women who fear that his example will be deleterious to the world and to them. The story is preceded by a long misogynistic harangue put in the mouth of the youth's father, and it ends with a literary trick of great cleverness. Incidentally, the theme of misogyny is prominent in *The Book of Delight* as well and must have been in vogue in the thirteenth century.

A third Barcelona author of the period, Abraham Ibn Ḥasdai, used the form of rhymed prose interspersed with short poems as the vehicle for a very influential work, *The Prince and the Monk*. Partly a translation from Arabic and partly original, the book is a collection of proverbs and philosophical discussions within a narrative framework derived from the story of the childhood of Buddha.

Works reaching Hebrew from India via Arabic had a vogue in this period. Jacob b. Eleazar of Toledo (twelfth–thirteenth centuries) translated *Kalila and Dimna,* a book of animal fables, into Hebrew rhymed prose. He also composed an original narrative work, a collection of stories of various types. Some are philosophical allegories of a type attested in Hebrew in Muslim countries at this time; others resemble more the European vernacular romances of the period.

The great variety of narrative types suggests the growing independence of Hebrew writers from Arabic models. With the important exception of Judah al-Ḥarizi, as we will see, we may say that in form, the Hebrew narrative prose of the period seems to look back to the symbiosis with the Arabic-speaking world, but in theme, it looks forward to a potential new symbiosis with the belles lettres of Christendom. Certainly, such a shift seemed possible at the end of the twelfth century.

The Almohad persecution had cut Andalusian Jewish culture off at the root. The Jews of Iberia would retain their link with Arabic for at least another century, but signs of change were evident almost as soon as the new Hebrew literature emerged in the triumphant Christian kingdoms. One such sign was the abrupt cessation of Judeo-Arabic literature in Spain. From the mid–twelfth century on, Hebrew predominated as the language of Jewish writing in Spain and soon became the sole language for internal purposes. A wave of translations of Judeo-Arabic works into Hebrew for the use of Jews in Christian Europe, as well as for Spanish Jews no longer familiar with Arabic, dates from this period. This trend is distinct from the stream of translations of philosophical and scientific works intended for the use of Christians.

This internal shift from Arabic to Hebrew reflects a significant change in the linguistic situation of the Jews. Throughout the Arabic-speaking world, the daily language of the Jews was merely a variety of the lan-

guage that also served as the medium of high culture. Although vernacular Arabic was not the same as learned Arabic, knowing the vernacular
gave access to the language of philosophical and scientific writings and
provided a solid foundation for learning the language of high literature;
moving from one register of the language to the other was no more difficult for Arabic-speaking Jews than for their Muslim neighbors. The situation was completely different in Christian Europe, where the Latin ver-
naculars had diverged so radically from Latin that knowing a Romance
language did not provide access to higher literature. Furthermore, the Islamic world boasted a class of scholars who were not clergy, so that there
was much that a non-Muslim could study without coming into contact
too intimately with religious scholarship.

In Christendom, scholarship was more tied to the Church and was almost exclusively in the hands of the clergy, so that it was much more difficult for a Jew to become learned in Christian high culture, even if he did
manage to learn Latin. With the spread of Christianity throughout the
Iberian peninsula, the linguistic, and therefore the cultural, situation of
Iberian Jewry became more like that of the Jews of the rest of Europe. But
this process was gradual and did not affect everyone equally. Even as late
as the fifteenth century, we still encounter Jews in Castile who are learned
in Arabic and Latin.

Catalonia had never been deeply Arabized and had close links to the
south of France. There, the Andalusians soon lost their connection with
Arabic and came under the influence of intellectual and cultural trends
from beyond the Pyrenees. By the thirteenth century, the Jewish culture of
the northeastern region of the Iberian peninsula had largely lost its Arabic
cast. Although philosophy and science were still being studied (but from
Hebrew rather than Arabic texts) and Arabic-style secular poetry continued to be written by such poets as Meshullam Dapiera (d. after 1260), the
emphasis was now on such intrinsically Jewish subjects as Talmud, which
was studied according to northern European methods, and kabbalah. The
academy of Gerona, which became a major center of both Halakhic and
kabbalistic writing in the thirteenth century, reflected this development.
Its greatest leader, Nahmanides (Rabbi Moses b. Naḥman, 1140–ca. 1270),
represents quite a different cultural type from the contemporaneous Jewish courtiers of Alfonso X in Castile, who, though no longer writing much
in Arabic, remained much more in the Judeo-Arabic cultural tradition.
Nahmanides' works are exclusively Halakhic, exegetical, and mystical;
although he tried to calm the passions of the anti-Maimunist movement,
he was opposed to the widespread study of philosophy. Individual Jews
continued to serve the Aragonese government as Arabic interpreters.

Meshullam Dapiera's poetry embodies some of the contradictions of
the age. Dapiera was a bon vivant who celebrated the pleasures of life in

his Arabic-style poetry, much as the poets of Andalusia had. But in matters of doctrine, he was a traditionalist, being both a friend of Nahmanides and close to the circles of the mystics of Gerona. He participated vigorously in the controversy that raged, beginning in 1232, over rationalism and Aristotelianism in Jewish philosophy, especially in the writings of Maimonides. Intellectuals from Spain and Provence took positions as pro-Maimunists and anti-Maimunists, and a significant body of writing accumulated, mostly formal epistles in rhymed prose, in which each side denounced the other. Dapiera's contribution to this ugly episode was a spate of Hebrew poems using Arabic prosody, by now an old tradition of Spanish Hebrew poetry no longer associated with the cosmopolitanism of its origins, denouncing the pro-Maimunists. He also exchanged verse epigrams with various anti-Maimunists.

Though reactionaries could be found in Castile as well, Castilian Jewry retained its ties to Arabic language and culture longer. Toledo had been a major center of Arabic civilization prior to its reconquest in 1085, and Arabic continued to be spoken there long after it was forgotten in Aragon. Jews in Castile continued to bear Arabic traditions: Meir Abulafia (d. 1244), a famous Toledan rabbi and a literarily prolific anti-Maimunist, wrote Hebrew secular poetry in Arabic forms and even translated a short poem by the eleventh-century Sevillian prince al-Muʿtamid Ibn ʿAbbad into Hebrew. Abraham Ibn al-Fakhkhār (d. 1240), a Jewish grandee and a patron of Hebrew poetry, wrote Arabic poetry considered good enough to be transmitted by Muslim sources; one is in praise of Alfonso VIII of Castile. Judah al-Ḥarizi was a major Hebrew writer who was notably untouched by new Romance influences. Active as a translator, he rendered many Judeo-Arabic works into Hebrew, including—a tour de force—the *maqāmāt* of al-Ḥariri, a notoriously difficult masterpiece of Arabic rhymed prose. He followed this achievement by composing his own collection of Hebrew *maqāmāt*, the *Taḥkemoni*. Here, he reverted to the narrative type of the pure Arabic *maqāma*, showing little interest in the new type of narrative cultivated by writers like Ibn Zabara or by his fellow Toledan Jacob ben Eleazar. Al-Ḥarizi left Spain and traveled, via Provence, to the Muslim East, where he was probably culturally more at home. The importance of his literary activity in Provence will be discussed.

Under Alfonso X El Sabio (1252–1284), Jewish activity in the field of translation took a new direction, for the king encouraged the development of the Castilian language, and under his patronage many works were translated into the vernacular, with Jews being prominent among the translators. This project, undertaken for the benefit of non-Jewish scholars, mainly involved scientific works, but Alfonso also sponsored the translation of Jewish and Islamic religious writings for the use of the Church. Hebrew literature also continued to flourish. Todros b. Judah Abulafia, a Jewish man of letters who was close to several of Alfonso's court Jews, left a huge *dīwān* (corpus of poetry), including some Hebrew verses addressed to the king. They were supposedly engraved on a goblet that Todros presented to Alfonso.

Todros's Hebrew poetry is mostly in forms derived from Arabic, but he experimented with verse forms derived from Romance, as in his Hebrew canzone, which is also dedicated to Alfonso. He also cultivated pattern verses, which became fashionable at this time. It is a sign of the times that the introduction to his *dīwān* and the headings to the poems describing the circumstances of their composition are in Hebrew rather than in Arabic. Particularly interesting is his love poetry, which includes, alongside salacious verse, poems that bespeak a more spiritual idea of the nature of love. In a radical break with the traditions of the Golden Age, he even has Love itself speak.

The worldliness of the courtiers of Castile was countered by the kabbalists' distaste for aristocratic pleasures and frivolous writing. Kabbalism was not, strictly speaking, a literary movement; but it must be mentioned here because its flourishing in Spain during the thirteenth century culminated in the composition of one of the most original Jewish works of the Middle Ages, the *Book of Splendor* (the *Zohar*), probably by Moses de Leon (ca. 1240–1305). The book appears to belong to the traditional genre of commentaries on the Torah, but it is actually very innovative. It is a pseudepigraph attributed to a second-century rabbi; it was written in Aramaic, a language not spoken anywhere in Europe and long abandoned by the Jews as a literary language; it is not a single book but several books interwoven with one another; and, above all, it is a work of a most original imagination. Although the ostensible purpose of the book is to propound certain esoteric doctrines, it does not teach its doctrines by means of exposition or even, really, of exegesis, though its form might make this seem to be the case. Rather, it manipulates the traditional exegetical system of rabbinic Judaism, turning it into a vehicle of the author's imagination. The language and imagery of the *Zohar* were eventually to have an important influence on Hebrew poetry, but mostly after the expulsion from Spain.

Provence

Since Provence had long been part of the Carolingian Empire, its Jewish cultural life resembled that of the Rhineland, with the emphasis on Talmud and rabbinic learning. But much of the territory fell to Catalonia in the early twelfth century, linking Provence with Spanish Jewry and resulting in an immediate rise of interest there in the sciences and language. The Barcelona astronomer and moralist Abraham bar Ḥiyya (d. 1136) spent considerable time in Provence, disseminating Arabic scholarship in Hebrew to a community ignorant of the contemporary language of scientific culture. He was one of the first Jewish scholars to use Hebrew for this purpose.

The influence of Hispano-Jewish culture on Provence was reinforced by the flight of Andalusian Jewish intellectuals from the Almohads, beginning in the 1140s. Abraham Ibn Ezra also spent some time in Provence, after his period in Italy, which will be discussed in the section "Italy." Provençal Jewish culture was enriched by the presence of these Arabic-speaking Jews. Kimḥi, with his grammatical works and commentaries on the Bible, mediated the exegetical and linguistic tradition; his son David (known as Radaq, 1160–1235) composed an extensive commentary on many of the books of the Bible that is widely studied to this day. Judah Ibn Tibbon (1120–after 1190), his son Samuel, and his grandson Moses translated Maimonides' *Guide,* Halevi's *Kuzari,* Saadia's *Beliefs and Opinions,* Bahya Ibn Paquda's pietist classic *Introduction to the Duties of the Hearts,* and other works, creating a corpus of philosophical works upon which later Provençal scholars were to build. Moses expanded the repertoire of Hebrew philosophical writing by translating many works of non-Jewish origin. Judah al-Ḥarizi, not a refugee from the Almohads like the Kimḥis and the Ibn Tibbons but an itinerant scholar, also visited Provence on his way to Iraq, as we have seen; he helped to satisfy the thirst of the Provençal Jews for the sciences by translating Jewish philosophical works like Maimonides' *Guide* from Judeo-Arabic. Provence became a major center of translations and a bridge between the Ashkenazic world and the Judeo-Arabic culture that continued to flourish in the Muslim world and, for a while, even in Christian Spain. Some Provençal translators found patrons for their activities outside the Jewish community, like Jacob Anatoli (1200–1250), who eventually joined the court of Frederic II in Naples, or Kalonymos b. Kalonymos (1287–1337), whose patron was Robert of Anjou.

Provence flourished as a center of Jewish culture from the end of the twelfth to the fourteenth centuries. The greatest Provençal-Hebrew poets were active in the thirteenth and fourteenth centuries. In many respects, they may be viewed as continuers of the Andalusian tradition; they employed the Arabic prosodic system pioneered by the Andalusians, and their themes remained close to those of Muslim Spain. But there were some distinguishing features and some distinguished poets.

Joseph Ezovi (ca. 1230) of Perpignan was the author of a collection of rhymed maxims called *The Silver Bowl* and fine liturgical poetry. His disciple Abraham Bedersi (Perpignan and Narbonne, second half of the thirteenth century) was a grammarian and author of a long poem entitled "The Revolving Sword," which, in part, is an invaluable survey of the history of Hebrew poetry in Spain and Provence; in an explicit recognition of the relationship between Hebrew poetry and that of the Jews' host cultures, he named four non-Jewish poets as well, two Provençal and two Arabic. He also organized "courts of poetry," poetic contests held in the presence of wealthy patrons, as was done among the Christian Provençal poets. Many of his poems are polemics against his contemporaries in the spirit of the Romance *tenso* (a kind of romance polemical poem). His poetry represents an extreme development of the manneristic style cultivated by Hebrew writers in Christian Spain. It is often based on artificial principles; he wrote a prayer in poetic style called "A Thousand Alefs," in which there are one thousand words, each beginning with the letter *alef*.

The third in this succession of masters and disciples was Bedersi's son, Yedaya ha-Penini (1280–1340). His fame as a writer rests on an ethical treatise, "The Contemplation of the World," and a didactic text, "The Prayer of the Mems," in which each word begins with the letter *mem*.

The most interesting of the Provençal poets was Isaac of Aire (known in Hebrew as ha-Gorni), whose life is obscure. He seems to have spent it as a wandering poet, since he is found in all the important towns of southern France, writing poetry for money. His is thus the nearest career to that of a jongleur that Hebrew literature has to offer. The series of *tensos* exchanged between him and Bedersi is troubadour-like. He is celebrated for his poems boasting of his amorous adventures and for his macabre reflections on death.

Kalonymos ben Kalonymos, who has already been mentioned as a translator, was also active as a Hebrew belletrist. He composed the first parody for Purim, a genre that became popular among Jewish writers in many lands, and a social satire in rhymed prose saturated with parody, *The Proof Rock*. The book's conclusion, written years after its main part, is a somber palinode reflecting the persecutions of the Shepherds' Crusade.

But the direction of cultural influence was not only from Spain to Provence. The twelfth century saw the rise of kabbalistic writing in Provence, apparently as a local development; this type of intellectual activity spilled over into Catalonia, along with Ashkenazic Halakhic influences. Both developments were connected to a generally traditionalist, antiphilosophical reaction against the influence of Judeo-Arabic culture, which, as we have seen, had become a powerful force in Provence. These traditionalist tendencies came to a head in the controversy over the writings of Maimonides, in which the rabbis of Provence played an important role.

Italy

With the arrival in Italy of such Iberian Jews as Abraham Ibn Ezra (1140) and of the lexicographer Solomon Parhon (before 1160?), Italian Hebrew literature may be said to enter a second phase, in which Hebrew writers experiment with forms derived from Arabic and, later, from Italian.

We have seen that Abraham Ibn Ezra introduced the Italian Jews to Arabic metrics in Hebrew. Ibn Ezra also attacked the tradition of liturgical poetry prevalent among the Italian Jews. In his commentary on Ecclesiastes, written in Rome, he included a tirade on the distinctive Hebrew diction of Palestinian liturgical poetry, insisting that only the supposedly pure biblical diction of the Andalusian poets had the requisite dignity and purity for prayer. With Isaiah de Trani (b. 1220) we have the first major Hebrew liturgical poetry by an Italian Jew written in the new Andalusian style; and Benjamin Anav (Di Mansi) composed a Hebrew work resembling a *maqāma,* a rhymed-prose satire entitled "The Prophecy of the Valley of the Revelation."

But the first major literary figure among Italian Jewry was Immanuel of Rome (1265–1330), the author of the *Maḥbarot.* This is a collection of narratives in rhymed prose interspersed with poetry, very similar in prosodic form and rhetorical technique to the *maqāmāt* of the Iberian Hebrew writers, but significantly different in narrative structure. Some of Immanuel's racy narratives are closer in spirit and structure to the Italian novella than to the Arabic *maqāma* that had inspired Iberian Hebrew poets like al-Ḥarizi. Yet there is no question that Immanuel considered his work to be the continuation of al-Ḥarizi's. Here is a clear case in which a classical literary form has been adapted to new cultural circumstances, resulting in a product with features of the old and new literary worlds. The same may be said of Immanuel's Hebrew sonnets, which are interspersed in the text of the *maḥbarot.* They are cunningly composed so that they may be scanned according to the rules of the Arabo-Hebrew quantitative meters, while at the same time, they satisfy the requirements of Italian versification. The sonnet was a new genre in Immanuel's time, having been invented only in the thirteenth century; Immanuel's thirty-eight sonnets are the first in any language other than Italian. The last of Immanuel's *maḥbarot* is called "The *Maḥberet* on Hell and Paradise," inspired by Dante's *Divine Comedy,* though far more modest in scope.

A more modest work attesting to the interest of Jews in the lore of Christian Europe is *King Artus,* composed in 1279, extant only as a fragment. It derives from a lost Italian Arthurian work deriving from old French romances. It covers the birth of King Arthur and the destruction of the Round Table.

Dante's most ambitious Hebrew imitator was Moses Rieti (1393–1460), the author of *The Little Sanctuary.* This work, making the first use in Hebrew of terza rima, surveys many philosophical and scientific ideas. It also describes, in the manner of Dante's *Paradiso,* a visit to the heavenly abode of the Jewish religious heroes. Despite the innovative character of

Rieti's verse form and the tribute paid by his book's form to Christendom's greatest poet, the work is conservative in the extreme, to judge by the figures excluded by Rieti from paradise. One passage from the poem, a prayer, became popular as an independent work and was eventually incorporated into the Italian rite.

Late medieval Italy, like all centers of Jewish culture, produced a quantity of new liturgical poetry, mostly *selihot*, as well as a major narrative of biblical history called *Sefer Hayashar*. But this second phase of Italo-Hebrew literature was only a preparation for the great flowering of Hebrew letters that would occur after 1500, past the period of this survey.

The Final Chapter in Spain

As the *reconquista* progressed into the mid–thirteenth century, the Christian rulers found themselves less in need of Jewish administrators and courtiers. With the completion of the conquest and the development of local culture, Arabic declined in prestige, and as Christians acquired linguistic skills, administrative experience, and scientific training, the Jews gradually lost their role as indispensable administrators and mediators of Arabic culture. At the same time, the anti-Jewish pressure from the masses and the Church mounted. By the end of the century, Spain was far less hospitable to Jews than it had been at the beginning. Jewish fortunes rose and fell until 1391, when pogroms and mass conversions heralded the collapse of the Jewish community. But individual members of the Jewish elite maintained the Arabic scholarly tradition and the Hebrew literary culture that was so closely tied to it. We hear of Jews, even in the fifteenth century, translating Arabic texts into Latin or Hebrew, and secular Hebrew poetry cast in Arabic meters and rhyme schemes was written in Spain right up to the expulsion in 1492.

A monument to the continuing prestige of Hebrew poetry within the Jewish community may be observed to this day in the El Transito synagogue in Toledo (dedicated in 1357), where the dedicatory inscription is in Hebrew verse, employing the Arabic metrics of the Golden Age. The synagogue's founder was Samuel Halevi, a financier to Pedro the Cruel (1350–1369). The use of a poem to commemorate the founder of a synagogue is consistent with the practice of Spanish Jewish grandees since the time of Hasdai Ibn Shaprut, four centuries earlier, as we saw in the epistle of Menahem.

One of Samuel's contemporaries, Shemtov ben Ardutiel, known in Spanish as Santob de Carrión, exemplified a potentially new development in the literary history of Iberian Jewry. Shemtov was distinguished as a Hebrew writer: He was the author of a lengthy poem of confession for Yom

Kippur that is still found in some prayer books, a kabbalistic treatise, and a charming Hebrew *maqāma* called *The Battle of the Pen and the Scissors*. He was also an expert Arabist who translated a Halakhic work into Hebrew. But he achieved fame in the wider world for the *Proverbia Morales*, dedicated to Pedro the Cruel. Written in Spanish just as the El Transito synagogue was under construction, this collection of proverbs was an important and influential contribution to the nascent Spanish literature. In it, Shemtov does not hesitate to call attention to his being Jewish.

As one who drew on both Hebrew and Arabic literary traditions while writing in Spanish, Shemtov is a pivotal figure in Iberian literary history. Other writers of Jewish origin made contributions to Spanish literature in this period, but Shemtov is the only belletrist known to us who was active as a Jew both in Hebrew and in Spanish.

Toward the end of the fourteenth century, a circle of poets appeared who revived the tradition of Hebrew literature in Spain. These poets were connected with the de la Caballeria family of Saragossa, an important Aragonese Jewish family of financiers and courtiers who were also devotees of Hebrew letters. Solomon Dapiera, a descendant of Meshullam Dapiera, served as Hebrew secretary to three successive heads of the family and exchanged poems with many of the distinguished Jewish leaders of the time. His literary circle included his disciple Vidal Benvenist, a member of the de la Caballeria family, who became his patron; Joseph ben Lavi; and Solomon Bonafed. These poets were among the members of a kind of poets' club known as the "The Congregation of Singers"; they engaged in poetic competitions and addressed poems to one another. They were, however, destined to endure the hard times of Spanish Jewry. The peninsula-wide pogroms and forced conversions of 1391 caused traumatic upheaval, which is reflected in the synagogue poetry of the period. Along with other leaders of the Jewish community, these poets were present at the fateful Tortosa Disputation in 1413–1414, in the wake of which many Jewish grandees converted to Christianity. Among the converts were Dapiera and Vidal Benvenist, while apparently Solomon Bonafed and Joseph ben Lavi remained Jewish. But their poetic relationship did not end; even after their conversion, several of them continued to exchange poems in Hebrew, with Bonafed using this medium for chastising the converts for their unfaithfulness. Thus, among the oddities of Spanish Jewry's last century, we find Christians writing poetry in Hebrew!

The poetry of this generation carries on many of the formal traditions of the Golden Age. The prosody remains completely in accordance with the Arabic practices adopted by Dunash four centuries earlier, and the poets frequently allude to poems of the classical period. Some of the genres cultivated by the earlier poets also remained intact. But there are new formal features, like the frequent practice of ending a poem by repeating or alluding to its opening words. This practice is not merely a technical device but a structural principle, for it lends many poems a closed, circular feeling that is different from the open-endedness of the monorhymed poetry inherited from Arabic by the Golden Age poets. Strophic Hebrew poetry on secular themes had become much less common in Spain—where it had originated—than in other Mediterranean lands, which had learned it from earlier Spanish Hebrew poets, or which were adopting new strophic forms from Italian. One has the impression that contemporaneous tendencies in Spanish literature left little mark on Hebrew poetry, but this topic has not been investigated sufficiently. Traditional Hebrew scholars have been content to label it epigonic, thereby discouraging serious investigation of an important creative moment in Hebrew letters.

In what was left of Muslim Spain, the Jewish community had been reduced by the Almohads to insignificance, never to recover. Jews returned to Granada after the establishment of the Nasrid dynasty in the thirteenth century, but we have little information about them. After the anti-Jewish riots and forced conversions that raged throughout Christian Spain in 1391, many *conversos* made their way to Muslim Granada, where they could return to Judaism. The last Hebrew poet of Muslim Spain was a Granadan Jew, Saadia Ibn Danan, who was among the Jewish exiles of 1492. He went to Morocco, where he wrote a treatise on the craft of poetry. Among the last Hebrew poets of Christian Spain was Judah Abravanel. In 1503, he wrote a long poem, still using the Arabic prosody first adapted for use in Hebrew by Spanish Jews four and a half centuries earlier to describe his experiences at the time of the expulsion and the dislocation he experienced thereafter. Under the name Leone Ebreo, he was to become famous among Italian writers of the Renaissance as the author of a treatise on love. He is thus a bridge figure into the Renaissance. But that is another chapter in the long and colorful history of Hebrew letters.

Suggested Readings

Carmi, Ted. *The Penguin Book of Hebrew Verse*. Harmondsworth, Eng.: Penguin Books, 1981.

Cole, Peter. *Selected Poems of Shmuel HaNagid*. Princeton: Princeton University Press, 1996.

Elbogen, Ismar. *Jewish Liturgy: A Comprehensive History*. Translated by Raymond P. Scheindlin. Philadelphia: Jewish Publication Society, 1993.

Pagis, Dan. *Hebrew Poetry of the Middle Ages and the Renaissance*. Berkeley: University of California Press, 1991.

Petuchowski, Jakob. *Studies in the Medieval Piyyut*. London: Routledge and Kegan Paul, 1978.

Scheindlin, Raymond P. *The Gazelle: Medieval Hebrew Poems on God, Israel, and the Soul*. Philadelphia: Jewish Publication Society, 1991.

Scheindlin, Raymond P. *Wine, Women, and Death: Medieval Hebrew Poems on the Good Life*. Philadelphia: Jewish Publication Society, 1986.

Stern, David, and Mark Mirsky, eds. *Rabbinic Fantasies*. Philadelphia: Jewish Publication Society, 1990.

7

Medieval
Jewish Philosophy

WARREN ZEV HARVEY

MY DISCUSSION OF JEWISH PHILOSOPHY will focus on three major medieval philosophers, Saadia Gaon, Judah Halevi, and Moses Maimonides. I also shall discuss one nonphilosophic book, the *Zohar*, the classic text of the medieval kabbalah; this strange book may be seen as a mythopoetic critique of philosophy.

Saadia Gaon (892–942)

Saadia ben Joseph al-Fayyumi, known as Saadia Gaon, was a prodigious scholar in many fields. He was the leading authority of his time in talmudic law and wrote important works on this subject. He composed the first known Hebrew dictionary. He translated the Bible into Arabic, and wrote commentaries in Arabic on several biblical books. He compiled an authoritative edition of the Siddur (the Jewish prayer book). He engaged in many polemics, in particular against the Karaites. He also wrote Hebrew poems. His one systematic philosophic work, written in Arabic, is called the *Book of Beliefs and Opinions (Kitab al-ʾAmanat wal-Iʿtiqadat*; Hebrew translation: *Sefer ha-Emunot ve-ha-Deʿot)*. Philosophic discussions are found also in his Arabic commentary on the old Hebrew mystical book, *Sefer Yeṣirah* ("Book of Creation").

Saadia was born in 892 in Fayyum, Upper Egypt. He lived also in Palestine, Syria, and Iraq. In 928, he was appointed the *gaon* (dean) of the great talmudic academy in Sura, near Baghdad. Baghdad was at the time a vibrant hub of Arabic culture and the world center of philosophy. Saadia died in 942.

Saadia was an eclectic philosopher. His *Book of Beliefs and Opinions* contains Platonic, Aristotelian, and Stoic elements. However, it is probably best seen as belonging to the school of Kalam (philosophical or dialectical theology). Although the Kalam was developed mostly by Muslims, it also had Jewish and Christian advocates. Saadia's philosophy is thus often classified as "Jewish Kalam." Saadia seems to have been influenced by his older contemporary, al-Jubbai (850–915), head of the Mu'tazilite school of Kalam in Basra. However, he was not noticeably influenced by al-Ash'ari (873–935), founder of the Ash'arite school of Kalam, or by Alfarabi (ca. 870–950), founder of the Arabic Aristotelian tradition, who lived for a while in Baghdad, and who had a great impact on Maimonides.

The *Book of Beliefs and Opinions* consists of an introduction and ten treatises. The introduction discusses the existential anguish caused by doubt and expounds a method for the attainment of certainty. Treatise 1 treats Creation, and Treatise 2 treats God. This is in accordance with a strategy common in the Kalam according to which the existence of God is proved from the creation of the world. Treatises 3–5 deal with the divine Law, that is, the Torah, its observance and transgression, and its rewards and punishments. Treatises 6–9 discuss the soul, resurrection, redemption, and the world to come. Treatise 10 discusses virtuous human conduct and criticizes various vulgar views on the nature of human happiness.

Although the book deals with many different themes, perhaps its central subject is legal and moral philosophy. One famous discussion is that concerning two different kinds of laws, the "rational" and the "auditory." This discussion is important in the history of the Theory of "Natural," or "Rational," Law. It is found in Treatise 3, chapters 1–3.

Before turning to Saadia's discussion, I should like to insert two brief comments, one about the meaning of rational or natural law, and one about a relevant talmudic discussion.

The Theory of Rational or Natural Law is usually associated with the Stoics. Cicero (*Republica* 3.22) set down three conditions for rational or natural law: (1) it is known by unaided human reason (*ratio*), since it agrees with nature (*natura*); (2) it is universal (i.e., it holds equally in Athens, Rome, and everywhere else); (3) it is eternal (i.e., it holds equally in the past, present, and future). Thus, to say that a law is "rational," or "natural," is to say that it is valid in every place and time, regardless of customs or traditions. In other words, moral laws are understood to be similar to physical laws: Just as the law of gravity is universal and eternal and cannot be abrogated, so the law against robbery or murder is universal and eternal and cannot be abrogated.

The rabbis in the Talmud did not speak about "rational" or "natural" law. However, a passage in the Babylonian Talmud (Yoma 67b; see also *Sifra* on Leviticus 18:4) deals with a somewhat similar notion. Interpreting Leviticus 18:4, the rabbis distinguish between "ordinances" (*mishpatim*) and "statutes" (*huqqim*). "Ordinances" are laws that, "had they not been written, should have been written"; they include the prohibitions of idolatry, sexual crimes, murder, robbery, and blasphemy. "Statutes" are laws that seem to be vain or purposeless; they include the prohibition of wearing a mixed wool and linen garment (Deuteronomy 22:11), the ceremony of removing the brother-in-law's shoe (Deuteronomy 25:5), and so on. The interpretation here of "ordinances" is similar to rational or natural law, although the terms *reason* and *nature* are not mentioned.

Let us now turn to Saadia's *Book of Beliefs and Opinions,* Treatise 3, chapter 1. Saadia distinguishes here between two kinds of laws: rational (Arabic: ʿaqliyyat; Hebrew: sikhliyyot) and auditory (Arabic: samʿiyyat; Hebrew: shimʿiyyot). Rational laws are required by unaided reason (Arabic: ʿaql; Hebrew: sekhel). They include gratitude to God; the prohibition of blasphemy; and the prohibition of aggression, for example, lying, robbery, murder, adultery. Auditory laws are those that are not required by unaided reason and are accepted only because they have been heard from the lawgiver.

Saadia's "rational laws" thus amount to (1) a *religion of reason,* or a *natural religion* (namely, the commands to show gratitude to God and not to blaspheme), and (2) a *rational morality,* or *natural morality* (namely, the prohibition of aggression). In other words, the foundations of religion and morality are common to all human beings; they are known to all human beings by means of their *reason* alone.

The "auditory laws," Saadia explains, are not required by reason alone. The auditory laws of the Torah were given by God "in order to increase our reward and happiness." Moreover, these laws, while not *rational* (required by reason alone), are generally *reasonable* (they are beneficial, they have utilitarian value).

In chapter 2, Saadia amplifies his discussion of rational and auditory laws. He gives arguments to show that murder, adultery, theft, and lying are irrational. For example, if murder were permitted, the human race would annihilate itself, thus contradicting all purposes; or if theft were permitted, there would be no private property and thus nothing to steal. He remarks that truth telling may be the basic rational law; that is, just as the law of noncontradiction (i.e., A cannot be both B and not-B) is the foundation of all rational thought (cf. Aristotle, *Metaphysics* 4.3.1005b), so it is the foundation of all morality. Saadia also addresses the argument of the hedonists, who justify murder and other crimes on the grounds that they give pleasure to the aggressor. He retorts that the pain of the victim outweighs the pleasure of the victimizer.

As examples of auditory laws, Saadia mentions inter alia laws of the Sabbath and the other holy days, the dietary laws, and various laws regulating sexual intercourse. These laws are not rational but are *reasonable.* Although reason does not require us to rest on the Sabbath, it is reasonable to set aside times for rest from work, study, and prayer. For Saadia, the prohibition of murder is known by unaided reason just as certainly as the proposition that $1 + 1 = 2$. The command to observe the Sabbath is not known by unaided reason and thus is not similar to mathematical propositions, but it is *reasonable*. We expect all human beings, regardless of their customs and traditions, to know the propositions of mathematics and morality; but we do not expect them all to know that they should rest on the Sabbath.

Saadia's distinction between "rational" and "auditory" laws differs from the talmudic distinction between "ordinances" and "statutes" in two important ways. First, it explicitly uses the philosophic term "reason," absent in the talmudic discussion. Second, it is an exhaustive distinction, while the talmudic distinction is not: all commandments of the Torah are either "rational" or "auditory"; but many (if not most) of them (e.g., those concerning the Sabbath and the other holy days) are neither "ordinances" nor "statutes."

In chapters 1 and 2, Saadia defends a strong version of the Natural Law theory. However, in chapter 3, he moderates his position.

Chapter 3 opens with a question regarding the theory of Rational Law expounded in chapters 1 and 2: If universal religion and morality are known by unaided reason, why did God need to send us prophets? Saadia answers, as we would expect on the basis of chapters 1 and 2, that prophecy is necessary for the auditory laws (in order to increase our reward and happiness). However, he then adds that prophecy is also necessary for the rational laws because their practice cannot be complete unless prophets show us how to perform them. For example, there is a rational law to show gratitude to God, but we do not know how to do this until a prophet teaches the commandment of prayer. Again, there is a rational law against theft, but we do not know what ownership is until a prophet sets down the appropriate rules. By affirming that prophecy is necessary for the rational laws, Saadia weakens the theory of Natural Law, which he had developed in chapters 1 and 2. The rational laws concerning religion and morality are now turned into general principles, whose concrete content is unclear.

Saadia applies his distinction between "rational" and "auditory" laws to the commandments of the Torah; thus the auditory laws are identified by him with "revelational," or "prophetic," laws. In fact, however, Saadia's distinction may be aptly applied to any legal system, divine or human: There are laws that are knowable by reason alone, and that we would expect to find in every legal system in every time or place; and there are other laws that are particular to a given legal system, and whose authority is not human reason, but only the word of the lawgiver. Using Saadia's distinction, one can analyze the laws of any legal system, for example, that of Russia, the United States, Israel. A person who holds a strong Natural Law theory will maintain that most laws should in fact be universal, that is, common to all legal systems; a person who holds a weak Natural Law theory will maintain that only a few laws are universal; and a person who denies Natural Law theory holds that no laws are universal. In any case, Saadia's discussion provides an excellent framework for debating questions concerning the theory of Natural Law.

Judah Halevi (before 1075–1011)

Judah ben Samuel Halevi is primarily known as a poet, perhaps the greatest Hebrew poet since biblical times. He wrote both secular and liturgical poetry. In some of his religious poems, he speaks of his own visions of the divine. One of his most famous poems is the *Ode to Zion*, a poem recited in many rites on the Ninth of Ab (the Fast Day commemorating the destruction of the First and Second Temples). However, Halevi is also known for a philosophical dialogue he wrote in Arabic, called the *Kuzari*.

Halevi was born in Tudela before 1075. He lived in Granada and later Toledo, where he worked as a physician. He completed the *Kuzari* in 1140 and left Spain for the Land of Israel in 1141. He debarked in Alexandria and spent several months in Egypt. It is not clear whether he ever reached the Land of Israel. According to a folk legend, he arrived in Jerusalem, and while kissing its stones and reciting his *Ode to Zion*, he was trampled to death by an Arab horseman.

The *Kuzari* is a philosophic (or antiphilosophic) dialogue set in the kingdom of the Khazars in the eighth century, when the king and the people converted to Judaism. The book is a fictionalized reconstruction of the king's conversations with a philosopher, a Christian scholar, and a Muslim scholar, but primarily with a Jewish rabbi. It is openly polemical, and its formal title is *The Book of Proof and Demonstration in Defense of the Despised People*. The main target of the polemic is Aristotelian philosophy, particularly the Andalusian school represented by Ibn Bajja (ca. 1070–1138). Secondary targets of the polemic include Christianity, Islam, and Karaism.

Halevi's critique of Aristotelianism is clearly influenced by Algazali (1058–1111), the famed Muslim mystic and critic of Aristotelianism. Halevi made much use of Avicenna (980–1037), especially (and maybe exclusively) in the last three parts of the *Kuzari*; Halevi's attitude toward him is fundamentally sympathetic, for although Avicenna was an Aristotelian, his Aristotelianism was tempered by a pious mysticism. Halevi was also influenced by Neoplatonic philosophy. He had a negative attitude toward the Kalam. In his view, the Kalamic theologians do not know

God, but merely know about Him, just as professors of poetry know about poetry, but cannot write a verse (*Kuzari* 5.16).

The *Kuzari* is divided into five parts. It begins with a dream that haunts the king of the Khazars night after night. In the dream, an angel appears to him, and says, "Your *intention* is pleasing to God, but your action is not" (*Kuzari* 1.1). To help him interpret this dream, the king summons a philosopher. The philosopher explains that what is important is contemplation, not action. The king deems the philosopher's advice irrelevant, since the dream had clearly required a change in *action* (1.1–4). He then summons a Christian scholar (1.4–5) and a Muslim scholar (1.5–9); and he finds that they disagree about many things but agree that at one time God had chosen the Jews and had spoken to the Jewish prophets. The common testimony of the Christian and the Muslim leads the king to summon a Jew (1.10). The Jew, a rabbi, states that Jews believe in the God of Abraham, Isaac, and Jacob, who liberated the Israelites from bondage in Egypt, and performed other miracles in history (1.11). Halevi emphasizes throughout the *Kuzari* that the Jewish religion is based on the God of history and experience, whereas the religion of the philosophers is based on the god of nature and reason (1.12, 25; 4.16–17). As opposed to the Aristotelians, Halevi argues the priority of *praxis* to *theoria*. The king is impressed by the rabbi's teachings concerning the importance of action, and he and his subjects convert to Judaism (2.1).

The king and the rabbi continue their discussions. The rabbi soon tells the king about the wondrous qualities of the Land of Israel, and the king asks him: If so, *what are you doing here?* You have embarrassed me, the rabbi replies meekly (2.9–24). At the end of the book, after much talk, the rabbi announces he is leaving for the Land of Israel. He explains that intention without action is insufficient (unless of course the action is impossible), and thus he must act on his intention to go to the Land of Israel (5.22–28). Suddenly we realize that the king's dream was not directed to him alone, but also to the rabbi! In leaving for the Holy Land, the rabbi shows that he has learned the lesson of the king's dream: Intention requires action! Previously he had known how to talk theoretically about action, but only now does he act.

The *Kuzari* treats of many topics. Having discussed Saadia's distinction between rational and auditory commandments, let us now look at Halevi's development of this distinction. Halevi accepts Saadia's distinction, but unlike Saadia, he argues that the most noble laws are the auditory ones, not the rational ones. In a brilliant rhetorical move, he identifies the rational laws with the "political" ones, and the auditory laws with the "divine" ones (*Kuzari* 2.48). He thus in effect belittles the rational laws. "Rational" may sound more noble than "auditory," but "divine" sounds more noble than "political." Following Plato (*Republic*, 1.351C), he observes that even a gang of robbers observes among itself the basic laws of justice (i.e., the rational laws). The rational laws, therefore, constitute the minimum, whereas the divine laws constitute the maximum (*Kuzari* 2.48). Halevi thus holds that there is a rational or natural law, but true religion is manifest primarily in the auditory laws, which transcend the rational ones (see also 3.7, 11).

Halevi emphasizes that we cannot rationally understand how the auditory laws are efficacious. However, he continues, we also do not really understand how the laws of the natural sciences are efficacious. In Kantian terms, we perceive only the *phenomena;* we cannot know the *noumena.* He illustrates this idea by referring to sex and animal sacrifices. The sex act and animal sacrifices seem both to be an absurd and silly preoccupation with the flesh; but after nine months a human being is born and the sex act is proved to be purposeful and sublime; similarly, when the divine Presence descends from heaven, the act of animal sacrifice is proved to be purposeful and sublime (3.53).

It should be noted that Halevi adds a new category to Saadia's "rational" and "auditory" laws; namely, the "psychic" laws (Arabic: *nafsiyyat;* Hebrew: *nafshiyyot*). These include the honor toward God required by the opening of the Decalogue (Exodus 20:1–7), plus the doctrine that God knows our actions and thoughts, and rewards and punishes us (*Kuzari* 3.11). It is not clear how Halevi understands the "psychic" laws in relation to the rational and auditory ones. He seems to consider them to be a third independent category. However, it is also possible that he has divided the "rational" laws into two classes: the political and the psychic.

Halevi's commitment to the Theory of Rational or Natural Law is illustrated by his famous parable of the king of India (1.19–25). Although the parable is told in order to make a theological point, it also reveals something about Halevi's political thinking. According to the parable, the just and virtuous behavior of the people of India would not prove that there exists a king of India, since their justice and virtue might be "natural." If however one were to be visited by messengers from the king of India, bearing gifts from him, this would prove his existence. So too, the philosophic "argument from design" does not prove the existence of God, since the design of the universe may simply be "natural." However, our knowledge of God is based on his sending messengers (the prophets), who brought us gifts from him (the Torah and its commandments). Halevi's position is clearly supernaturalist: The God of religion is not the god of nature, and similarly true religion transcends nature. At the same time, Halevi is saying that philosophy (i.e., unaided human reason) cannot prove the God of religion, and human beings do not need religion in order to live justly or virtuously. The divine law, the Torah, is concerned with raising human beings above nature (see 2.29–42).

Thus, religious experience, according to Halevi, concerns a "divine order" higher than reason. In a few regrettable passages (almost exclusively in parts 1 and 2), Halevi explains this divine order as being transmitted by heredity from Adam through Noah, through Abraham, Isaac, and Jacob, and to their offspring (1.27, 63, 75; 2.12). In doing so, he borrowed a dubious argument from certain Muslim theologians and appropriated it for Judaism.[1] However, in more significant passages (e.g., 4.3, 16–17), Halevi identifies this suprarational realm with experience, imagination, and *taste* (Arabic: *dhawq*; Hebrew: *ta'am*), as it is written: "Taste and see that God is good!" (Psalms 34:9). Whereas the Aristotelians held that God is known by the intellect, Halevi teaches that he is known by taste; that is, by the immediate experience of our external and internal senses. The association of the religious experience with direct sensual and imaginative experience is also found in many of Halevi's poems.

Moses Maimonides (1135/8–1204)

Moses ben Maimon, known by acronym in Hebrew as Rambam (Rabbi Moses ben Maimon), and in Latin as Maimonides, was without doubt the most influential Jewish philosopher of the medieval period. His *Guide of the Perplexed* revolutionized Jewish philosophy and had a strong impact on Christian philosophers, such as Albert the Great and Thomas Aquinas. Like Saadia, Maimonides was also a great rabbi; indeed, he was probably the foremost authority on Jewish law since the talmudic period. His works on Jewish law include the *Commentary on the Mishnah* and the *Book of the Commandments*, both written in Arabic, and the *Mishneh Torah*, his monumental fourteen-volume code of Jewish law, written in Hebrew. He wrote two philosophic books, both in Arabic: an *Introduction to Logic*, which he wrote as a young man; and the *Guide of the Perplexed* (Arabic: *Dalalat al-Ha'irin*; Hebrew translation: *Moreh ha-Nebukhim*), completed in the last decade of his life. In addition, he wrote scores of epistles and responsa on rabbinic subjects and many important books on medical subjects.

Maimonides was born in Cordoba in 1135 or 1138. After the intolerant Almohads conquered the town in 1148, the Maimon family was forced into exile. Maimonides wandered in Spain, Morocco, and the Land of Israel, before settling in Egypt in 1165. In Egypt, Maimonides served as a physician in the court of Saladin and was head of the Jewish community. His opinions on Jewish law were sought by Jews throughout the world.

The *Guide of the Perplexed* was written for outstanding young students, "perplexed" by the apparent contradiction between religion and philosophy (as he said in the dedication, "Epistle Dedicatory to Joseph ben Judah"). In Maimonides' view, religion and philosophy are not contradictory, but complementary. Religion requires philosophy; for the divine Law commands the knowledge and love of God, which can be truly achieved only by the scientific study of the universe. Conversely, philosophy requires religion; for it explains that the divine Law is of great utility in leading human beings to the true goals of peace and knowledge (*Guide* 2.40; 3.27).

The *Guide* is divided into three parts. Part 1 presents a critique of the errors of the imagination, beginning with crass anthropomorphism (1.1) and concluding with the sophisticated but (at least in Maimonides' judgment) sophistic doctrines of the Kalam (1.71–76). The difference between the Kalamic theologians and the philosophers, according to Maimonides, is that the former try to make the world fit their ideas, whereas the latter try to make their ideas fit the world (1.71); this description of the Kalam might, if one wishes, be applied equally to ancient Greek sophism or to modern ideology. If part 1 destroys unphilosophic religion, part 2 constructs a philosophic one in its place. It offers Aristotelian proofs of the existence, unity, and corporeality of God (2.1–2), and explains creation (2.13–31) and prophecy (2.32–48) in Aristotelian terms. However, the confident rationalism of part 2 is shattered in part 3. Its discussions of Ezekiel's vision of the chariot (3.1–7) of Job (3.22–23) raise grave doubts about the possibility of certainty in metaphysics or even in physics; its analysis of the problem of evil (3.8–14) is antianthropocentric and antiteleological; its examination of the commandments of the Torah is detached and sociological, explaining them against the background of ancient Canaanite idolatry (3.25–50); and its famous discussion of the love of God is not Aristotelian but mystical, influenced by Sufism (3.51). Its final chapter (3.54) teaches that despite everything, the true human excellence is that of the intellect, and the political activity of the excellent individual is *imitatio Dei*.

The *Guide* is an esoteric book, a book of puzzles. Since it seeks to replace naive faith with reasoned conviction, it risks causing profound harm to some readers, namely, those who understand enough to lose their naive faith, but not enough to acquire reasoned conviction. In order to hide the potentially subversive doctrines of the *Guide* from unprepared readers, Maimonides uses various methods of indirection (see Introduction to *Guide*); for example, he purposely affirms contradictory propositions, one being argued logically (for the sake of the philosophic reader, who accepts only logic), the other being stated rhetorically (for the sake of the unphilosophic one, who is moved only by rhetoric). Studying the *Guide* thus means solving its puzzles, trying to discover its esoteric teachings hidden beneath its exoteric ones. These puzzles make the *Guide* an especially exciting book.

The *Guide* begins (1.1) with a discussion of the biblical term "image of God." What does the Bible mean when it says that human beings are created in the divine image (Genesis 1:26–27)? Maimonides explains that the term "image" (Hebrew: *ṣelem*) denotes Aristotelian form, not physical form or shape, and concludes that the divine image of the human being is the intellect.

Maimonides next (*Guide* 1.2) discusses the Garden of Eden story (Genesis 2:8–3:22). His novel exegesis is in essence adopted by Spinoza in his *Ethics* 4.68. Maimonides uses the story as a "state of nature" parable that illustrates how politics and law come into being. His interpretation is based on a radical distinction between the concepts "true" and "false" and the concepts "good" and "bad." True and false are objective concepts, *intelligibilia*: "true" means corresponding to existence, and "false" means not corresponding to it. Good and bad, however, are subjective concepts, popularly accepted opinions: "Good" means corresponding to one's purpose (cf. *Guide* 3.13), and "bad" means not corresponding to it. Our judgments of true and false are theocentric or cosmocentric (from the impartial point of view of God or nature); but our judgments of good and bad are egocentric (from our own partial point of view). True and false thus are the same for all human beings, but good and bad vary: What is good for me may be bad for you. Notions of "good" and "bad" arise in the imagination (on the imagination, see *Guide* 1.73, proposition 10; and *Eight Chapters*, 1–2). Since they are not *intelligibilia*, they could not even be conceived by a purely rational person. According to Maimonides' exegesis, Adam and Eve were created with perfect intellects ("in the image of God"), knowing true and false, and having no notions of good and bad; but they forsook the way of Reason, went after their imaginary desires, and began to judge the world in terms of "good" and "bad" (that is, they ate from the Tree of Knowledge of Good and Evil). Adam and Eve thus sinned by forsaking objective scientific knowledge (true and false) for subjective egocentric opinion (good and bad). Before they rebelled, they had no need for fig leaves; for they regulated their sex life rationally, that is, in accordance with an impartial evaluation of their combined true biological needs; but after their rebellion, they needed the fig leaves to protect themselves from their selfish imaginary desires. The sexual relation between man and woman represents the beginning of society; and the fig leaf symbolizes the beginning of law. If human beings were purely rational (like Adam and Eve before their rebellion), there would be no need for law. Rational Adam could not even think of raping Eve, but egocentric Adam was a threat to her, and society had to provide protection: namely, the fig leaf. The political problem begins when imagination conquers intellect and egocentrism conquers cooperation.

With regard to the question of Rational, or Natural, Law, it is clear that Maimonides, as opposed to Saadia and Halevi, does not think that moral norms are "rational" or "natural"; rather he considers them to be popularly accepted opinions. In a discussion in the *Eight Chapters*, 6, he explicitly rejects Saadia's description of the moral commandments as "rational." In Maimonides' view, our laws (like the fig leaf) come into being precisely when human beings cease to be rational. They aim to help us live more rationally, but they themselves are not rational, and thus they are not universal. However, since irrational behavior is part of human nature, law may be said to fulfill a natural human need. In this sense, law has something to do with nature but is not "natural" (2.40).

It is interesting to compare Maimonides' parable of the weak moneychanger (1.46) with Halevi's parable of the king of India. If the big bully does not rob the weak moneychanger, it is only because there is a ruler in the city. Similarly, if there is order in the universe, it must have a ruler.

Maimonides distinguishes between two kinds of political law: nomic law (from the Greek *nomos*, "law") and divine Law. The two are distinguished by their goals. The goal of a nomic law is the establishment of peace. The divine Law sees the establishment of peace as its intermediate goal, but its ultimate goal is scientific knowledge, that is, the knowledge of God. The Torah is divine Law, since it seeks to promote both physical and spiritual welfare, that is, peace and truth. There may be many divine laws, but the Torah of Moses is the original one (2.40; 3.27–28). The messianic era refers to the time when the Torah will finally succeed in creating a community of peace and knowledge (3.11).

Questions of law and politics have an important place in the *Guide*, and the *Guide* may well be defined as primarily a book of legal or political philosophy. However, the book is famous also for its discussions of God.

Maimonides holds the extreme position that there is absolutely nothing that can be literally predicated of God. All descriptions of him are figurative. "The Torah speaks according to the language of human beings," that is, according to imaginative language, not philosophic language (1.29, 46). Even the statement "God exists" is not literally true, for how can the creator of existence be said to exist? The term *existence*, explains Maimonides, is used in a purely equivocal sense with regard to God (1.56). According to Maimonides' uncompromising *via negativa* (use of negative definitions) (1.59), we can say what God is not, but not what he is. Ultimately, all attributes of created things are to be negated of God; and thus the upshot of the *via negativa* is that *God is not the created universe.*

For more than 800 years, Maimonides' *Guide of the Perplexed* has fascinated, challenged, enraged, and perplexed readers. Studying it remains a singular philosophic experience.

The *Zohar* (late thirteenth century)

The *Zohar* is a mythico-mystical midrash on the Pentateuch and other parts of the Bible. It is written in Aramaic, the language of the Talmud, and purports to contain the esoteric discussions of the second-century Rabbi

Simeon bar Yohai and his circle in the Galilee. In fact, it was written eleven centuries later in Spain. Rabbi Moses de Leon (ca. 1240–1305), a philosopher and mystic from Guadalajara, was active in copying and distributing the *Zohar*. After his death, when his widow was asked about the whereabouts of the ancient manuscript from which he had supposedly copied the *Zohar*, she replied: "He wrote it entirely from his own head!" Her attribution of the *Zohar* to her husband has been accepted by most modern scholars, although some think he was merely one of a group of coauthors. Some thirteenth-century kabbalists held that in a mystical sense both Rabbi Simeon bar Yohai and de Leon wrote the *Zohar*: that is, de Leon mystically united in spirit with Rabbi Simeon and his companions, they dictated the *Zohar* to him, and he wrote it by means of "automatic writing."

Zoharic myth is extravagant and wild, but far from being primitive or naive. It may be described as postbiblical and postphilosophic myth. Both the biblical and the philosophic traditions are basically antimythological. The biblical God, unlike the gods of ancient mythologies, fights no bloody wars with other gods and has no sordid love affairs with seductive goddesses. He creates the world by speech alone: "Let there be light!" (Genesis 1:3). Similarly, the philosophic tradition replaced the colorful and fascinating gods of the sea, the winds, and so on, by the "principles" *(archai)* of water, *pneuma*, and so on. Thus, a Jewish philosopher in the thirteenth century belonged to two antimythological traditions: the biblical and the philosophic. He had before him Maimonides' *Guide of the Perplexed*, a Jewish book and a philosophic book, which methodically pushed both antimythical traditions to an extreme. Of course, it might be argued that life without myths is arid, banal, boring, and spiritually deprived. The great thirteenth-century kabbalists seem to have thought this. In any case, they boldly sought to revive mythology. They believed that myth could take them beyond the intellectualism of Maimonides' *Guide*. Kabbalah, they asserted, begins just where philosophy ends. Where the philosopher's *ratio* (reason) stops, the kabbalist's imagination takes over.

Maimonides had taught that one cannot speak about God. The kabbalists agreed that one cannot speak about God, the *En Sof* (Infinite), but they added that one can indeed speak about God's presence in the universe. They explained that God is present in the universe by virtue of ten *sefirot* (manifestations or emanations; singular: *sefirah*). As monotheists, they could not speak about wars or romances between the gods, but they could speak about wars and romances *inside* God; that is, they could speak about wars and romances among the *sefirot*. There are ten *sefirot*: one suprasexual, five masculine, and four feminine. They are as follows:

1.   Keter (Crown), no sex, the indescribable first emanation from *En Sof*, known also as Nothingness (ʾayin).

2. Hokhmah (Wisdom), male, the primordial point.
3 . Binah (Understanding), female, the spiritual womb of all existence.
4. Hesed (Love), male, the right arm.
5. Geburah (Power), female, the left arm.
6. Tiferet (Beauty), male, the torso.
7. Nesah (Eternity), male, the right leg.
8. Hod (Majesty), female, the left leg.
9. Yesod (Foundation), male, the penis.
10. Malkhut (Kingdom) or Shekhinah (Presence), female, the presence of God in history.

The *sefirot* constitute an anthropomorphic portrait of God, but they are also independent powers, each having his or her own loves and hates.

In order to show how the *Zohar* "goes beyond" philosophy, let us look at its exposition of the first verse in the Bible (*Zohar* 1.15a)[2]. This verse is usually translated: "In the beginning *[be-reshit]*, God *[Elohim]* created *[bara²]* the heaven and the earth." The first word *"be-reshit"* had already been interpreted in the classical Midrash as meaning "by means of Wisdom," in accordance with Proverbs 8:22 ("The Lord made me [Wisdom, *hokhmah*] the beginning *[reshit]* of His way"). The rabbis had identified this "Wisdom" with the preexistent Torah. The *Zohar*, however, now identifies it with the second *sefirah*, named "Hokhmah." Thus, *"be-reshit"* is to be understood: "by means of the *sefirah* Hokhmah." The word *"Elohim"* is taken by the *Zohar* to be the direct object of the verse, not the subject. This is because in the Hebrew text the word *"bara²"* precedes *"Elohim."* *"Elohim"* is held to refer here to the third *sefirah*, namely, Binah. Thus, the verse now reads: "By means of the *sefirah* Hokhmah, [. . .] created the *sefirah* Binah. The verse therefore does not speak about what *Elohim* created, but rather it speaks about the creation of *Elohim!* The *Zohar* has transformed the God of Genesis 1:1 from Creator to Created! It has mythologized the verse. But what is the subject of the verse? It is either the ineffable and unknowable first *sefirah* (Keter) or the ineffable and unknowable *En Sof*. But since Keter and *En Sof* are ineffable and unknowable, they cannot appear in our verse or in any other text. The verse thus has no subject. The grammatical defect is a theological boon. The Infinite God *(En Sof)*, as indeed the philosophers had taught, is beyond words or understanding, but, affirm the kabbalists, the Bible never tried to speak about the Infinite God. The Bible speaks only about God's created presence in our universe. The first verse of Genesis tells us about the creation of God's presence in the universe, that is, the creation of the *sefirot*. By means of the primordial point, the *sefirah* Hokhmah, the *En Sof* created the *sefirah* Binah and the seven other *sefirot* (i.e., the heaven and the earth). Hokhmah is masculine and Binah feminine, and the creation of *Elohim* has a sexual interpretation: The masculine divine being emanated the feminine divine being and then impregnated her with the divine seed *(zera')*, which is also the divine light *(zohar)*.

Not surprisingly, many students of the Bible and philosophy are outraged by the *Zohar*. Nonetheless, since the *Zohar* is postbiblical and postphilosophic myth, it can be truly appreciated only by students of the Bible and philosophy.

A Final Word

I have discussed briefly some views of three major Jewish philosophers who lived at different times and in different places and who differed on fundamental questions; I have also discussed briefly the mystical *Zohar*. It is hoped that these brief discussions will have given the student a taste of the rich tradition of Jewish philosophy and encourage further study.

Notes

1. See S. Pines, "Shi'ite Terms and Conceptions in Judah Halevi's *Kuzari*," *Jerusalem Studies in Arabic and Islam* 2 (1980), pp. 165–251.

2. D. C. Matt, *Zohar, the Book of Enlightenment* (New York: Paulist Press, 1983), pp. 49–50.

Suggested Readings

Husik, Isaac. *A History of Medieval Jewish Philosophy*. New York: Atheneum, 1973.
Lewy, Hans, Alexander Altmann, and Isaak Heinemann, eds. *Three Jewish Philsophers: Philo, Saadya Gaon, Judah HaLevi*. New York: Atheneum, 1969.
Matt, Daniel. *Zohar, the Book of Enlightenment*. New York: Paulist Press, 1983.
Scholem, Gershom. *Major Trends in Jewish Mysticism*. New York: Schocken, 1941.

8

Modern
Jewish History

DAVID E. FISHMAN

The Early Modern Period (1500–1750)

The expulsion of the Jews from Spain, in 1492, culminated the gradual process through which the Jews were expelled from Western and much of central Europe in the Middle Ages. In its aftermath, the centers of Jewish life shifted eastward: to Italy and the Ottoman Empire (including the Land of Israel) for the Sephardim (Jews of Iberian origin), and to Poland for the Ashkenazim (Jews of northern European origin). Because of continued eastward migration (in the sixteenth century) and natural increase (in the seventeenth and eighteenth centuries), 80 percent of the world's 2.5 million Jews lived in the Near East and eastern Europe in 1800.

In many respects, Jewish life in the lands of resettlement continued along medieval lines: Jews were legally a separate category of inhabitants; their internal affairs were governed by Jewish communal bodies (the *kahal*) recognized by the Crown; and the revealed and binding nature of Jewish religious law remained the cornerstone of Jewish social values. Jewry was bound together by a shared liturgical and literary tongue—Hebrew—and by a common messianic faith in their eventual return to the Land of Israel.

In many respects, the Jews' separateness, distinctiveness, and traditional religious culture not only persisted but actually intensified in the sixteenth to eighteenth centuries. With their geographic shift eastward, the Jews' spoken languages now differed greatly from that of their non-Jewish neighbors, with Ashkenazim speaking Yiddish—a Germanic language—in a Slavic environment, and Sephardim speaking Judezmo—a Romance language—in Turkey. The Catholic Counterreformation led to more strictly enforced physical segregation of Jews in Italy and Poland.

(In Italy, the enclosed Jewish quarters were known as *ghettos*.) Jewish messianic fervor flourished among the Sephardim in the aftermath of the Spanish expulsion, an event that aroused popular hopes and mystical speculations of imminent redemption. In 1665 and 1666, most of world Jewry embraced with excited enthusiasm the claims of a Jewish mystic from Smyrna, Turkey, named Shabbetai Zevi, that he was the Messiah. His eventual conversion to Islam disabused them of this belief. Nearly a century later, in Poland, a powerful Jewish mystical and pietistic movement called Hasidism arose, which stressed religious joy and faith in the salvationary powers of holy men called zaddikim. Seen from the perspective of these developments, the period between 1500 and 1750 can be considered the "late Middle Ages" in Jewish history.

But in other important respects, the period marked the beginning of social, political, and cultural transformations. In the early seventeenth century, the geographic pendulum began to shift westward. Groups of Spanish and Portuguese New Christians settled in Holland in the 1590s, and by the 1610s they were publicly conducting Jewish religious services in Amsterdam, which became one of the most vibrant Jewish communities in Europe. At about the same time, in southern France, groups of New Christian "Portuguese Merchants" began to revert to Judaism, without being expelled or persecuted by the local authorities. And the Jews were formally allowed to reenter England in 1656, following appeals from Dutch Rabbi Manasseh Ben Israel and deliberations by the government of Oliver Cromwell. Jews also settled in the Dutch, French, and British colonies in the New World—most notably in Dutch New Amsterdam (later called New York), in 1654.

This Jewish resettlement in the West was made possible by the decline of traditional Christian theological thinking about the Jews—and by the rise of pragmatic economic considerations. In the era of mercantilism, the Jews' long-standing involvement in international commerce and banking came to be viewed as desirable assets. In a related development, the idea of religious tolerance began to take hold in western Europe and was articulated with specific regard to the Jews by a number of prominent jurists and political thinkers.

Early capitalism and mercantilism enabled a small elite of Jewish bankers to rise to positions of prominence and power in the surrounding societies. In 1697, 12 of the 124 reserved seats on the London Stock Exchange were held by Jews. In the German principalities, "Court Jews" served in a combination of capacities—as financiers, purveyors, and close advisers—to dukes and monarchs. Living at court, rather than in a Jewish community or enclosed ghetto, they adopted many of the styles and behavior patterns of the Christian aristocracy, becoming quite lax in their Jewish religious observance.

Skepticism and religious laxity crept into Jewish society, particularly in Holland, England, and Italy. Ambivalence toward Judaism was characteristic of many of the ex-Marranos (Jewish converts to Christianity) and their descendants who had lived as Christians on the Iberian peninsula, before emigrating and professing Judaism. Many of them could not adjust to traditional Jewish practice and faith. The most prominent Jewish heretic and naturalist philosopher of the seventeenth century—Benedict (Barukh) Spinoza—was a Dutch Jew with Marrano ancestors.

The Enlightenment and the Jews

The ideas of the European Enlightenment, which proclaimed the supremacy of reason and equality of all men, had a complex impact on modern Jewish history. On the one hand, Enlightenment thinkers, such as Montesquieu, advanced the idea of Jews being equal human beings and condemned their persecution as the barbarous product of religious superstition and the abuses of the Church. The German writer G. E. Lessing wrote a number of dramatic works (e.g., *Nathan the Wise*) that revolved around virtuous and heroic Jewish characters in order to show his readers that such Jews could and did exist, and to argue on behalf of religious tolerance. On the other hand, Judaism itself was viewed with distaste by Enlightenment philosophers such as Rousseau and Voltaire, who considered it a superstitious and narrow-minded religion that bred immorality. The men of the Enlightenment, as antagonists of Christianity and the Church, ascribed many of the latter's "depravities" to Judaism, its mother religion, as well.

This ambivalent legacy of the Enlightenment first began to have impact on social and political realities in central Europe, in Germany and Austria, in the 1770s. The admission of Moses Mendelssohn into Enlightenment circles in Berlin, the close friendship that developed between him and Lessing, and his rise to a central position in German philosophy and letters signaled the beginning of the integration of Jews into European society. To the astonishment of his contemporaries, Mendelssohn mastered the German language, literature, and social manners, but remained an observant Jew. He rejected several public challenges to the effect that, as a man of reason, he ought to convert to Protestantism. He responded in his book *Jerusalem* that the state and society should afford equal tolerance toward the followers of all religions, as long as they conformed to "natural law," and that Judaism was, in any event, the religion most compatible with the Enlightenment, since it was itself tolerant and commanded laws, not irrational dogmas of faith. Mendelssohn thus attempted to combine and synthesize Judaism and the European Enlightenment. Because of his attachment to two communities and cultures—a duality that was to become a central feature of the modern Jewish experience—he came to be considered the father of modern Jewry.

Under Mendelssohn's model and inspiration, there developed a Jewish Enlightenment movement in Germany, called the Haskalah. It urged Jews to learn and use the language of their non-Jewish neighbors, to acquire general scientific knowledge, to eschew social separatism and religious superstition, and to consider themselves loyal subjects of their lands of residence. It also called for the productivization of Jewish economic activity, that is, their adoption of crafts and agriculture in place of commerce. Nevertheless, the Haskalah did not advocate the abandonment or radical alteration of Jewish religious practice, and its members embraced the study of the Bible and the literary use of Hebrew. Implicit in its ideology was the anticipation that the modernized Jew would be accepted into surrounding society and would be afforded an equal legal status with Christians.

The first partial realization of this hope came in the Edict of Toleration, issued by the enlightened emperor Joseph II of Austria, in 1782. This edict sought to bring down some of the legal barriers separating Jews from surrounding society. It abolished several (though not all) long-standing restrictions on Jewish residence and occupations, and it eliminated special Jewish taxes and signs (such as the "Jewish hat"). It required Jews either to send their children to state public schools or to create analogous *Normalschulen* of their own, and it prohibited the use of Hebrew and Yiddish in business records. In subsequent years, Joseph II also required Jews to serve in the Austrian army and abolished Jewish judicial autonomy.

Enlightened Jews, such as Mendelssohn's associate Naftali Hertz (Hartwig) Wessely, greeted Joseph's reforms as beneficent acts to bring Jews out of their backwardness and isolation, and to grant them a higher status, similar to that of Christian subjects. Wessely composed a pamphlet, *Words of Peace and Truth,* that called upon Jews to reform their elementary school (the *heder*) in accordance with Joseph's directives. But traditionalist Jews, led by Rabbis Raphael Ha-Cohen of Hamburg and Ezekiel Landau of Prague, viewed these measures with suspicion and trepidation. For them, Joseph's reforms were evil decrees that interfered in the Jews' internal autonomy (education, courts, business) and that threatened to weaken Judaism by enticing and forcing Jews into Gentile society. This conflict between Enlightened and traditionalist Jews was to persist over the next several generations, first in central Europe, and then in eastern Europe. In Germany and Austria the momentum was unmistakably on the side of the Enlightened camp.

Emancipation and Reform

The French Revolution of 1789, which created the modern nation-state, also radically altered the relation of France's Jews to the State. Despite the revolution's "Declaration of the Rights of Man and the Citizen," Jews were not incorporated immediately into the French citizenry. After Jewish delegations submitted petitions, the French National Assembly debated the issue of Jewish enfranchisement, or, as it would later be called, Emancipation.

Opponents argued that Jews were a foreign nation, that they prayed for their return to their ancestral homeland, and that they followed their own laws and considered Frenchmen to be strangers; therefore, they should be treated as resident aliens, not as citizens. Indeed, it was claimed that the Jews' religion (particularly the dietary laws and Saturday Sabbath) prevented them from assuming the responsibilities of French citizens and that their moral depravity disqualified them from this honor. Supporters of Jewish Emancipation, such as Stanislas de Clermont-Tonnerre, argued that the principle of religious liberty championed by the revolution was at stake; denying citizenship to people who had lived in France for centuries just because they "wore beards, were circumcised, and followed a different religion" would make a mockery of the Declaration of the Rights of Man. Abbé Grégoire argued that Jewish depravities were themselves the consequence of Christian persecution, and that Jewish separatism and messianism would whither away if the Jews were admitted into the citizenry. In the end, the Sephardic Jews of southern France were emancipated in January 1790, and the Ashkenazim of Alsace-Lorraine one and a half years later, in September 1791.

Emancipation meant that the Jews no longer existed as a separate legal category in the eyes of the State. In practical terms, all sorts of professional, educational, and social opportunities were opened up to them. However, Emancipation also meant the dissolution of the legally mandated Jewish community (kahal) with its administration, taxes, and courts. Clermont-Tonnerre had stated in the National Assembly's debate, "The Jews should be denied everything as a nation, but must be granted everything as individuals. There cannot be a nation in a nation." Abolition of the kahal system meant that religious observance and indeed identification with the Jewish community altogether became a matter of individual, voluntary choice.

Most Jews welcomed the granting of Emancipation: some viewed it in nearly messianic terms, as the end to Jewish suffering in exile and a form of political redemption. Attainment of Emancipation was the primary political goal of Europe's Jews for most of the nineteenth century; its spread was uneven and dependent upon local political conditions and social attitudes toward Jews. At first, Emancipation was advanced by the conquests of Napoleon's armies in Holland (in 1796), in southern Germany and northern Italy (in 1806–1807). But Napoleon himself considered rescinding the Jews' Emancipation and convened an Assembly of Jewish Notables from throughout his empire in 1806, as well as a rabbinic synod (Sanhedrin), to extract solemn oaths of loyalty to France, its laws and inhabitants.

The most difficult struggle was in Prussia, where Jews acculturated rapidly but did not secure equal civil and political rights until very late. Emancipation was first granted in 1812, then retracted at the Congress of Vienna in 1815, reinstated by the revolutions of 1848—only to be abolished by the postrevolutionary reaction. It was finally granted in 1869. During the course of this protracted struggle, German Jews redefined their identities and produced a variety of modern Jewish ideologies.

Among upwardly mobile German Jews, one solution to the frustrations of second-class status was conversion to Christianity. Four of Mendelssohn's six children converted, as did the parents of Karl Marx and the German poet Heinrich Heine, who declared that "the baptismal font is the ticket of admission to European Society." Most, however, redefined Judaism rather than abandoning it altogether. They relegated Judaism to the synagogue service while eagerly joining the ranks of the German urban bourgeoisie.

Associated with this was the rise of Reform Judaism, which transformed Jewish religious practice as well as doctrine in accordance with the new spirit and demands of the nineteenth century. In the first Reform Temple (a term used instead of "synagogue"), founded in Hamburg in 1818, and in its successors, much of the liturgy was recited in German, and the "national" prayers for the return to the Land of Israel were deleted. A choir, accompanied by an organ, was introduced and the donning of the Jewish prayer shawl (talit) and head covering was discontinued. Strict formal decorum was maintained. The service became more decorous and dignified—and resembled more closely the form of prayer in a Protestant church.

The leading thinker of Reform Judaism, Abraham Geiger, emphasized the universalist aspects of Judaism and contended that its essence was Ethical Monotheism—the moral teachings of the prophets and faith in one God. Many religious laws and rituals (such as the complex dietary laws) were expendable externalities, products of more primitive times. In a few more-radical Reform congregations, the Sabbath service was shifted to Sunday and the practice of circumcision was discontinued. This form of Judaism, which minimized the areas of tension and conflict with the dominant culture while accentuating its lofty moral teachings, was most attractive in a period when Jews were struggling for social acceptance and political Emancipation.

More traditionally disposed rabbis accused the reformers of bartering away Jewish tradition in exchange for Emancipation. In a famous incident, Rabbi Zacharias Frankel walked out in protest from a Reform rabbinical conference in 1843, after a dispute with Abraham Geiger over the importance of Hebrew in Jewish prayer and religious education. Frankel created the movement for "Positive-Historical" Judaism (later called Conservative Judaism), which affirmed traditional religious practices but recognized their historical evolution over time and the legitimacy of adjusting them to new circumstances. A third religious trend, called Neo-Orthodoxy, was led by Samson Raphael Hirsch of Frankfurt; it combined a dogmatic adherence to traditional doctrines and practices with an embrace of German culture and the adoption of some "aesthetic" reforms in the synagogue service.

Jews in European Society and Modern Anti-Semitism

During the course of the nineteenth century, Jews became a highly urbanized group. By 1905, 86 percent of the Jews in Prussia lived in cities, and 70 percent of France's Jews lived in Paris alone. Jews were heavily—and disproportionately—concentrated in small business, manufacturing, and the professions. In 1861, more than half of all Prussian Jews were shopkeepers. In Berlin, where Jews made up 4.8 percent of the total population in 1881, 12 percent of the physicians were Jewish, as were 8.6 percent of all writers.

As an urban, middle-class group, subject to various legal disabilities, most Jews sympathized with European liberalism and the struggle for democracy and individual rights. Heinrich Heine and Ludwig Boerne were among the most prominent spokesmen of German liberalism in the mid–nineteenth century. Jews widely sympathized with the revolutions of 1848, and their participation on the barricades and in political events was quite striking. In Vienna, Adolph Fischoff and Joseph Goldmark were the de facto heads of state during the revolution; in Prussia, Gabriel Riesser was elected second vice president of the Frankfort Assembly; and in Paris, Adolphe Crémieux became minister of justice. The appearance of Jews in positions of political authority during the brief "springtime of nations" was an important historical milestone.

Much smaller, but more visible, was the upper-class stratum of Jewish investment bankers. The house of Rothschild, headed by five brothers in London, Paris, Vienna, Frankfurt, and Naples, was one of the most successful banking establishments in Europe, issuing bonds and credits to several European governments. The Rothschilds' overriding interest was in the political stability of existing regimes and states, and they offered loans to Metternich to help crush the Austrian revolution of 1848. One of the family's members, Sir Moses Montefiore of England, actively utilized his financial clout to intercede with the authorities on behalf of the persecuted Jewish communities in Czarist Russia (where he met with Nicholas I in 1846) and in Damascus, Syria (where a group of Jews were accused of the blood libel in 1840).

With the influx of Jews into the mainstream of society, there came a reactionary backlash in the form of modern anti-Semitism, which typically
ascribed society's ills to the Jewish "invasion." One of the features of the
new, modern anti-Semitism of the mid–nineteenth century was its overtly
radicalist character, its contention that Jewish depravity was biologically
innate. Whereas in the Middle Ages, Jewish converts to Christianity were,
in theory, considered "the most beloved children of Christ," for modern
anti-Semites, the abandonment of Judaism and conversion to Christianity
were no solution to the "Jewish problem." On the contrary, converts and
their descendants were the most dangerous peril of all because they cor-
roded an unknowing society from within with their "Jewish" traits.

One of the early exponents of this anti-Semitic view, the German composer Richard Wagner, argued in his widely read essay "Jewry in Music"
(1850) that the entry of Jews such as composer Felix Mendelssohn and
Heinrich Heine into German arts was the cause of Germany's cultural de-
generation, since Jews were inherently the antithesis of beauty. The term
anti-Semitism was coined by Wilhelm Marr, one of its leading exponents,
precisely to emphasize its racial (rather than religious) nature.

Anti-Semitism could be and was wedded to a remarkable variety of so-
ciopolitical ideologies. The French Utopian Socialist Alphonse Toussenel
warned that Jewish bankers and financiers were the true rulers of France,
and the young Karl Marx, in his essay "On the Jewish Question," blamed
the Jews for the evils of modern capitalism, declaring "the bill of exchange is the true God of Israel." Furthermore, conservatives ascribed the
weakening of Christian values to Jewish influence and blamed them for
the hardships encountered by the German middle class.

In the 1870s, anti-Semitism became an organized political force in Germany. Marr founded the "League of Anti-Semites," whose goal was to
roll back Emancipation, and political parties emerged which incorporated
anti-Semitism into their platforms. In 1880, a petition with 225,000 signa-
tories was submitted to the chancellor, Otto von Bismarck, calling upon
Germany to exclude Jews from the civil service, ban them from teaching
in public schools, and cut off Jewish immigration to Germany.

The Russian-Jewish Experience (until 1881)

The modernization of Russian Jewry occurred both later and differently
than that of German and French Jewries. Throughout the sixteenth, seventeenth, and eighteenth centuries, the Muscovite state had banned and
expelled Jews from its midst. Ivan the Terrible refused to allow Polish-
Jewish merchants to visit Muscovy for the purposes of trade, and the 1655
Russian invasion of Poland was accompanied by massacres and expul-

sions of Jews. In the eighteenth century, there was a period of Jewish "infiltration" across the border, only to be followed by Empress Elizabeth's expulsion order of 1742, at which time she declared, "I desire no profit from the enemies of Christ."

Russia first acquired a sizable Jewish population, of nearly one million, through the partition of Poland (1772, 1793, 1795). Russian policy, initiated by Catherine II's decrees of 1791 and 1794, was to restrict Jewish residence to the former Polish provinces and "New Russia"; an area that was called the "Pale of Jewish Settlement." As a result of this policy of geographic containment, which was fully abolished only in 1915, the vast majority of Jews lived in regions that were populated predominantly by Poles and Ukrainians—and not by Russians. Inside the Pale, and the Russian-controlled Kingdom of Poland, most Jews lived in cities and towns, where they constituted the majority or the largest single ethnic group. Combined, these factors contributed toward a slow pace of social and cultural integration with Russia.

During the reign of Nicholas I (1825–1855), official hostility and suspicion toward the Jews reached a peak. The conscription of Jewish youths into the Russian army, introduced in 1827, was utilized by the regime as a device to draw the conscripts away from Judaism and induce them to convert to Christianity. The fact that the task of filling the conscription quotas was assigned to Jewish communal leaders created severe tensions between the elite and masses of the Jewish community. Traditional Judaism was assaulted through other state measures as well: the forced closing of most Hebrew printing presses in the empire in 1836, a campaign by the Ministry of Education, begun in 1840, to create a network of obligatory Crown schools for Jewish children, and the abolition of the *kahal* in 1844.

The Haskalah (Jewish Enlightenment movement) first gained strength in Russia through its support for and involvement in the system of Jewish Crown schools, which included State Rabbinical Seminaries in Vilna and Zhitomir. Mindful that they were a small minority of Russian Jewry and that through persuasion alone they would be unable to realize their program of cultural and social change, *maskilim* ("enlighteners"), such as Isaac Ber Levinsohn, "the Russian Mendelssohn," allied themselves with the state and applauded its program of compulsory Enlightenment. This position brought them into sharp conflict with traditionalist Jews.

In eastern Europe, the Haskalah's attachment to Hebrew and to creating a humanistic Hebrew culture was more pronounced than in Germany. The poetic works of J. L. Gordon, the historical treatises of S. J. Fuenn, and the polemical essays and autobiography of Moshe Leib Lilienblum stand out as the pinnacles of Haskalah literature. In an effort to reach out to a broader reading audience, Russian *maskilim* also took to writing in Yiddish, despite the fact that they despised the "corrupt jargon" and looked forward to its disappearance. The Yiddish satirical novels of Mendele Moykher Seforim, the pen name of S. Y. Abramovitsh, many of which were set in a prototypical shtetl called Glupsk ("Foolstown"), were extremely popular and influential.

The era of the great reforms of Alexander II was a period of hope and dynamism for Russian Jewry. The *rekruchina* (conscription) and other oppressive measures were terminated, and various categories of Jews were allowed to reside outside the Pale of Settlement—merchants, artisans, and university graduates. For the first time, a significant number of young Jews enrolled in Russian gymnasia (secondary schools) and universities, and sizable Jewish populations appeared in such Russian cultural centers as Odessa and St. Petersburg—and were influenced by their ambiance. In these cities, there emerged a Russian-Jewish intelligentsia and bourgeoisie that identified with Russian culture and loyally supported the empire on the Polish question. As early as the 1870s, parts of this intelligentsia (and of the Hebrew-writing Haskalah) came under the influence of Russian radical and nihilist literature.

Despite the growth of modernizing and integrationist trends, traditional Jewish religious culture remained quite vibrant inside the Pale of Settlement. The Hasidic courts in Lubavitch, Talnoe, and Gora Kalvaria (in Yiddish: Ger) were bastions of mystical and pietistic activity; academies for the study of the Talmud (yeshivot) flourished in Belorussia and Lithuania (in Volozhin, Mir, Slobodka); and the *Musar* movement, aimed at moral introspection and rejuvenation, captured the imagination of rabbinic circles. Thus, Russian Jewry, divided by social class, legal status, geocultural environment, and ideological orientation, was a highly differentiated community.

The Emergence of Zionism

The wave of pogroms that swept across the Ukraine in 1881–1882 came as a great shock to the Jewish intelligentsia, which had been confident that Russia and its Jews were marching down the path of Enlightenment and Emancipation. Their sense of isolation and vulnerability was heightened by the fact that both the czarist regime and the revolutionary circles of Narodnaia Volya blamed the violent outbursts on Jewish abuses. The authorities responded by issuing the "temporary laws" of May 1882, which resulted in the large-scale expulsion of Jews from the Russian countryside.

The trauma of the pogroms led *maskilim* such as M. L. Lilienblum and Russified intellectuals such as Leon Pinsker to conclude that Emancipation was a hopeless cause. For them, the only solution to the Jews' precarious condition was their settlement in a territory of their own, preferably in their ancestral homeland in the Land of Israel. Groups of Jewish university students departed for Palestine, where they founded collective agricultural colonies. Pinsker and Lilienblum founded the "lovers of Zion" organization in 1883, which propagated the Palestinophilic idea and raised funds on behalf of the colonies.

A similar dynamic developed in central and western Europe more than a decade later. Theodor Herzl, a relatively assimilated Jew who worked as the Paris correspondent of a Viennese newspaper, was shocked by the anti-Semitism exhibited by the trial of Captain Alfred Dreyfus, a Jew who was convicted of trumped-up charges of treason and espionage against France. Convinced that anti-Semitism was a permanent and dangerous feature of European society and politics and that assimilation was an impossible dream, Herzl proposed a national solution to the Jewish question in his epochal pamphlet "The Jewish State" (1896). He organized the First Zionist Congress, held in Basel, Switzerland, in August 1897, at which the goal of securing a home for the Jewish people in Palestine based on public law was proclaimed.

The Zionist idea generated much controversy within European Jewry. The established leadership of western Jewries viewed Zionism as a dangerous movement that added fuel to the flames of anti-Semitism by confirming that Jews were aliens in their lands of residence. Meanwhile, in eastern Europe, the traditional rabbis viewed Zionism as a rebellion against God, a rejection of the traditional religious doctrine that the ingathering of the exiles would take place in the end of days, with the coming of the Messiah. But despite these circles of opposition, the Jews' deteriorating political and social position in czarist Russia made Zionism an increasingly popular movement among East European Jews. The affirmation of Jewish nationhood and quest for statehood also fit well in a region where numerous groups were undergoing national revivals.

Herzl engaged in active diplomatic efforts to secure a charter for Jewish migration to Palestine, negotiating with the Turkish sultan, Kaiser Wilhelm of Germany, the pope, British officials, and even Russian minister Vyacheslav von Plehve. Others in the movement, called "practical Zionists," advocated focusing energies on building and strengthening the Jewish settlement in Palestine proper. A third, highly influential stream was "Spiritual Zionism," led by Ahad Ha'am (pseudonym of Asher Ginzberg), which viewed the movement's main goal to be the strengthening of the Jewish national spirit. According to Ahad Ha'am, the Land of Israel was to serve as the cultural center of Jewry, where Hebrew language and literature would flourish and an integral modern Jewish culture would grow, free of the danger of assimilation. Spiritual Zionists devoted much of their energy to work in the Diaspora: establishing nationally oriented Jewish schools and supporting Hebrew literature and scholarship.

The Zionist movement faced a crisis in 1903, when Herzl, reacting to the lack of progress with the Turks and the outburst of a bloody Easter pogrom in Kishinev, negotiated an offer from the British government to designate the British colony of Uganda as a territory for Jewish settlement. The issue of whether to accept, even temporarily, a territory other than the Land of Israel divided the Fifth Zionist Congress, with leaders of the Russian Zionist movement walking out in protest against Herzl's proposal. The Uganda project was ultimately rejected by the Zionist movement in 1905.

Other Solutions:
Emigration, Radicalism, Diaspora, Nationalism

During the period between 1881 and 1914, the economic and political position of Russian Jewry deteriorated dramatically. The Jewish small-town economy entered an extended crisis owing to the emancipation of the serfs and the growth of the railway system, and Jewish rural businesses (mills, distilleries, taverns) were largely eliminated by the "temporary laws" of May 1882 and subsequent state measures. Jews flocked in great numbers to the cities of the Pale of Settlement and Russian-controlled Poland but faced great economic difficulties there as well. Quotas on Jewish students in the universities, introduced in 1887 and tightened in 1901, limited the entry of Jews into the professions. The civil service did not accept Jews. Laws on Sunday rest forced Jewish shops to be closed two days a week, rather than one, thereby decreasing their income. The overall trend was toward pauperization.

The Jews' sense of political precariousness was heightened by events such as the violent expulsion from Moscow in 1891, the rise of right-wing organizations, such as the Union of True Russian People and the "black hundreds," and the scores of pogroms perpetrated between 1903 (Kishinev) and 1906, with a climax in October 1905. The 1911–1913 show trial of Mendel Beilis in Kiev on charges of using Christian blood for ritual purposes added a macabre and foreboding feeling to the political atmosphere.

The most widespread response to the economic and political crises was emigration westward, mainly to the United States. Between 1881 and 1914 more than 2 million Jews went from Russia to the United States. Smaller numbers settled in England (105,000 between 1881 and 1905 alone), France, South Africa, and Canada (100,000 between 1901 and 1914). The Russian authorities did not prevent or discourage Jewish emigration, much of which was conducted illegally. As Count Ignatiev told a Jewish delegation in 1882, "The Eastern border is closed to you [i.e., the Pale of Settlement will not be abolished]; the Western border [i.e., emigration] is open."

This massive social movement was facilitated by an international network of Jewish social service organizations. In Germany, committees provided food, shelter, medical care, and pocket money to refugees and directed them to Hamburg and other ports. In part, the German Jews' aid was motivated by self-interest: to ensure that their impoverished and "backward" eastern brethren moved on and did not settle in Germany and fester into a social problem, which would fan the flames of anti-Semitism.

Attempts were made to control and direct the migration. In 1891, Baron Maurice de Hirsch founded the Jewish Colonization Association and announced ambitious plans to settle Russian Jews on farms and rural areas in Argentina. American Jewish leaders attempted at one point to settle thousands of migrants in Texas. But despite these efforts, the great stream of migration continued to the major cities on the eastern coast of the United States. In the years following the 1905 revolution, more than 100,000 Russian Jews arrived in New York City annually.

As a result of the great migration, the United States became the preeminent Jewish center in the world. Its Jewish population increased from 271,000 in 1880 (3.5 percent of the world total) to 5,556,000 in 1939 (or 33.5 percent of the world total). Because of the strong personal, ethnic, and cultural bonds between the U.S. Jews and those of Russia/Poland, the provision of material aid to East European Jewry and political interventions on its behalf became important features of American Jewish communal life.

Meanwhile, the migration barely diminished the Jewish population of czarist Russia, which remained stable at slightly above 5 million. For the Jews who remained in the czarist empire, the revolutionary movement, with its promise of a new world of equality and justice, became increasingly popular. In 1897, 25 percent of all political arrestees in Russia were Jewish. Social democracy was particularly attractive, because of its universalist ideology of the brotherhood of all workers and its openness to Jews participating in its ranks. Young Russified Jews found in Social Democratic circles a milieu in which they could realize their aspiration for social acceptance and cultural assimilation. Some of them, such as Leon Trotsky (Lev Davidovich Bronstein) and Yulii Martov (originally: Tsederbaum), rose to leadership positions in the Russian Social Democratic Labor Party (RSDLP).

The development of a Jewish proletariat, whose members were overwhelmingly employed by Jewish bosses, led to the emergence of a Jewish workers' and socialist movement, which propagated its ideas in Yiddish. In

1897, the representatives of Jewish Social Democratic groups, led by Arkady Kremer, met clandestinely in Vilna to establish the General Jewish Workers' Union of Lithuania, Russia, and Poland, or the Bund. The Bund was extraordinarily successful in organizing workers' *kassas* (unions) and spreading socialist literature in Yiddish among the Jewish masses. It helped found the RSDLP (in 1898) and worked closely with the latter.

At first, the only specifically Jewish point in the Bund's platform was its call for equal civil rights for Jews. But in 1901, the Bund endorsed the principle of Jewish nationality and adopted a platform calling for cultural autonomy for all nationalities in Russia. This, in turn, created an ideological rift between the Bund and the RSDLP, whose leaders—including Trotsky and Martov—declared the idea of Jewish nationality reactionary. This issue and others led the Bund to secede from its mother party (perhaps more correctly called its daughter party) in 1903. (It rejoined in 1906.)

In the ensuing years, the Bund's national orientation grew: It organized Jewish self-defense units against pogromists and supported the development of modern Yiddish cultural institutions. At the same time, the Bund was stridently anti-Zionist and opposed emigration as a solution to the Jews' problems, enunciating a doctrine of *doikayt* ("hereness"). Bundists were staunch anticlericalists and advocated the cultivation of a secular Jewish identity based on the language of the working masses—Yiddish. In general political and tactical matters, the Bund adhered to the program of the RSDLP.

In between the Bund and Zionism there was a sizable ideological middle ground of smaller parties and trends. The prominent Jewish historian Simon Dubnow founded the Folkspartei, which proclaimed Jewish national autonomy in the Diaspora as the cornerstones of its program, and which supported the Constitutional Democratic Party on general political questions. The idea of national autonomy was even endorsed as an interim measure by the Russian Zionist movement as its 1906 conference in Helsinki. Socialist Zionism also straddled the fence between the two main rival camps. Although it set as its ultimate goal the creation of a Jewish socialist state in Palestine, it affirmed the need for national and revolutionary struggle in Russia as well. The movement was divided between Marxist and non-Marxist parties, headed by Ber Borokhov and Nahman Syrkin respectively.

An integral part of the national revival at the turn of the century was the flourishing of Jewish culture: of Hebrew and Yiddish literature, the Yiddish press and theater, and Russian-language publicists and historical scholarship. Spiritual Zionists established modern Jewish schools, which used Hebrew as a spoken language. Yiddish also came to be viewed as a valued resource and was declared a national language of the Jewish people at a 1908 conference in Czernowitz.

World War I: Devastation and Hope

During World War I, European Jewry was divided between the Axis and Allied powers and Jews served in the armies of both sides. Much of the Great War was waged in the lands between Germany and Russia, where Jews were most heavily concentrated, and they suffered greatly along with the other local inhabitants. But they were also the victims of specifically anti-Jewish violence: In 1915–1916, the Russian military expelled all Jews from the provinces near the front (first Lithuania, later Galicia and Bukovina) on the suspicion that they were spying for the Germans, an act that created a stream of tens of thousands of refugees into inner Russia. Toward the end of the war, Polish legionnaires perpetrated bloody pogroms in numerous cities under the pretext that Jews supported their enemies (the Ukrainians, Bolsheviks, and/or Lithuanians). By far the bloodiest massacres, in which an estimated 50,000 Jews were killed, took place in the Ukraine in 1919, by the "Whites," Ukrainian nationalist forces and various other bands.

The Zionist movement was divided over the position it should take in the war. Some urged support for Germany, which would liberate the Russian Jews from czarist oppression and prevail upon its ally, Turkey, to protect the Jewish settlement in Palestine. Others urged support for England, in its struggle against German imperialism, on behalf of the principle of self-determination by small nations. Officially, the World Zionist Organization declared its neutrality; unofficially Zionist leaders in Germany and England tried to extract pro-Zionist commitments from both sides, in exchange for the movement's support.

The leader of the pro-British faction, Chaim Weizmann, engaged in negotiations that led to a breakthrough. On November 2, 1917, the British foreign minister, Sir James Balfour, issued a declaration that Britain supported "the establishment in Palestine of a national home for the Jewish people." The motives for this declaration were a combination of sympathy for the plight of the Jews and the Zionist cause, coupled with wartime realpolitik. Britain had its own imperial goals of establishing a protectorate over Palestine; it also hoped to sway Jewish public opinion in Russia and the United States to support the Allies' war effort. Soon thereafter, the Balfour Declaration became more than just words on paper; in early 1918, British troops conquered Palestine, and Sir Herbert Samuel, a Jew, was appointed high commissioner. Hopes for the realization of the Zionist ideal were higher than ever before.

Another momentous and hopeful event for Jews to emerge from the war period was the Russian Revolution of February 1917. On April 2, 1917, the Provisional Government officially removed all legal restrictions based on religion and nationality, thereby finally emancipating the Jews of Russia. In the honeymoon period between February and October, Jewish cultural and organizational life flourished, elections were held to establish democratic Jewish *kehiles* (communities), and plans were made to convene an all-Russian Jewish congress. The Bolshevik coup, which was condemned by all the Jewish political parties, brought most of these endeavors to an abrupt halt.

The American Center

The United States was the one Western country in which Jewish Emancipation was never debated or granted by special enactment. The principles of religious liberty and equality before the law were enshrined in the American Constitution without any particular attention to the Jews (who were, at the time, very few in number). The multiethnic composition of the mass migrations of the nineteenth century, which brought people from all parts of Europe to the shores of the New World, facilitated the "benign neglect" of the Jews as a distinct "problem." Not surprisingly, many of the German Jews who settled in America between the 1840s and 1860s, and the East Europeans who came between the 1880s and 1920s, saw their immigration in terms of the biblical story of the Exodus from Egypt—from slavery to freedom, from the House of Bondage to the Promised Land.

The German and East European immigrants transplanted their divergent social and cultural traditions in America. The "Germans" were a middle-class group that experienced rapid socioeconomic mobility. They were best known for their role in establishing the first large American department stores (Macy's, Gimbel's), but they also established Reform Judaism as the predominant form of Jewish religious life in America, creating a network of congregations and an institution for the training of rabbis, the Hebrew Union College. In nineteenth-century America, Reform assumed a more universalist posture than it had in Europe. The platform distinguished between the moral and social parts of biblical legislation, on the one hand, which it declared sacred, and the national and most of the ritual parts, which it declared outdated.

The East Europeans settled in dense ethnic neighborhoods such as the Lower East Side of Manhattan, in New York, and worked overwhelmingly as laborers in the garment industry. They created a distinctive social and cultural milieu in which associations of Jews from the same town or region *(landsmanshaftn)* served as primary social units and helped new immigrants find fellowship, work, housing, and loans. These associations also served as the bases for thousands of small synagogue/congregations. The Yiddish press and theater became the public outlets for expressing the immigrants' common concerns, memories, and ideals. As an urban proletariat, the immigrants developed a strong Jewish labor movement, whose federation of unions, the United Hebrew Trades, had 250,000 members in 1917.

Until World War I, the organized leadership of American Jewry was made up exclusively of German Jews who did not have any sympathy for the East Europeans' cultural foreignness—whether it be their old-fashioned religion or their Yiddish language—and for their aggressively activist politics (whether Socialist or Zionist). Tensions between the two groups abounded. But a distinctly American synthesis of these two Jewish subcultures began to emerge, with the maturation of the first generation of American-born children of East Europeans.

In religion, this synthesis led to the rise of Conservative Judaism, whose rabbis were trained at the Jewish Theological Seminary of America (founded in 1886 and headed by Solomon Schechter beginning in 1902). Conservative congregations offered more traditional ritual and more Hebrew liturgy than Reform congregations, but introduced innovations that made religious practice more compatible with American ways, such as mixed seating of men and women and after-dinner Friday night services. The American (especially the Conservative) synagogue became a multifaceted Jewish communal center, which incorporated within it a religious school for children (on Sundays and/or weekday afternoons, after public school instruction), as well as social and recreational activities for families and adults.

Zionism was also transformed and Americanized, especially once the leadership of the American Zionist Federation was assumed in 1914 by Louis Brandeis, the first Jew to serve on the United States Supreme Court. Brandeis argued that there was no conflict between Zionism and Americanism. Its goal was to attain liberty and social justice—quintessentially American values—for the persecuted Jews of Europe through the building of a free and progressive Jewish homeland in Palestine. This version of Zionism made Palestine/Israel an object of philanthropic and political support and a source of ethnic identification and pride for American Jews.

The generation of the children of immigrants was Americanized through the agency of the public schools, and a very high proportion of them went on to university education. The children of poor garment workers became small businessmen, -women, and professionals (accountants, lawyers, journalists, academics), and the socialism of the fathers was transmuted into the liberalism of the sons, in the form of support for the New Deal, advocated by President Franklin D. Roosevelt. Along the path of upward mobility, the second generation did encounter some obstacles, owing to the prevalence of anti-Jewish attitudes among the country's Anglo-Saxon elites. In the 1920s, prestigious universities, such as

Harvard, established strict quotas on the admission of Jewish students, and major law firms and hospitals refused to hire Jewish professionals, who were considered "aggressive upstarts." Anti-Semitic images also played a role in the "Red Scare," which warned of Communist subversive plots against America, and in the Nativist movement, which brought an end to mass migration in the 1920s.

The Growth of the Yishuv in Palestine

Much like American Jewry, the Jewish community in Palestine, known as the Yishuv, arose as a result of immigration, referred to as aliyah (Hebrew for "ascent"). In 1890, at the conclusion of the First Aliyah (wave of migration), 25,000 Jews lived in Palestine, amounting to roughly 5 percent of the total population. By 1914, after two waves of aliyah, the number of Jews had grown to 85,000. The most significant numerical increase took place in the interwar period; by 1939 the size of the yishuv had reached 450,000.

The Second Aliyah, between 1904 and 1914, which consisted primarily of emigrants from Russia, had a formative impact on the social and political portrait of the Yishuv. Its members were adherents of the socialist trend within Zionism and were endowed with a distinct pioneering spirit. Their mentor was A. D. Gordon, who propagated the idea of the Jews' return to physical labor and the soil. They endeavored, through labor, to revive the desolate Land of Israel, transform their own way of life, and, most important, to forge a new type of self-reliant Jew. In 1910, members of the Second Aliyah established the first collective agricultural settlement, or kibbutz, in Deganya. Several pioneers of the Second Aliyah subsequently assumed leadership in the State of Israel, including David Ben-Gurion, Israel's first prime minister.

The 1917 Balfour Declaration gave political legitimacy to the Zionist enterprise and raised the prospects for its realization. In 1922, the Balfour Declaration was endorsed by the League of Nations, which assigned to Great Britain a mandate to administer Palestine, with the object of creating on its territory a "Jewish national home." In accordance with the terms of the mandate, Hebrew was recognized as one of the official languages of Palestine, and official status was afforded to the Zionist organization and, later (in 1929), to the Jewish Agency for Palestine to participate in administering the socioeconomic affairs of the Jewish population. Britain was to facilitate Jewish migration, while at the same time protecting the civil rights of Muslim and Christian inhabitants.

The Balfour Declaration and establishment of the British Mandate spurred the growth of national consciousness among the Palestinian

Arabs. An Arab congress that was convened in 1919 called for the declaration's repeal; it was followed by an Arab uprising in 1920–1921, which stunned the Yishuv and the British administration. Confronted with intensifying, violent Arab opposition, Britain attempted to retreat from its commitments to the Zionist movement. The British minister for colonial affairs, Winston Churchill, issued a 1922 "White Paper," according to which support for a Jewish national home in Palestine meant merely assisting the development of the land's existing Jewish community. According to the new turn in British policy, the Yishuv was to remain a part of a united Palestine under British control.

During the course of the next twenty-five years, the cycle of events between 1920 and 1922 repeated itself several times. After a wave of Jewish immigration, there followed a series of Arab protests and disturbances, which in turn led to shifts in British policy in a direction more favorable to the Arabs.

The Zionist movement entertained a wide range of prospective solutions to the Arab-Jewish conflict. The left wing of the Yishuv, including such organizations as Ha-Shomer Ha-Tza'ir (Young Guard) and Brit Shalom (Covenant of Peace), supported creation of a binational Jewish-Arab state. The mainstream of the Zionist movement, led by Chaim Weizmann, agreed to the idea of partitioning Palestine into two states, which was proposed by a British Royal Commission in 1937. The Zionist Revisionists, headed by Vladimir Jabotinsky, insisted upon creation of the Jewish state within the ancient historical borders—"on both banks of the Jordan river."

The migration to Palestine of middle-class Jews from Poland (in the 1920s) and Germany (in the 1930s) led to the urbanization and industrialization of the Yishuv. Tel Aviv, which was established by a small group of pioneers in 1909 as "the first Jewish city in the Land of Israel," had developed into a city of 160,000 inhabitants by 1939. In this period, the General Federation of Hebrew Workers in the Land of Israel (Histadrut ha-Ovdim) emerged as a powerful organization, providing for the medical, social, and cultural needs of Jewish agricultural and urban workers and of the Yishuv at large. The Histadrut Labor Federation established enterprises for construction and food products, sponsored schools and newspapers, and served as a central nation-building agency in interwar Palestine.

Interwar Europe

The redrawing of the map of Europe at Versailles resulted in the creation of several new nation-states, including Poland, where Jews constituted 10 percent of the overall population. In June 1919, Poland and the Allies signed the "Minorities Treaty," which guaranteed full equal civil rights for the members of minority ethnic and religious groups, and which recognized their group rights in the administration and public funding of schools with instruction in minority languages, religious affairs, and charity. The treaty stipulated that a proportional share of state funding be allocated to Jewish schools and ensured the protection of the Jews' right to Saturday rest.

Poland signed the treaty reluctantly, under international pressure, and did not honor its provisions. In the fiercely nationalist atmosphere of revived Poland, the Jews were treated as an alien element, which threatened the country's economic and cultural sovereignty. The combination of pervasive anti-Semitism with electoral democracy and the freedom of assembly and expression made interwar Poland a fruitful breeding ground for Jewish national politics and culture.

The Jewish political movements competed freely in election campaigns and chose deputies to the Polish Assembly, Senate, and city councils, where they pursued divergent strategies. The Zionists, led by Yitzhak Gruenbaum, were the most aggressive in demanding Jewish civil and national rights. In the 1922 elections, Gruenbaum organized the Minorities' Bloc of Jewish, Ukrainian, and German parties, which scored remarkable electoral success in the face of a discriminatory curial system. This high-risk confrontational tactic intensified the crisis in Polish-Jewish relations and was eventually abandoned. The Bund, in contrast, boycotted Poland's national elections as undemocratic and allied itself with the Polish Socialist Party on the municipal level. But the two movements disagreed sharply over whether the solution to the Jews' plight was assimilation or national rights. Meanwhile, Orthodox Jewry organized a powerful party of its own, Agudat Yisrael, which was staunchly anti-Zionist and pursued a strategy of quiet supplication and deal making with Polish political parties. Agudat Yisrael succeeded in securing Jewish religious liberties and special privileges for its own institutions, but it did not press for civil rights (e.g., equal access to universities and government employment) or national rights (e.g., state recognition and funding of Jewish institutions).

The political movements became dominant forces in Jewish social and cultural life in Poland. Each party established its own newspaper, school system, youth movement, publishing house, loan fund or bank, and cultural association. Polish Jewry was one of the most mobilized and organized communities in history.

Yiddish-language culture reached its greatest strength, with an explosion of newspapers and theaters and the emergence of highbrow magazines on cultural and social affairs. The establishment of the Yiddish Scientific Institute (YIVO) in Vilna in 1925, with divisions of history, philology, demographics-statistics, and pedagogy-psychology, represented a high-water mark in this regard. Nonetheless, there was a gradual process of linguistic Polonization, with slightly more than half of the Jewish children attending Polish public schools, including special schools that did not conduct classes on Saturdays.

The other great European arena was Weimar Germany, where assimilation and integration seemed all but complete in the years after the end of the Great War. Between 1921 and 1927, 45 percent of all marriages of Jews in Germany were intermarriages with Christians. A minority movement for the renewal of Jewish learning and culture, outside the framework of the established religious denominations, was led by the Jewish philosophers Martin Buber and Franz Rosenzweig. Its crowning achievement was the Jewish Lehrhaus (House of Study) in Frankfurt, where classical Jewish texts were studied by groups of laymen and professional scholars in both critical and personal religious terms.

Meanwhile, the power of the anti-Semitic Right, which blamed Jews for Germany's humiliation in the Great War, grew steadily. The assassination of the country's Jewish foreign minister, Walter Rathenau, in 1922, by a right-wing group was an early omen. Anti-Semitic pamphlets by Alfred Rosenberg were reprinted in scores of editions and were a formative influence on Adolf Hitler and his Nazi Party. In *Mein Kampf,* Hitler declared the "removal" and "elimination" of Jews from Germany to be one of his primary goals. And as Germany's economic crisis deepened, the Nazi Party's electoral popularity grew, until it garnered 14 million votes (33 percent of the total) in the 1932 elections and seized power.

Nazi policy toward the Jews went through several stages. At first, a brief reign of extralegal terror was instigated by the party and its paramilitary arms: Jewish businesses were vandalized, then boycotted; Jews were expelled from the bar, the civil service, and from much of public life. In 1935, the Jews' exclusion from German society was codified in the form of the Nuremberg Laws, which denied Jews the rights of citizens. A person with one Jewish grandparent was defined by the law as Jewish. These developments were accompanied by the introduction of medieval trappings of Jewish subjugation, such as the Jewish badge—a yellow Star of David—and a ban on sexual relations between Jews and Germans.

Throughout the 1930s, Nazi policy had as one of its goals to induce Jews to emigrate from Germany, and indeed, over 300,000 German Jews left the country between 1933 and 1939—more than half of the total number. But the possibilities for emigration were severely limited by the British White Papers regarding Palestine and by American immigration restrictions. A July 1938 international conference at Evian, France, on solving the plight of Jewish refugees led to expressions of sympathy—but to no tangible results. The inaction of the West emboldened Germany, which proceeded to forcibly deport 50,000 resident Polish Jews to the border. The Nazis instigated a nationwide eruption of anti-Jewish violence on November 9, 1938, which came to be known as "Kristallnacht" (the night of the broken glass). In one night, 100 Jews were killed, 191 synagogues were destroyed, 7,000 Jewish businesses were looted, and 30,000 Jewish men were sent to concentration camps.

Meanwhile, Germany's Jewish policy had a profound impact on Poland as well, especially after the rise to power of a military regime in 1935. The government supported a massive economic boycott against Jewish businesses and allowed a wave of 150 pogroms to sweep across the country. Adding insult to injury, it passed a law prohibiting the slaughter of kosher meat and instituted separate "ghetto benches" in the classrooms of Polish universities. As Jewish desperation and anger grew, so did the popularity of the militant Revisionist Zionism of Vladimir Jabotinsky, which called for the immediate evacuation of Jews from Poland to Palestine and which glorified military might and discipline.

The Holocaust

The German invasion of Poland in September 1939 was swift, and roughly 350,000 Jews managed to flee eastward, to the Soviet Union, its annexed territories, and Lithuania. The remainder were forced into sealed ghettos, where they were kept under inhumane conditions and used as slave labor. In each ghetto, the Germans appointed a *Judenrat* (Jewish Council) to maintain order and implement their policies. These included supplying labor contingents and exacting tributes. The tremendous congestion in the ghettos—in Warsaw, 500,000 Jews were crowded into 1,500 buildings—the meager food rations, and the poor sanitary conditions led to mounting problems of disease and starvation. The Jews attempted to cope with these overwhelming problems directly through social welfare agencies and house committees and, indirectly, through cultural institutions (schools, theaters, and libraries, many of them clandestine), which lifted morale and created a semblance of normalcy.

The ghetto inhabitants sought to persevere, make themselves useful to the Nazis through their labor, and outlive the enemy. Physical resistance was considered "foolish heroism," since the Germans took reprisal against hundreds of Jews for the act of a single resister.

The systematic large-scale murder of Jews began during the German attack on the Soviet Union in June 1941. Specially trained killing squads *(Einsatzgruppen)* attached to German army units rounded up Jews, took them to large pits, and stripped and shot them. The most famous site of this kind was Babi Yar, where 52,000 Jews of Kiev were killed in two days' time. In the roundups and shootings, the Nazis were assisted by local inhabitants (Lithuanians, Ukrainians, Romanians).

At a conference of high-ranking German officials in Wahnsee, Germany, in January 1942, the plan for the "final solution of the Jewish question" was adopted. It called for the construction of five death camps at Chelmno, Belzec, Sobibor, Treblinka, and Auschwitz, which would carry out technologically efficient mass murder using gas chambers and dispose of the bodies through crematoria. By April of that year, the death camps were fully operational, and the ghettos began to be "liquidated," as their inhabitants were deported. By the end of September 1942, only 45,000 Jews were left in the Warsaw ghetto. French Jews were rounded up by the collaborationist Vichy regime and were sent by rail, along with German, Austrian, Czech, and other Jews, to the death camps in Poland.

The "final solution" was implemented in strict secrecy, under the cover of "resettlement to the East." Although escapees and eyewitnesses reported back about the death camps, many in the ghettos and in the Western world considered such systematic genocide incredible and counterproductive to the German war effort.

The *Judenrat*s were made responsible for choosing which Jews would be awarded work passes and thereby avoid immediate deportation to the death camps. As Jews hid in underground bunkers and sewage drains, the Germans conducted *"Aktzionen,"* raids into the ghettos, and then performed "selections" to determine which Jews should be sent to the death camps. When it became clear to the head of the Warsaw Judenrat, Adam Czerniakow, in July 1942, that the German plan for total annihilation was unavoidable, he committed suicide.

The movement for armed resistance gained strength only once the ghettos were severely depleted and it had become clear that certain death awaited the remainder as well. The resistance movement was organized by members of the various Jewish youth movements, from Communist and Bundist to Labor Zionist and Revisionist Zionist. Its goal was not to rescue lives or score military victories against the Nazis but to "die like men of honor and not like sheep to the slaughter," in the words of Mordechai Anielewicz, the leader of the April 1943 Warsaw ghetto uprising. The Warsaw uprising lasted three weeks and was not defeated until the Germans burnt the entire ghetto to the ground, building by building. Similar uprisings were conducted in most major ghettos, as well as in concentration camps.

It is estimated that 6 million Jews perished in the Holocaust—4 million in the death camps and concentration camps (1.5 million in Auschwitz alone) and 2 million in the ghettos and in the mass shootings by the *Einsatzgruppen*. This figure represented more than one third of the world Jewish population. The Germans considered the "Final Solution" to be one of their highest wartime objectives, and siphoned off significant manpower and resources to it even after they were in retreat from the Allied forces.

The Allied governments downplayed the degree and unique nature of Jewish suffering in the war, so as not to lend credence to the German claim that it was a "Jewish war." Numerous warnings to the West about the mass murders went unheeded. A member of the Polish underground, Jan Karski, was smuggled into the Belzec death camp in 1942, where he saw the gas chambers in operation. He subsequently reported to British Foreign Secretary Anthony Eden and to American President Roosevelt on the death camps but was unable to extract a commitment from them to stop the genocide by bombing the camps. The U.S. State Department was annoyed by the subject, whereas the British worried that highlighting the Jewish issue would complicate their situation in Palestine.

Postwar Years (1945–1950)

The conclusion of the war in Europe left several hundred thousand Jews in "displaced persons" camps in Germany. These Jews had no homes to return to (their homes had been destroyed or were occupied by others) and had nowhere to emigrate. A few hundred thousand Polish Jews returned to Poland from the Soviet Union in 1945–1946 but were received with hostility. A 1946 pogrom in Kielce, which killed forty-one Jews, sent shock waves through the remnants of Polish Jewry and stimulated many of them to seek emigration.

As the enormous proportions of the Holocaust became known to the world public, the problem of Jewish "displaced persons" and refugees festered. The Zionist movement organized the *bericha*, an illegal migration movement from Europe to Palestine, using ships from Italian ports. But the British refused to let the ships dock in Palestine, sending many of them to Cyprus, where the passengers were kept in internment camps. In a famous incident, the ship *Exodus 1947* was sent back to Hamburg, Germany, with its 4,200 passengers.

Against this background, the conflict between the Yishuv and the British authorities grew, with the main Jewish defense organization, the *hagana*, resorting to sabotage against British military installations and railways. The Revisionist Irgun Zvai Leumi (National Military Organization) engaged in assassination attempts and acts of terror, such as the bombing of the King David Hotel. The British, in retaliation, arrested the Executive of the Zionist movement, headed by David Ben-Gurion.

The intertwined issues of the European Jewish refugees and the future of Palestine led U.S. President Harry Truman to exert diplomatic pressure on the British and to declare in September 1946 his support for "a viable Jewish State in a part of Palestine." In April 1947, Britain turned the entire question over to the United Nations, where the Soviet representative, Andrei Gromyko, spoke out in favor of the creation of a Jewish state. With both superpowers in agreement, the United Nations passed a resolution partitioning Palestine into two states, one Jewish and one Arab (with an internationalized Jerusalem), by a vote of thirty-three to thirteen, on November 29, 1947.

Civil war between Palestinian Jews and Arabs broke out immediately, and the British quickly removed their forces and administration. The State of Israel declared independence on May 14, 1948, with Ben-Gurion as its first prime minister, and Weizmann its first president. The new state was immediately attacked by the neighboring Arab states. In the ensuing war, 650,000 Arab refugees fled from the territory of Israel to Egypt and Jordan, where they were settled in refugee camps. Jerusalem was divided between Israel and Jordan, as was the remainder of the territory designated for the Palestinian Arab State.

In the three years immediately following Israel's War of Independence, its Jewish population doubled, from 750,000 to 1.5 million, because of an influx of European Holocaust survivors and Jews from Arabs lands (especially Iraq, Yemen, and Morocco). The migration altered the ethnic composition of Israel to roughly half Ashkenazic and half Oriental. One of the first laws to be passed by the Knesset (Israel's parliament) was the Law of Return, which recognizes the right of every Jew to immigrate to Israel and obtain Israeli citizenship.

Meanwhile, American Jewry emerged from the war as by far the largest and most secure and influential Diaspora community. Not only was American Jewry left intact, unscathed by the devastation of war, but its social position in America was enhanced. The large-scale participation of young Jews in the U.S. armed forces broke down social barriers between them and other Americans. The battle against a common enemy, which Jews had particular reason to fight, strengthened the consciousness of shared values. Judaism gained greater respectability in American society and came to be viewed as America's third religion (after Protestantism and Catholicism).

In the postwar years, American Jews participated in the massive stream of migration from large cities to neighboring suburbs, and from the Northeast to the southern and western parts of the country (in particular, Florida and California). The proportion of Jews in the new suburban settlements was much less than in the old urban neighborhoods, and formal institutions began to take the place of the "natural" ethnic milieu in perpetuating Jewish identity. American Jews were heavily involved in the process of community building in the late 1940s and 1950s, as they constructed synagogues, Sunday Schools, and new branches of Jewish organizations in the suburban and "sunbelt" areas of settlement.

The American Jewish community reacted with euphoria to the establishment of the State of Israel, but it refused to view America as a land of Jewish "exile" (*galut*), in accordance with classical Zionist ideology. Ben-Gurion caused a public furor among the leaders of the American Jewish community when, on his first state visit to the United States, he gave speeches predicting the eventual decline and assimilation of American Jewry and urged Jews to emigrate to Israel. Eventually, Ben-Gurion and David Blaustein, president of the American Jewish Committee, agreed upon a relationship of mutual noninterference in the others' affairs, and de facto parity between the world's two major Jewish centers.

Suggested Readings

Dawidowicz, Lucy. *The War Against the Jews*. New York: Holt, Rinehart and Winston, 1975.

Katz, Jacob. *Out of the Ghetto*. Cambridge, Mass.: Harvard University Press, 1972.

Mendelsohn, Ezra. *On Modern Jewish Politics*. New York: Oxford University Press, 1995.

Mendes-Flohr, Paul, and Jehuda Reinharz, eds. *The Jew in the Modern World*, 2nd ed. New York: Oxford University Press, 1995.

Meyer, Michael. *Response to Modernity*. New York: Oxford University Press, 1988.

Sarna, Jonathan, ed. *The American Jewish Experience*. New York: Holmes and Meier, 1986.

Stanislawski, Michael. *Tsar Nicholas I and the Jews*. Philadelphia: Jewish Publication Society of America, 1983.

Vital, David. *Zionism: The Formative Years*. New York: Oxford University Press, 1988.

Wertheimer, Jack, ed. *The Modern Jewish Experience: A Reader's Guide*. New York: New York University Press, 1993.

9

History of
Soviet Jewry

ZVI GITELMAN

THE HISTORY OF THE JEWS in the Soviet Union and its successor states is replete with paradoxes, complexities, and ironies. At the beginning of the twentieth century, the 5.2 million Jews of the Russian Empire constituted the largest Jewish population in the world; by the end of the century the number of Jews in the former Soviet Union will be smaller than that in either of the two countries to which most Russian/Soviet Jews migrated en masse during the century, Israel and the United States. It was in the Russian Empire that all the modern Jewish political movements and ideologies—several variants of Zionism, Bundism, territorialism, Yiddishism—emerged. Yet, all were suppressed by the Soviet government and were invisible for about seventy years. Only in the late 1980s were Soviet Jews reconnected to the Jewish world. They had to "catch up" to religious, political, social, cultural, and ideological developments among world Jewry.

A further irony is that when the Bolsheviks came to power in 1917, they reaffirmed the commitment of the Provisional Government to guarantee civil and political rights to the Jews and grant them the educational and vocational opportunities denied to them by the czars. But by the end of Communist rule, most Jews perceived themselves as second-class citizens and were seen as such in many sectors of Soviet society. Finally, the Soviet state, which was always a bitter critic of Zionism and from 1967 a leader of the anti-Israeli camp in world affairs, "exported" more Jews to the State of Israel than any other, though it must be acknowledged that of the 1,215,000 Jews who emigrated, nearly 30 percent left between 1992 and 1994, after the Soviet Union had collapsed, and 73 percent left between 1989, when radical changes occurred in the system, and 1994. When one considers that, like all Soviet citizens, Jews experienced two world wars, two revolutions, a civil war, radical alterations in their economic and cultural lives, Stalinist purges and collectivization, and the political vicissitudes of the past forty years—and that, as Jews, they also experienced the horrors of the Holocaust and the privations of governmental and societal anti-Semitism—one can begin to appreciate the turmoil experienced by several generations in this century.

Before the Revolution

Jews had been barred by law from residence in the Russian Empire, though some had managed to live there nevertheless, until the Russian annexation of eastern Poland in the late eighteenth century. When Poland was divided among Russia, Prussia, and Austria, the czars were confronted with a dilemma: They wanted to rule over Polish territory, but that area contained nearly a million Jews. Since this was before genocide and "ethnic cleansing" had been perfected, the solution devised by the czars was to keep the territory and its population, but to confine the Jews to what became the fifteen western provinces of the Russian Empire. These lands constituted the "Pale of Settlement"—roughly, present-day Lithuania, Belarus, western Ukraine, Moldova, and northeastern Poland. In 1897, about 97 percent of the Jewish population lived there. The Pale was abolished only in 1915, not because the government wanted to relax its restrictions on the Jews, but because the authorities suspected them of disloyalty and, fearing they would collaborate with the invading Central Powers, drove them from their homes in the western borderlands, exiling them to the deep interior of the empire.

In the czarist period the Jews were also restricted in other ways. At a time when 80 percent of the empire's population was dependent on agriculture for its livelihood, Jews were generally barred from owning land, though from time to time the czars would grant a small number of Jews the right to acquire land, especially in newly acquired areas of Ukraine and southern Russia. This restriction created a Jewish occupational profile that was radically different from that of the rest of the population. The Jews had no landowning aristocracy and hardly any peasantry. The great majority were urban dwellers, and the rest of the population was overwhelmingly rural. Jews were about a third of the urban population in Ukraine and about a half in Lithuania and Belarus. In 1897, about two thirds of the Jews were craftsmen, artisans, storekeepers, petty traders, or peddlers. *Luftmenshen* (people of the air), those without a stable means of earning a living, were counted as 8 percent of the Jewish population—though in some communities they were said to be as many as 40 percent—and 12 percent were classified as manual laborers, domestic and private employees. Though not as poor as most peasants, most Jews lived in painfully modest circumstances. In 1898 nearly 20 percent of the Jewish population in the Pale applied for assistance in making the Passover holiday. In 1900 over 60 percent of the Jewish dead in Odessa, a rather wealthy community, were buried at communal expense. Little wonder that about 1.5 million Jews emigrated from Russia between 1897 and 1914, about 70 percent of them going to the United States.

Jews were restricted in education as well. The czarist governments imposed a numerus clausus, or quota, which restricted the number of Jews to 2 or 3 percent of the students in higher education and even in the secondary schools. This restriction effectively barred Jews from the free professions, and many Jews who aspired to higher education went abroad to seek it. When the czarist authorities did encourage Jews to enter government schools, Jews regarded this, correctly, as a ploy to wean them away from Judaism and win them over to Russian Orthodoxy. Nevertheless, in 1897, over 30 percent of Jewish men and 16 percent of Jewish women could read and write in non-Jewish languages, at a time when only 21 percent of the general population could do so. The proportion literate in Hebrew or Yiddish was much higher.

Another attempt to convert Jews to Christianity was made in what became known as the "Cantonist" episode. In 1827, Czar Nikolai I decreed that each Jewish community supply a certain number of Jewish boys to what was already one of the largest standing armies in the world. These boys would be assigned to special military districts (cantons) far from the Pale and would serve terms of twenty-five years. The aim was clearly not so much military as to wean the recruits away from their faith, since they would be far from their families, teachers, and supportive environment. It is estimated that 70,000 Jewish boys—some as young as thirteen—were drafted in this way, and around 50,000 did, indeed, leave the Jewish fold. Marxist historians have argued that this was the beginning of class struggle among the Jews because the *kehilla*, or organized Jewish community, charged by the government with delivering the quota of the recruits, would snag the poor and the ne'er-do-wells, while protecting the children of the wealthy and the learned. There is no doubt that great social tensions were aroused by this episode and that these lingered for many years.

Jews were blamed for the assassination of Czar Alexander III in 1881, and a wave of pogroms swept over Ukraine. The May Laws, which imposed further restrictions on Jews, sent a clear signal to them that they would continue to be treated as an alien element. Together with the pogroms, the new restrictions spurred further Jewish emigration. In a sense, the Jews gave up on Russia. Some other Jews who had acculturated into the Russian milieu and had been drawn into the *narodnik* (populist) movement were shocked when their revolutionary comrades approved of the pogroms on the grounds that although the peasantry might have missed the target in venting their spleen on the Jews, at least the peasants had been aroused from their torpor and this newfound activism might be mobilized to change the social, political, and economic order. Some of these radical Jews, disillusioned by the behavior of their comrades, gave up on the peasantry as the engine of revolutionary change and were drawn into the nascent Marxist movement, which pointed to the proletariat as the revolutionary class. Moreover, Marxism assured its adherents that the revolution did not depend on voluntaristic actions but was the inevitable result of the clash of inexorable social forces.

Still other Jews gave up not only on Russia and on *narodnichestvo* (populism), but on the Diaspora as a whole. They were drawn to the emerging Zionist movement, which postulated that there was no solution to the "Jewish problem" (which was, after all, as much a problem of Gentile attitudes and actions as it was a problem inherent in the Jews) other than the establishment of an independent Jewish state whose sovereignty would guarantee the Jews the ability to develop economically and culturally and to defend themselves. The bankruptcy of czarism was illustrated generally by Russia's poor military performance during World War I and, for Jews, by the insistence of the czarist regime in prosecuting Mendel Beilis, a poor Kievan Jew accused of murdering a Christian child for ritual purposes, even after a Russian court had acquitted him. Little wonder that when the czarist regime collapsed in February–March 1917, its demise was greeted with universal enthusiasm among the Jewish population.

The Promise of the Revolution

The Provisional Government abolished all restrictions on the Jews, who set about feverishly to reconstruct their communal and personal lives. *Kehillas*, now with a broader franchise and more democratic in their operations, were formed in most localities. Plans were made for an all-Russian Jewish congress, where representatives of all communities would chart the future course of Russian Jewry. Jewish political and cultural organizations became very active. Since the British government announced in November that "His Majesty's government view with favor the establishment in Palestine of a national home for the Jewish people" (the "Balfour Declaration"), the Zionist idea, which had been dismissed as unrealistic by Bundists and "reactionary" by Bolsheviks and Mensheviks, gained credibility. Zionists won control of most *kehillas* in local elections and emerged as the single largest political grouping among Russian Jews. The Jewish Labor Bund, founded in 1897—the same year as the world Zionist organization—was its main rival. The Bund was a Marxist organization; it had helped organize the Russian Social Democratic Labor Party in 1898 but was expelled from that party in 1903 because the Bund insisted on a federated party with the nationalities retaining their own organizations and on national-cultural autonomy in a future socialist state. Lenin argued that these demands weakened the unity of the drive against czarism and impeded Jewish assimilation, which, according to him, was the only realistic and "progressive" solution to the "Jewish problem." Other Jewish parties active at this time were non-Marxist socialist parties, religious (Orthodox) parties, and parties representing middle-class aspirations for civil rights and equal economic opportunity.

When the Bolsheviks mounted their coup d'état in October–November 1917, the Bund, echoing the Menshevik position, criticized them for seizing power "prematurely" in a country that had not yet gone through the capitalist stage of history and was therefore not ready for a proletarian revolution. Most Jews saw the Bolsheviks' hostility to Zionism, religion, and private enterprise as inimical to their interests. Contrary to popular myth, propagated both in Russia and abroad, before and even during the revolution, Bolshevism had little support among the Jewish masses. In a census of Communist Party members taken in 1922, only 958 Jews were identified as having been "Old Bolsheviks," that is, members of the party before 1917. Considering that the Bund had 35,000 members in 1917 and that the Zionists had about 300,000 nominal members, the number of Jewish Bolsheviks, in a Party that claimed 23,600 members in January 1917, was tiny indeed. However, in the Bolshevik leadership there was a high proportion of people of at least partially Jewish origins. Thus, of 21 members of the Bolshevik Central Committee in August 1917, 6 were of Jewish origin. At Party congresses held between 1917 and 1922, 15 to 20 percent of the delegates were Jews.

Those Jews who did join the Bolsheviks in the early days were largely "non-Jewish Jews," in Isaac Deutscher's phrase. That is, they were among the small minority born outside the Pale (e.g., Yakov Sverdlov) or were half Jews or converts to Christianity (e.g., Lev Kamenev, Grigory Zinoviev). Lev Davidovich Trotsky, who became a Bolshevik only in 1917, was born on a farm in Kherson province—his parents were among the few Jews who were granted the possibility of owning land—and told in his autobiography how alienated he was from Jewish religion, culture, and even people. Such Jewish Bolsheviks were "doubly alienated." They were estranged from the Jewish milieu, and when they discovered that they were not accepted into Russian society, they found a counterculture in Bolshevism, which promised that in socialist society ethnicity and religion would not matter, indeed, would cease to exist. No doubt, this idea was attractive to those who had a highly ambiguous sense of ethnic identity. Despite the unpopularity of Bolshevism among the Jewish masses, the myth of a "Judeo-Bolshevik" conspiracy was propagated by the

White leadership during the Civil War and by those hostile to Bolshevism in Europe and America.

Ironically, what drove Jews into the ranks of the Communist Party and the offices of the Soviet government were the pogroms of the anti-Bolsheviks, on the one hand, and the opportunities given to Jews by the Soviet government, on the other. In 1918–1921, in the course of the Civil War, at least 35,000 Jews were murdered, mostly in Ukraine, primarily by Ukrainian nationalists, White armies, and bandits. There were some pogroms carried out by Red Army units, but these actions were counter to Bolshevik policy and were condemned by the Party leadership. The pogroms confronted the Jews with the "dilemma of the one alternative." The only armed force not attacking the Jews was the Red Army, and therefore many ideological opponents of Bolshevism—socialists, Zionists, religious Jews—joined its ranks. Jews were also considered "reliable" elements for police and counterrevolutionary work, since there was no danger that they would be secret supporters of the White forces or Ukrainian nationalists. Jews such as Isaac Babel joined the security forces partly out of a desire for revenge against those who had murdered their families and fellow Jews. Trotsky, commissar of war, warned against admitting too many Jews to the ranks of the Red Army because, he pointed out, they were joining for the "wrong" reasons—to defend themselves, their families, and their homes, rather than to fight for Bolshevik ideals.

Jews also found that the Bolsheviks had opened the doors to educational and vocational opportunities that they had been denied previously. They could now enter institutions of higher education as long as they had academic qualifications; they could become policemen, government officials, factory managers, and army officers, all positions unavailable to them under the czars. Even those who had religious or political reservations about the Bolsheviks could not deny that the latter had opened hitherto closed doors to them.

Among Jewish socialists, opposition to Bolshevism began to erode when they observed what they interpreted as revolutions in Germany, Hungary, and elsewhere in Europe. Some became persuaded that world revolution was imminent and that the Bolshevik seizure of power was not premature. It was such people who constituted the left wings of socialist parties, which now split over the issue of support for the Bolsheviks. By 1921, the issue was moot because the Bolshevik regime had driven all other parties out of existence and forced the left wings of the Bund; Fareynigte, a Jewish socialist party; and Poalei Tsion, a Zionist-socialist party, to merge with the Bolsheviks. These mergers brought badly needed personnel into the ranks of the Jewish Sections (*Evsektsii*) of the Communist Party.

In 1918, the government established a Commissariat for Jewish Affairs, headed by Semen Dimanshtain, one of the very few Old Bolsheviks who knew Yiddish and had an intimate knowledge of Jewish culture (he had even been ordained a rabbi by the Lubavitch/Habad Hasidic movement). The Jewish Commissariat (Evkom) tried to establish a monopoly "on the Jewish street" by abolishing the *kehillas* and taking over all Jewish communal institutions. Evkom was hampered by a lack of qualified personnel willing to work with the Bolshevik government. The same was true of the *Evsektsii*. When the Bolsheviks attempted to publish a newspaper in Yiddish, they could not find people willing to write for or edit it, despite the fact that Yiddish was the mother tongue of the vast majority of Soviet Jews. However, when ex-socialists and even Zionists entered the ranks of the Communist Party, it suddenly gained experienced politicians, editors, writers, and organizers, most of whom labored under the burden of having "come late to the revolution" and seemed to feel they had to compensate for their tardiness by exhibiting great zeal in the pursuit of the Party's goals.

Revolution on the Jewish Street

The *Evsektsii* assumed the lead in making the "revolution on the Jewish street." Acknowledging that among Jews there was still little genuine support for Bolshevik ideals and programs, *Evsektsii* activists were determined to "revolutionize" the Jewish population by destroying the institutions and uprooting the traditional values of Jewish society. In the 1920s, they identified three targets and mounted campaigns against each of them: Zionism, Judaism, and the Hebrew language. The campaigns against Zionism and religion were of a piece with general party-government struggles against non-Bolshevik political movements and parties, on one hand, and religions, on the other. But the campaign against Hebrew was an *Evsektsii* initiative and represents a continuation of the prerevolutionary Kulturkampf, which had pitted the adherents of Yiddish, most of them socialists, against the promoters of Hebrew, most of them Zionists.

Zionism had long been considered a "petit bourgeois, reactionary nationalist" ideology by the Bolsheviks because Lenin regarded it as attempting to "isolate" the Jewish proletariat and preserve its national consciousness, thus artificially retarding the progression of Jews toward full assimilation into the peoples among whom they lived. Assimilation would be a great achievement, in Lenin's view, because Jews would show the way to other peoples in creating a world without nations, as Karl Marx had prescribed for the postcapitalist era. In the 1920s, with the exception of a tiny party called the Evreiskaya Kommunisticheskaya Partiya–Poalei Tsion, all Zionist organizations and activities were outlawed and many activists were arrested. Some were sent into exile in the Urals,

Siberia, and Central Asia, whereas others were allowed to emigrate to Palestine. Some Zionist agricultural communes were permitted to exist, since they were practicing "progressive" forms of agriculture, but by the end of the decade they too were closed down.

The attack on Judaism was, of course, an integral part of the attack on religion generally. However, unlike Russian Orthodoxy, Judaism had never been part of the czarist order. But its leaders had generally adopted conservative social and political positions, to the extent that they were involved with such issues at all, for fear of bringing down the wrath of the czarist government on the Jews. The Bund had criticized this conservatism and the tendency of most rabbis to side with Jewish capitalists rather than with Jewish workers, but the Bund was more anticlerical than it was antireligious. Now, however, the *Evsektsii* mobilized the full force of state power against Judaism and its practitioners. Over 600 synagogues and over 1,000 religious schools were closed down in less than a decade. The *Evsektsii* used four tactics in the campaign against Judaism: (1) They employed agitation and propaganda, which included show "trials" of Jewish rituals such as the Passover seder (a ritual meal and recitation of the story of the Exodus of the Israelites from Egypt), ritual preparation of (kosher) food, and religious holidays. (2) There was feigned accession to the "will of the masses." Public meetings were held in which Bolshevik supporters would demand that synagogues or religious schools be turned over for use as workers' clubs, or that religious properties be seized. (3) There were Bolshevik substitutes for traditions and rituals. Thus, there were attempts, highly unsuccessful, to create a "Living Synagogue" (parallel to the "Living Church") and "Red Passover Seders" complete with a "Red Haggadah" (the book which is used at the seder). (4) Coercion was used to seize religious properties and arrest and deport rabbis, ritual slaughterers, religious teachers, and cantors.

Hebrew was defined by the Jewish Communists as "the language of the class enemy." As they argued to the somewhat puzzled Commissar of Enlightenment Anatoly Lunacharsky, Yiddish was the language of the proletarian masses and Hebrew was used only by clerics, Zionists, and pretentious members of the bourgeoisie. Therefore, Hebrew was an alien and enemy tongue, whereas Yiddish should be supported by the state of the working people. The Jewish Communists emphasized that Yiddish was not an end in itself but only an instrument for conveying the Bolshevik message to the Jewish masses. It would disappear once those masses learned Russian. On the one hand, no other state in history has supported Yiddish schools, newspapers, journals and magazines, theaters, and research institutes to the extent that the Soviet state did in the 1920s and early 1930s. On the other hand, Hebrew remained probably the only language to be cast into a kind of political imprisonment or exile. Despite the fact that there were many Hebrew writers, poets, and dramatists in the USSR, none was allowed to publish in that language, though, thanks to the intervention of Maxim Gorky's wife, some of the most prominent Hebrew writers were allowed to emigrate. For those who stayed behind, even "writing for the drawer" was a dangerous enterprise. No instruction in Hebrew was given anywhere except for a short while in Central Asia, where Yiddish was unknown, and in a few tightly controlled courses in universities in Leningrad and Tbilisi. The Jewish Communists tried to eliminate even the Hebrew elements in Yiddish—perhaps 20 percent of the language—and to reform Yiddish orthography in such a way that Hebrew words that could not be easily substituted for would be respelled phonetically in Yiddish. Thus, Communist Yiddish came to have a distinctive form, setting it apart from the Yiddish written in the rest of the world.

Although religious practice and knowledge faded quickly among Soviet Jews, it is likely that this was due more to urbanization and industrialization, coupled with the unavailability of religious instruction and materials, than to the *Evsektsii*'s antireligious campaigns. As Jews moved out of the *shtetlekh* and to the larger cities, like their relatives who had migrated abroad, they abandoned their language (Yiddish), changed their clothes and foods, developed new social networks, celebrated new holidays, and generally changed their ways of life. Customs, traditions, and beliefs fell by the wayside as Jews traveled from one milieu to another. However, surveys of Soviet Jews and Soviet Jewish émigrés over the past twenty years show that religious belief, as opposed to knowledge and practice, was not eliminated by the Soviet experience. This result seems to imply the possibility of a religious revival among some segments of Jews in the former Soviet Union.

Similarly, although Zionist organizations and ideas were forbidden by the Soviet regime, when conditions were conducive to their revival and expression, as they were after 1967, they revived remarkably. The study of Hebrew was revived by the small dissident circles of the 1970s, and after 1989, when mass emigration to Israel began, Hebrew study became very popular as a means of preparing for immigration to the Jewish State.

Postrevolutionary Construction

According to both Lenin and his *Evsektsii* disciples, once the Jews had abandoned their "outmoded, medieval superstitious and reactionary beliefs," they were to blend in with the peoples among whom they lived and abandon their particular culture and ethnic consciousness. However, the Bolsheviks realized that this process would be more gradual than originally anticipated. They were prepared to take what they considered intermediate steps, which would involve the construction of a socialist, secular, Soviet substitute for the culture that was being destroyed and abandoned. Within the *Evsektsii* there were three schools of thought on the future of Soviet Jewry. Some believed that Jews could move directly to assimilation, and therefore no "Jewish work" by the Party was necessary. Others took a "neutralist" position, arguing that it was impossible to tell how quickly Jews would assimilate; as long as Jews had cultural and economic needs specific to them, "Jewish work" was justified. The third faction held that Jews would retain a distinct identity for the foreseeable future and that they had pressing needs, so "Jewish work" would have to accelerate and be continued for quite a while. The Party's policy of *korenizatsiia*, which entailed "implanting" Bolshevik ideas among the non-Russian peoples, by bringing the message of Marxism-Leninism to them in their native languages, strengthened the second and third schools of thought. Soviet and Party institutions were now to operate in local languages, and the flowering of non-Russian cultures, many of which had been suppressed under the czars, was to be encouraged. This allowed the *Evsektsii* to expand their role from agitation and propaganda to economic planning and organization and a wide range of cultural activities.

The Jewish Sections promoted three programs in the attempt to bring the Bolshevik message to the Jewish masses and to rehabilitate them economically and remake them culturally. Yiddishization was the main cultural program adopted. The *Evsektsii* advocated Yiddish schools, newspapers, theaters, research institutes, and journals and pushed for the use of Yiddish in local and regional soviets, trade unions, and even Party organizations. These would simultaneously weaken the Hebrew language, bring Bolshevik ideas to the masses until such time as they could learn Russian, and preserve Jewish cultural consciousness. The number of Yiddish books and brochures published went from 76 in 1924 to 531 in 1930. Whereas there were 21 Yiddish newspapers in 1923–1924, there were 40 in 1927. In 1923–1924 there were 366 Yiddish schools, but by 1930 there were approximately 1,100. The number of students in these schools increased from 54,173 to 130,000 in the same time period. Almost half the Jewish children attending school in Belorussia and Ukraine were enrolled in a Yiddish school, though, significantly, in Russia, which was outside the old Pale area, only 17 percent of Jewish schoolchildren were in Yiddish schools. Just as significant was the fact that about 40 percent of the Jewish children in Ukraine and between a quarter and a half of the children in Belorussia attended no school at all.

By 1930 there were 169 soviets operating in Yiddish, most of them in Ukraine, in areas where about 12 percent of the Jewish population lived. In 1931, there were 46 Yiddish courts in Ukraine, 10 in Belorussia, and 11 in the Russian Soviet Federated Socialist Republic (RSFSR). Whereas in 1924 there was not a single Communist Party cell operating in Yiddish, by 1926 there were 25 such cells in Belorussia and 55 in Ukraine. Nearly 60 trade union cells conducted their business in Yiddish.

Impressive as these numbers might seem, they represented "Yiddishization from above," rather than an organic growth of institutions genuinely rooted in the masses. For example, the schools wrestled with the problem of Jewish content. Once one removed religion, traditions, and the idea of a historically unified Jewish people—rejected by Communists as a petit bourgeois notion that negated the principle of class differentiation and class conflict—what was left, save the Yiddish language? In fact, since the antireligious teachings in the Yiddish school were directed against Judaism, whereas parallel teachings in Russian, Ukrainian, and Belorussian schools were focused mainly on Christianity, many traditional Jewish parents preferred to send their children to non-Yiddish schools because there, at least, they would not be exposed to as much anti-Judaism propaganda. Moreover, Yiddish schools had to teach several languages: Yiddish, Russian (the language of "international communication"), Ukrainian or Belorussian, and a foreign language, usually German. That was an unrealistic burden that few schoolchildren (and perhaps their teachers) bore successfully. Perhaps the greatest weakness of the Yiddish school was that it did not prepare its students to compete on equal terms with graduates of Russian schools in the competition to gain admission to higher education, since the entrance examinations to higher educational institutions were given only in Russian. Jewish parents who had higher educational and vocational aspirations for their children were reluctant to send them to Yiddish schools and were often compelled to do so by zealous *Evsektsii* activists.

Yiddish courts did not work very well, because Jewish legal terminology was derived from rabbinic law, anathema to the Communists. There were few Yiddish-speaking lawyers, since Jews had been very restricted in this profession before the revolution. Procurators and the militia rarely referred cases to Yiddish courts. Moreover, there were no appeals courts operating in Yiddish.

Most Jewish Communists, thinking of themselves as "progressive" and the "vanguard of the proletariat," shunned Yiddish in favor of Russian. Of 45,000 Jewish members of the Party in the late 1920s, 18,000 listed Yiddish as their mother tongue *(rodnoi iazyk)*, but only 2,000 (2.2 percent) were members of cells said to operate in Yiddish. The trade unions were the weakest link in the chain of Yiddishized institutions. One calculation showed that of 1,696 trade union cells with a majority of Jews (35,523 members), only 57 cells conducted business in Yiddish. The reason was that Jewish workers and others associated Yiddish with the shtetl and its poverty and backwardness, and Russian with science, industry, progress, high culture, and the future. As one porter explained when asked why he so adamantly opposed union work in Yiddish: "For many years I have carried hundreds of *pood*s [thirty-six pounds] on my back day in and day out. Now I want to learn some Russian and become a *kontorshchik* [bank teller]." Just as their American cousins insisted on speaking broken English rather than the Yiddish of the "old country," as they attempted to become accepted into American society, so did Soviet Jews jump at the chance to learn Russian, become Russianized, and hence be accepted into Russian society—or so they thought.

The second type of constructive activity promoted by the *Evsektsii* was economic rehabilitation of the Jewish population. War, revolution, civil war, nationalization of private property and business, and emigration had left the *shtetlekh* economically devastated. In 43 Belorussian *shtetlekh* studied in the mid-1920s, only a quarter of the 91,000 inhabitants had an identifiable vocation. The Jewish Communists debated whether the *kustars*, or small craftsmen, should be regarded as a "petit bourgeois" or "proletarian" element, deciding that they were at least potential proletarians and that they should be assisted in entering cooperatives such as *artels*. Credit cooperatives and savings-and-loan associations were organized for the poor and middle-level *kustars*. The hope was that they would work in cooperative settings or move on to larger industrial enterprises. In 1926, 15 percent of the Jewish population were classified as workers, 23 percent as salaried employees, 19 percent as *kustars*, and 12 percent as petty traders. About 9 percent were peasants, whereas 91 percent of Ukrainians and 52 percent of Russians in Ukraine were classified as peasants.

Agricultural work for Jews had been made into an ideal by the Zionist movement and had been the goal of several non-Zionist Jewish movements in the late nineteenth and early twentieth centuries. The *Evsektsii* saw in agricultural work a solution to several problems: It would right the imbalance in the Jewish social structure, provide work for the unemployed and those without a fixed vocation, dispel the notion that Jews were too lazy to work the land and were a parasitical element, and offer an alternative to Zionism. In 1926, a committee was established to settle the Jews on land (*Komzet* in Russia and *Komerd* in Yiddish). A plan was devised to settle 100,000 Jewish families, that is, about a quarter of the entire Jewish population, on the land. *Ozet* (*Gezerd* in Yiddish) was formed as a non-Party organization to recruit potential colonists and rally financial and political support abroad. Jews began to settle in old Jewish agricultural colonies in Ukraine and established new ones in Ukraine, Belorussia, and Crimea. By 1928, it was estimated that 220,000 Jews had settled on the land as peasants.

The problem was that the colonies did not attract the déclassé and unemployed as much as they drew those already employed. Of 15,000 families in Ukraine who registered for settlement in 1925, 71 percent could be classified as "productive." The colonies lacked the cultural and physical amenities that an urban population was used to. Local peasants, especially in Ukraine, were resentful of Jewish settlers whom they saw as "taking over our land." There was a lack of machinery and livestock, though foreign sympathizers tried to supply these, along with agricultural expertise. The Organization for Rehabilitation and Training (ORT); an agricultural agency of the Joint Distribution Committee, Agro-Joint; and the Jewish Colonization Society (ICOR) were foreign organizations that sponsored Jewish colonies and assisted Jewish peasants. Some Jews used the colonies to "hide" from the authorities and conduct a more religious life in the colonies than they could in the cities, and some colonies served as a mask for Zionists, training people for agricultural work in Palestine.

Two developments effectively halted the experiment in agriculture. The collectivization campaign initiated in 1928 brought with it "internationalization," meaning the consolidation of many colonies with neighboring villages so that the specific Jewish character of the colony was lost. Collectivization also alienated many Jewish peasants, as it did the peasantry as a whole. Moreover, the Party—probably Stalin himself—decided to open up an area in southern Siberia, Birobidzhan, to Jewish colonization. Bordering on Manchuria and threatened by Japanese and Chinese incursions, the area was sparsely settled. Jewish colonization would beef up the Soviet presence and would also lessen tensions between Jews and others in the European areas where colonies had been established. Whatever Stalin's motives, the declaration of Birobidzhan as a potential future Jewish republic—"The Land of Israel in our very own country," as an enthusiastic Jewish woman was reported to have cried at a meeting in Belorussia to recruit settlers—meant that resources and settlers were diverted away from the colonies in Belorussia, Crimea, and Ukraine. However, since the area was so remote from traditional places of Jewish habitation and was so underdeveloped—nothing was done to prepare the region for mass settlement—half the initial arrivals left almost immediately and a year later 60 percent of the initial settlers were gone. The *Evsektsii* endorsed the Birobidzhan scheme, of course, but there is strong evidence that most *Evsektsii* activists covertly opposed it as unrealistic and harmful to the preservation of a compact Jewish population.

Some colonies survived in Ukraine and Crimea until the Nazi invasion, when they were easy targets for the *Einsatzgruppen*, whose mission was to murder Jews and Communists. None of these colonies were reconstituted after the war. In Birobidzhan, Jews never constituted more than 10 percent of the population, and many of the agricultural colonists moved to the cities. Nevertheless, in 1934 the government declared Birobidzhan the "Jewish Autonomous Oblast." In 1939, there were 17,695 Jews living in that oblast. In 1959, there were 14,269 Jews in Birobidzhan. Their numbers have steadily declined, and after 1991 there has been a significant emigration from Birobidzhan to Israel and the United States. Most observers believe that the Birobidzhan scheme was deliberately designed to fail and to simultaneously cripple the agricultural settlement of Jews in the European USSR.

The "high road" to the modernization of Soviet society was industrialization. Many more Jews entered the factories and plants than settled on the land, since they were already an urban element, unlike most of the other Soviet peoples. Between 1926 and 1935 the number of Jewish wage and salary earners seems to have increased more than two and a half times. The number of manual workers appears to have trebled. At the same time, owing to opportunities in higher education, the number of Jewish professionals, especially engineers and technicians, increased rapidly, so that by 1939, the number of manual workers, which had shot up earlier in the decade, was actually declining. Migration to the cities broke family ties and drove the migrants, especially the younger ones, further away from traditional ways of life. Yiddish was largely abandoned; religion was observed by the older generation, if at all; Hebrew could not be studied; and Jews married non-Jews at much higher rates than ever before.

Like all Soviet citizens, Jews were victimized by the purges. There is no evidence that they were especially singled out, and a substantial proportion of the secret police, the NKVD, and functionaries of the Gulag were of Jewish nationality. However, the last vestiges of Jewish cultural autonomy were erased. The *Evsektsii* were abolished in 1930, *Komzet* and *Ozet* were abolished later in the decade, many Yiddish schools were closed, and several Yiddish newspapers ceased publication. The Institute of Jewish Proletarian Culture in Kiev was thoroughly purged and reduced to a small department. The leaders of the *Evsektsii*—Semen Dimanshtain, Alexander Chemerisky, Rakhmiel Veinshtayn, Esther Frumkin, Yankl Levin, and many others—were arrested, almost all of them perishing in the Gulag. At the same time, like other Soviet citizens, many Jews threw themselves enthusiastically into what they saw as the construction of socialism, believing that in the course of this process "proletarian internationalism" was being achieved and that they would enjoy full equality with everyone else in the reconstructed society. These illusions were rudely shattered by the invasion of the German armies in 1941.

The Holocaust and the "Black Years" of Soviet Jewry

In 1939, the Soviet Union and Nazi Germany signed a nonaggression pact whose secret codicils divided some of the lands in Eastern Europe between the two totalitarian states. The USSR invaded eastern Poland sixteen days after the German armies' September 1, 1939, attack on Poland. The USSR then took over the three Baltic states, Estonia, Latvia, and Lithuania, and took Bessarabia and Bukovina from Romania, creating the Moldavian Soviet Socialist Republic (SSR) out of the former and adding the latter to the Ukrainian SSR. These territorial acquisitions added about 1.5 million Jews to the Soviet Union. During the years 1939–1941 they were subjected to the same antireligious and anti-Zionist policies their coethnics in the USSR had experienced twenty years earlier. Many political and religious leaders were arrested and deported to the Soviet interior. The Soviet government thereby inadvertently saved the lives of those who were able to survive forced labor and incarceration; had they remained in their home territories, they would have fallen victim to the Nazis.

Since the Jews from the Baltic states, Poland, and Romania were still strongly connected to traditional Jewish culture and to modern Jewish ideologies and movements, they exposed Soviet Jews to these ideas and ways of life that had already disappeared in the USSR. Though Soviet ideals and institutions were quickly forced upon the newcomers, the latter managed to preserve some of their values, ideals, and practices and, at great risk, sometimes transmitted them to Soviet Jews. This knowledge was especially significant in the 1960s when Jewish national consciousness revived and Zionist activity reemerged, led in part by the "*Zapadniki*" (Jews of the new western territories).

By the time the Soviet army entered eastern Poland, the Baltic states, and Bessarabia-Bukovina, all of them had been under dictatorial and increasingly anti-Semitic regimes. In Poland, Jews had been restricted in higher education, the military, and the professions, and there was an effective boycott of Jewish shops and manufacturers. Physical attacks on Jews became more frequent. Political groupings, including the military oligarchy that controlled the government, became explicitly anti-Semitic. In Romania, the Iron Guard fascist organization was flexing its political muscle against an already anti-Semitic regime, and in the Baltic states, all of which were dictatorships by the mid-1930s, fascist groups were becoming more prominent. Little wonder that when the Soviet army entered these areas some Jews, especially younger people who had no attachments to religion or Zionism, welcomed it as a liberating force. Among the Soviet soldiers were Jewish men and officers. The Soviets quickly sent Yiddish cultural figures into the "liberated" territories. Local Jews were impressed by the fact that Soviet Jews had the kinds of positions that they could not attain in their own countries.

The fact that some Jews welcomed the Soviet invaders impressed itself forcefully on the local populations, the great majority of whom saw the Soviets not as liberators but as imperialist invaders depriving them of the independence that they had enjoyed for barely twenty years. For them, the Jews' actions confirmed the idea of a *"zydokomuna,"* that is, that communism and Jewishness were somehow organically related. Despite the fact that Communists were a tiny fraction of the Jewish population—less than 1 percent of the Polish Jewish population and perhaps 1 percent of Lithuanian Jewry—and despite the efforts made by the Soviet authorities to keep down the number of Jews in local politics and administration, the image of Jews as Communists became very popular. The fact that Jews constituted about a quarter of the people deported from Lithuania by the Soviets, when they were less than 10 percent of the population of Lithuania, did not keep many Lithuanians from seeing the Jews as Soviet collaborators. So although some Jews saw the Soviet army as rescuers from oppression, the non-Jewish populations saw it as a foreign invading force and the Jews as traitors and collaborators.

These divergent perceptions had tragic results. When in June 1941 the Soviet army retreated hastily from the German onslaught, in parts of Poland that had been renamed West Ukraine and West Belorussia and in Lithuania and Latvia, local people attacked Jews even before the Germans could initiate their plans for the systematic annihilation of the Jews. In Kaunas, for example, about 3,000 Jews were killed in the streets by Lithuanian "partisans" before the Germans had full control of the city. The events of this period reinforced the image among some Jews of the local nationalists as fascists, especially after many of the locals enlisted in Nazi police forces and SS divisions, and reinforced the image among some segments of the local populations of Jews as Communist sympathizers.

The 3 million German troops who invaded the USSR quickly occupied main centers of Jewish population in Belorussia and Ukraine. The Nazis had long been explicit about their consuming hatred for both Bolsheviks and Jews, whom they equated with each other. General Von Manstein wrote: "More strongly than in Europe, [Jewry] holds all the key positions in the political leadership and administration. . . .The Jewish-Bolshevist system must be exterminated once and for all. The soldier must appreciate the necessity for harsh punishment of Jewry, the spiritual bearer of the Bolshevist terror."[1] However, many Soviet Jews were not fully aware of Nazi atrocities against Jews, because the Soviet media had ceased reporting and criticizing these following the August 1939 pact with Germany. Older people remembered Germans as "decent people" from their encounter during World War I. Many were therefore unprepared for the actions of the four *Einsatzgruppen,* or mobile killing squads, who liquidated much of Soviet Jewry by machine-gunning them in or near their hometowns. Other Jews were confined in ghettos, such as in Minsk, Vilnius (Vilna), and Kaunas, most of which were liquidated, along with their inhabitants, by 1941–1942. Within five months, the *Einsatzgruppen* had killed about 0.5 million Jews. The Wehrmacht, the regular German army,

also participated in killing operations, claiming that since Jews were Bolsheviks who encouraged partisan warfare against the Germans, killing
Jews was a military measure. The *Einsatzgruppen* numbered only about
3,000 men, but they were assisted by larger numbers of Lithuanian, Lat-
vian, Estonian, and Ukrainian collaborators. All told, about 1.5 million or
more Jewish civilians were killed in the USSR, and about 200,000 of the
500,000 Jews who served in the Soviet armed forces died as well.

Soviet historiography generally downplayed or ignored the Holocaust
of Soviet Jewry, though no consistent line was followed. It was not denied
that 6 million Jews had been murdered by the Nazis and their local collaborators, but the Holocaust was seen as part of a larger phenomenon—
the murder of civilians—which was said to be a natural consequence of
racist fascism. Monuments to victims of fascism rarely mentioned Jews,
but only "peaceful Soviet citizens." At Babi Yar, in Kiev, where over
33,000 Jews had been shot to death on September 29–30, 1941, and where
no monument at all stood until 1959 when Russian writer Viktor
Nekrasov protested plans to build athletic fields and a housing project on
the site, the inscription on the monument finally erected reads: "Here in
1941–1943, the German fascist invaders executed more than 100,000 citizens of Kiev and prisoners of war." When Evgeny Yevtushenko protested
the absence of a monument in his poem "Babi Yar," he was roundly criticized by officials of the Soviet Writers Union. When Dmitri Shostakovich
included the poem in his thirteenth symphony, the symphony was
banned after its premiere in Moscow.

The Black Book, a compilation of eyewitness accounts of the murder of
Soviet Jews, edited by Ilya Ehrenburg and Vassily Grossman, was ready
for publication in 1946 and had already been printed when orders came
not to distribute any copies. Indeed, only in 1993, after the breakup of the
Soviet Union, was it published in that part of the world—but in Vilnius—
long after its appearance in Israel and the United States. Soviet school
texts ignored the Holocaust. In other works the nationality of Jewish partisans and fighters was often ignored. S. S. Smirnov, in a popular multi-
volume history of the war, described the defense of the Brest fortress and
mentions its heroes as "the Russians Anatoly Vinogradov and Raisa
Abakumova, the Armenian Samvel Matevosian, the Ukrainian Aleksandr
Semenenko, the Belorussian Aleksander Machnach . . . the Tatar Petr
Gavrilov" and even "the German Viacheslav Meyer." The only hero
whose nationality was not mentioned was Efim Moiseevich Fomin, who
was described as "short . . . dark-haired with intelligent and mournful
eyes," from Vitebsk, where his father was a smith and his mother a seam-
stress. An extensive history of Ukraine, published in 1982, does not mention Jews even once, not even in connection with the Holocaust, though
Jews have lived there for nearly a millennium. In a documentary collec-

tion on Lithuania, a German document is reproduced where it says clearly that 4,000 Jews were given "special handling" (the Nazi euphemism for killing) in the Panierai death camp, whereas the translation in Russian says, "the Hitlerite security police report: another 4,000 *people* [emphasis added] have been killed." On the other hand, a study of wartime Estonia, where there were only 5,000 Jews before the war, presents a sympathetic portrayal of Jewish suffering during the Holocaust and an undistorted account of Jewish participation in the armed struggle against the fascists, acknowledging also that some Estonians participated in atrocities against the Jews. The literature in Yiddish throughout the postwar period often and explicitly discussed the Holocaust, but that was, of course, literature accessible only to a very small part of the population, basically older Jews.

Whatever the reasons for this peculiar treatment of the Holocaust, it managed to avoid raising the embarrassing issue of collaboration with the Nazis on the part of some Soviet citizens—all of whom were dismissed as "bourgeois nationalists" who had fled to the West—but it led Jews to wonder about the motivations of their government. After all, every single Jew had been affected by the Nazi occupation, and to ignore the fact that Jews were killed just for being Jews meant that the Soviet regime was deliberately overlooking an important part of their history and not condemning the greatest genocide suffered by the Jewish people in their long history. Perhaps that oversight explains why in the 1960s one of the first activities of younger Jews determined to assert their ethnic identity was to make pilgrimages to sites of mass killings of Jews—Panierai, Rumbuli, Babi Yar, areas near Minsk and Kharkov—and to try to hold memorial meetings and construct memorials there, despite KGB efforts to prevent this. Because part of the local population had collaborated with the Nazis, Jews also learned to distrust some of their neighbors. They certainly were disillusioned about Soviet claims to have achieved *"druzhba narodov"* (friendship of peoples) and *"bratstvo narodov"* (brotherhood of peoples). Establishing the historical record and confronting some painful issues of the wartime experience are high on the agendas of Jews and others in post-Soviet Lithuania, Ukraine, Latvia, and elsewhere. For the first time since the war, archives are open to researchers so that the full story of the Holocaust in the USSR may eventually be told.

During the war, the government established the Jewish Anti-Fascist Committee, whose purpose was to rally support among foreign Jews for the Soviet war effort. To that end, prominent Jewish cultural figures, the dramatist Shlomo Mikhoels and the poet Itsik Feffer, were sent to the United States and other countries to raise funds for the Soviet military. A Soviet Yiddish newspaper, *Einigkeit* (Unity), was published, picking up a thread lost when the last Yiddish newspaper from before the war, *Emes* (Truth), had ceased publication in 1938. The Jewish Anti-Fascist Committee was erroneously regarded by Soviet Jews as representing them. It became a clearinghouse for those seeking relatives who disappeared during the war, and its leaders saw as part of their mission planning the rehabilitation of the Jewish population after the war. They put forth a plan to create a Jewish population center, perhaps even a Soviet republic, in Crimea.

These plans were cut short by a campaign against Soviet Jews launched "from the top." Beginning in 1948, when Shlomo Mikhoels was murdered in a staged "accident" in Minsk, Jewish cultural institutions were shut down one by one. The Jewish Anti-Fascist Committee was dissolved, the last Yiddish publishing house was closed and even its Yiddish type was melted down, and the State Jewish Theater was closed. Not a single Yiddish book, journal, or newspaper appeared, with the exception of the provincial newspaper of the Jewish autonomous region, *Birobidzhaner Shtern*. Many Yiddish writers, actors, and researchers were arrested as "bourgeois nationalists," and more than twenty of the most prominent—including writers Dovid Bergelson and Perets Markish and poet Itsik Feffer—were shot in August 1952. At the same time, a campaign was launched against "rootless cosmopolitans," that is, Jews. The campaign began with attacks on Jewish literary and drama critics, who, it was said, could not possibly understand Russian culture, because they were alien to the Russian people and its culture, even though they had assumed Russian names and had nothing to do with Jewish culture. This was a clear signal that not even *sblizhenie* (closeness), let alone *sliianie* (assimilation), had been achieved as far as Jews were concerned. Thousands of Jews were dismissed from their jobs or demoted, and most found it very difficult to be admitted to institutions of higher education. There were reports of physical attacks on Jews, and many people freely insulted Jews in public.

The climax came in November 1952 when a headline in *Pravda* announced that a plot by "murderers in white coats" had been uncovered among Kremlin physicians whose aim was to murder medically top Soviet leaders. These doctors, almost all of whom were Jewish, were said to be agents of the American Jewish Joint Distribution Committee, a philanthropic organization that was accused of being a front for U.S. intelligence services. The Kremlin doctors were arrested. Mass hysteria against Jewish medical personnel, and then Jews in general, spread to many parts of the country. Aleksandr Solzhenitsyn reports in his *Gulag Archipelago* that new barracks were being built at this time in labor camps, apparently in expectation of a large number of deportees. Ilya Ehrenburg recalled that he was told to sign a petition to Stalin in which prominent Soviet Jews acknowledged their collective "guilt" and asked to be punished accordingly. Stalin's death in March 1953 put a halt to these plans. One month later Soviet newspapers announced that the doctors had been falsely accused and were being released. The fear of mass governmental persecution of the Jews abated.

During the "Black Years," 1948–1952, what was left of Yiddish culture and institutions was destroyed, along with any remaining illusions about the benevolence toward the Jews of the Soviet government and Communist Party. As a result of public insults and official criticisms, the loss of jobs, and very restricted access to institutes, universities, and responsible positions, most Jews became convinced that they were, at best, second-class citizens. Although Nikita Khrushchev denounced Stalin in his "secret speech" at the Twentieth Party Congress in February 1956, he explained the 1952 "Doctors Plot" as a personal caprice of Stalin's, and that Stalin had been preparing a purge of the top leadership. Khrushchev did not mention the anti-Semitic element in, or consequences of, the "plot." Furthermore, while denouncing the deportation of the Volga Germans and other nationalities, Khrushchev made no mention of Stalinist anti-Semitism. De-Stalinization was welcomed by most Jews, but it stopped far short of addressing past injuries suffered by them. It certainly made no commitments to restoring the Jews to the position of equality they had enjoyed in the first decade after the revolution, though they had been forcibly deprived of most of their religious and cultural traditions. Thus, Jews were now in the position of being forcibly acculturated—with no access to their own languages and culture, they had become fully Russianized—without being allowed to assimilate, that is, to change their identities from Jews to Russians or any other nationality. Not a single Jewish school of any kind existed anywhere in the country. There was no central religious body for Jewish believers, as there was for other religions, and close to nothing was published on Jewish history, traditions, and culture. Not surprisingly, Jews had become mostly Russians culturally, but they were still Jews legally and socially, since they were identified as Jews on their internal passports and regarded as Jews, not Russians, by the rest of society.

"Invalids of the Fifth Category"

Though the Khrushchev period brought relief from the threat to their physical survival, Jews were increasingly marginalized in the Soviet system. Where once they had been advantaged by their urban residence and propensity to pursue higher education, other peoples of the USSR had "caught up" to the Jews, and the latter no longer played as crucial a role in the advanced sectors of the economy. As Khrushchev explained to some foreign visitors, "Now we have our own cadres." The implication was that Jews were not "our own." Increasingly, Jews saw themselves as disadvantaged by their identification as such in the fifth paragraph of their internal passports. They joked sardonically that they had become "invalids of the fifth category." In 1965, Prime Minister Alexei Kosygin declared, "There is no and there never has been anti-Semitism in the Soviet Union." But unofficial and unacknowledged restrictions on Jews' vocational and educational mobility continued to exist, and several political campaigns had a negative impact on them.

Between 1957 and 1964 Khrushchev tried to reinvigorate the drive against religions. Several hundred remaining synagogues were closed. Although campaigns against Christianity and Islam pointed to no specific nationality (because Christianity and Islam were transnational religions), the campaign against Judaism clearly implicated the only nationality that practices Judaism, the Jews. Though the vast majority of Jews had long ceased to practice their religion, they were associated in the popular mind with the attacks on Judaism and with the closing of synagogues on the grounds that they had become "nests of speculators." Traditional anti-Semitic stereotypes were employed liberally by Soviet cartoonists and writers: Jews with hooked noses and wearing religious garb were shown counting and hoarding money, exploiting naive Russian peasants, and following the lead of their American and Israeli capitalist masters. The Ukrainian Academy of Sciences gave its imprimatur to Trofim Kichko's *Iudaizm Bez Prikras* (Judaism Without Embellishment), published in Kiev in 1963, whose rhetoric reminded many of Nazi propaganda. Many other works in a similar vein were published in Russian, Ukrainian, Moldavian, and other languages that non-Jews could read, so that the campaign against Judaism was not necessarily conducted among Jews.

A second campaign that had a negative spillover effect for Jews was that against Zionism. Accelerated after Israel embarrassed the USSR by defeating its Soviet clients in the June 1967 war, the campaign clearly linked Jews everywhere to Israel and Zionism. Zionism, the movement that held that Jews are a nation that should have its own state in the historic homeland of the Jewish people, Israel, was defined by Soviet authorities as a fascist movement. As one Soviet commentator put it: "There are many forms of fascism. Zionism is one of them and it is no better than Nazism." In light of the suffering of Soviet and other Jews under Nazism, such an equation could not but arouse great revulsion even among those who had no sympathy for Zionism or Israel. Israel was classified as a racist state, along with South Africa, and was considered a leader of the "imperialist" camp. Soviet images of Zionism are captured in the titles of some of the very many works critical of Israel and Zionism: *Fashizm pod*

Goluboi Zvezdoi (Fascism Under the Blue Star), published in Russian in 1971; *Ostorozhno, Sionizm!* (Caution, Zionism!), published in several languages in 1970; *Sionizm-Protivnik Mira i Sotsial'nogo Progress* (Zionism—Enemy of Peace and Social Progress), published in Kiev in 1984; and *Prestupleniem i Obmanom: Metody i Sredstva Sionizma v Osuchchestvlenii Politiki Neokolonializma* (By Crimes and Lies: Methods and Means of Zionism in the Implementation of the Policy of Neocolonialism), Kiev, 1989.

Most works like those went beyond political polemic and criticism; much of their content could fairly be described as anti-Semitic. Indeed, in February 1989 Soviet political commentators Rogov and Nosenko admitted, "This critique blurred the border between the concepts of a 'Zionist' and a Jew when it treated Judaism as the most misanthropic of world religions and declared virtually any display of Jewish national self-identification as a Zionist caper." The equation of Judaism and Zionism with anyone of Jewish nationality began under Khrushchev and continued during the "years of stagnation," until the end of the 1980s.

Jews tended toward the sciences and technology because these were the least politicized fields, whereas journalism, the military, the Party, and secret police work—all areas where Jews were once quite prominent—were generally closed to Jews. Against this background of continued restrictions and direct and indirect criticism, when Jews saw their country line up unequivocally with the Arab states against Israel in 1967, supplying arms, ammunition, military training, and political and economic assistance to countries that declared their intention of eliminating Israel from the map of the Middle East, some decided that they could no longer live in the USSR. A small trickle of Jews had been permitted to leave the Soviet Union for Israel, but after 1967 many Jews made public demands that they be allowed to do so. Some were so desperate that they attempted to hijack a Soviet plane and were caught and tried, drawing world attention to their cause.

Despite the fact that the USSR had signed three international conventions guaranteeing the right of free emigration, Soviet authorities were extremely reluctant to allow Jews (or any others) to leave. However, beginning in March 1971 substantial numbers were allowed to emigrate, perhaps in the mistaken belief that if the leaders of the emigration movement were to depart, the movement would die a natural death. Instead, the success of the first émigrés inspired others to follow their lead. In 1971 nearly 13,000 immigrated to Israel, but in each of the next two years over 30,000 did so. Between 1968 and 1980, 160,000 Jews left the Soviet Union for permanent residence in Israel. Beginning in 1974, following another war in the Middle East, increasing numbers of Jews left the USSR for Israel but changed their destination at the Vienna transit point (the USSR had broken relations with Israel in 1967 and refused to allow direct flights there); and more and more immigrated to the United States. Following the Soviet invasion of Afghanistan in 1979 and the worsening of relations with the United States, Soviet authorities turned down thousands of applications to emigrate, thereby signaling their displeasure with the West. In 1986, for example, only 914 Jews were permitted to leave the country. By the end of the 1980s, it was estimated that there were about 11,000 "refuseniks," people who had been refused permission at least twice to emigrate. Of those who were allowed to leave, in the 1980s almost 90 percent immigrated to the United States.

Glasnost, Perestroika, and Their Impact on Soviet Jewry

The reforms introduced in the late 1980s by Mikhail Gorbachev changed the situation of the Jews radically, as they changed the system and society generally. Glasnost allowed people to express themselves more freely than they ever had. Many nationalities, including Jews, took advantage of the new freedoms to express their grievances and to articulate their demands and aspirations. Perestroika allowed the formation of "informal" organizations—those not sponsored by the government or Party—and many nationalities began organizing "people's fronts" and cultural organizations. In 1988, the first Jewish schools were founded in Riga, Moscow, and a few other localities. At the same time, Jewish cultural organizations were being organized spontaneously in the larger cities. In the fall of 1989 a national roof organization calling itself the *Vaad* (committee or council)—echoing *Vaad Arba Aratsot*, the name of the regional body of Polish-Lithuanian Jewry in the sixteenth–eighteenth centuries—was formed. It claimed to represent Soviet Jewry at home and abroad. This was the first independent national Jewish organization in Soviet history. Within a year or two, between 400 and 500 local Jewish cultural organizations had been established, 40 Jewish newspapers were being published, and 27 full-day Jewish schools and nearly 200 supplementary Jewish schools had been organized. With very few exceptions, these institutions had not existed before 1988.

This sudden eruption of Jewish communal and cultural activity seemed to indicate that despite the widespread acculturation of Jews, Jewish national consciousness remained strong, though perhaps it had been sustained mostly by negative pressures. However, two developments suddenly threw into question the revival and development of Jewish life. These were the massive emigration that began in the latter half of 1989 and the breakup of the Soviet Union in late 1991.

Glasnost and pluralization of Soviet political life allowed spontaneous, rather than government-guided, expressions of anti-Semitism. This change was part of the general assertion of ethnic feelings and prejudices that came with freer expression. In February 1988 the struggle between Armenians and Azerbaijanis broke out in Nagorno-Karabakh. In 1989 in the Baltic republics there were public calls for declarations of sovereignty and even independence. In Russia a group calling itself *Pamyat'* adopted stridently anti-Semitic slogans and warned of attacks on Jews. Ironically, as economic reforms were implemented and new political groupings appeared, and as the tight grip of government and Party on society was relaxed, Jews and others began to fear that order, always a cherished Soviet value, was crumbling and that "dark forces" could gain control of the country. Rumors were rife that mass pogroms would take place in connection with the celebration of the millennium of Christianity in Slavic lands. In the event, nothing of the sort occurred and what grassroots anti-Semitism appeared was mostly verbal. But the number of Jewish emigrants went from 8,155 in 1987 to 18,965 in 1988 and then ballooned to 71,217 in 1989. Growing instability in the USSR, and the presence of so many relatives and friends in Israel and the United States, escalated emigration to unprecedented heights. In late 1989 the U.S. government announced new restrictions on the number of immigrants to be admitted from the USSR; as a result, the bulk of those leaving went to Israel, which has no restrictions on Jewish immigration. Thus, in 1990, 213,042 Jews and their non-Jewish relatives left the USSR, 181,759 of them going to Israel. In the next two years emigration declined somewhat, but between 1991 and 1994 about 0.5 million Jews left the USSR and its successor states. Obviously, this vitiated attempts to rebuild public Jewish life in the country, especially since younger people were overrepresented in the emigration, as they usually are.

The collapse of the USSR led to a splintering of the *Vaad* into republic-level coordinating bodies. The local Jewish cultural organizations began to operate in environments that had become increasingly differentiated and in states whose economic and political characters varied widely. Jews in the Central Asian republics, like Europeans, sensed a rise in what is loosely called "Muslim fundamentalism" or at least in Asian ethnocentrism, and many of them decided to leave for Israel. The Lithuanian Jewish community was shrunk considerably by emigration. Though Ukraine has consistently maintained itself as a civic state for all its peoples, rather than an ethnic state exclusively for Ukrainians, large numbers of Jews have emigrated from there, possibly because of the difficult economic situation in the early 1990s or because they are overwhelmingly Russophone and thus may feel doubly uncomfortable in a Ukrainian state, as Jews and as Russian speakers.

Another challenge to the reconstruction and continuity of the Jewish community is demographic. The Jewish population has been declining steadily since the turn of the century, owing to wars, emigration, the Holocaust, low fertility, and high rates of intermarriage. In 1989, there were 1,445,000 Jews in the USSR. Since then, over 750,000 Jews have emigrated. The ratio of births to deaths among Jews is said to have reached 1:7, and the median age of Jews in Russia and Ukraine is over fifty. In what may be the final irony in a long history, just when political conditions are propitious for the unfettered development of the Jewish people and its culture in the former USSR, that people is experiencing dramatic decline.

Notes

1. Zvi Gitelman, ed., *Bitter Legacy: Confronting the Holocaust in the USSR* (Bloomington: Indiana University Press, 1997).

Suggested Readings

Altshuler, Mordechai. *Soviet Jewry Since the Second World War: Population and Social Structure*. New York: Greenwood Press, 1987.

Gilboa, Yehoshua.*The Black Years of Soviet Jew*ry. Boston: Little, Brown, 1971.

Gitelman, Zvi. *A Century of Ambivalence: The Jews of Russia and the Soviet Union, 1881 to the Present*. New York: Schocken, 1988.

Gitelman, Zvi. *Jewish Nationality and Soviet Politics*. Princeton: Princeton University Press, 1972.

Gitelman, Zvi, ed. *Bitter Legacy: Confronting the Holocaust in the Soviet Union*. Bloomington: Indiana University Press, 1997.

Kochan, Lionel, ed. *The Jews in Soviet Russia Since 1917*. Oxford: Oxford University Press, 1970.

Pinkus, Benjamin. *The Jews of the Soviet Union*. Cambridge: Cambridge University Press, 1988.

Pinkus, Benjamin. *The Soviet Government and the Jews, 1948–1967*. Cambridge: Cambridge University Press, 1984.

Ro'i, Yaacov, ed. *Jews and Jewish Life in Russia and the Soviet Union*. London: Frank Cass, 1995.

Ro'i, Yaacov, and Avi Beker, eds. *Jewish Culture and Identity in the Soviet Union*. New York: New York University Press, 1991.

10

Modern
Jewish Literature

DAVID G. ROSKIES

Jewish Literature or the Literatures of the Jews?

We are living at a time when it is ever more difficult to determine the boundaries of a national literature. What do Chaucer, Shakespeare, Milton, Wordsworth, and Dickens have in common with English writing in the United States, Canada, Australia–New Zealand, India, and South Africa? Should American literature include within its purview the writings of Native Americans, Hispanics, and other ethnic groups? Is Franz Kafka a marginal figure in German literature, or does he represent its very core? The multicultural experience of the Jewish people may cast a new light on these vexing issues.

For one thing, Jewish culture has proved to be almost infinitely adaptable, whether one points to the influence of Hellenism on the Books of the Maccabees and on the *Guide of the Perplexed* or to the symbiosis with Arab culture that produced the Golden Age of Hebrew poetry. Closer to our own times, the European Enlightenment gave rise to a cultural revolution in Jewish life. So new were these forms of self-expression that their entire repertory could be described only in borrowed terms, beginning with *"Literatur"* itself, a loanword into Yiddish from German. The purveyors of European culture among the Jews, who called themselves *maskilim*, hoped to legitimate this new medium, literature, by basing the Hebrew name for it on the (very obscure) word for "record," *sifrah*, found in Psalms 56:9. Coined by Sholem Yaakov Abramovitsh (1836–1917), the current term *sifrut* did not come into being until 1865, and even the great Abramovitsh never found a Hebrew equivalent for his very favorite genre, the *roman* (novel). With amazing rapidity such terms as mise-en-scène, novella, feuil-

leton, reportage, humoresque, monologue, biography, autobiography, po-
ema, ballad, epic, lyric, satire, realism, romanticism, symbolism, futurism
began to appear in literary fora never before seen in Jewish society—al-
manacs, newspapers, journals, political pamphlets, and volumes containing nothing but secular verse, prose fiction, or plays. "My purpose in writing this novel," Sholem Aleichem (1859–1916) instructed his Yiddish
readers in the preface to *Stempenyu* (1888), "was to create three persons, or
as they are called [in German] *hoypt-heldn* [main characters]." To make this
first of his "Jewish novels" seem more *heymish,* or familiar, he cast the
whole preface in the form of a letter to his "beloved grandfather Reb
Mendele Moykher Seforim," Abramovitsh's pen name. Nothing could
hide the novelty of Sholem Aleichem's venue, however: a literary miscel-
lany consciously styled to imitate the Russian "thick" journal.

A second characteristic of Jewish culture is its internal bilingualism.
Prior to the Enlightenment there existed a division of labor between Hebrew-Aramaic, a language reserved for canonical works of Jewish law
and lore, and the various vernacular languages. Maimonides, for example, wrote the *Mishneh Torah,* his monumental code of Jewish law, in Hebrew but produced his philosophical *Guide of the Perplexed* in Arabic. On
the European continent, Yiddish served to mediate the Hebrew-Aramaic
classics for the common folk and also provided the folk with light entertainment. Because the assumption was that no one language could fulfill
all one's spiritual and intellectual needs, a coherent "polysystem" came
into being, which allowed for parallel and complementary developments,
both at the center and at the periphery of Jewish culture.

From 1800 on, however, the sudden explosion of new literary forms
and fora was accompanied by linguistic fragmentation. The "sacred
tongue" was being increasingly used for avowedly secular ends and the
possibility of creating high literary works in Yiddish was becoming ever
more apparent. Moreover, the absorption of Jews into the Christian body
politic suggested a third and even more radical solution: using the coter-
ritorial language to address a Jewish and non-Jewish audience alike. In
order to reach the totality of one's potential Jewish readership, intellectuals now had to translate *the same work,* pay to have it translated, and otherwise learn to adapt to an audience differentiated as to language, class,
educational level, ideological outlook, and geography. Thus Abramovitsh
became the "grandfather" of two literatures by translating his major Yiddish novels into a modern Hebrew style of his own invention. Sholem
Aleichem gained an international following by writing primarily in Yiddish but also in Hebrew and Russian. Abraham Cahan (1860–1951),
whose first literary language was Russian, learned the craft of fiction
writing for the *Commercial Advertiser,* a "progressive" English-language
newspaper in New York City, before becoming the czar and chief architect

of the American-Yiddish press. Until 1914 a Jewish writer limited to a single language was the exception rather than the rule.

So thoroughly had a European sensibility taken hold of Jewish literary culture that at the turn of the nineteenth century, when many Jewish intellectuals experienced a crisis of faith in the Enlightenment, they found themselves cut off from the sources of their own past. Launching a countermovement to reclaim "lost" Jewish forms in the name of cultural renewal, I. L. Peretz (1852–1915) discovered the beauty of Yiddish love songs, medieval romances, and Hasidic tales; Sholem Aleichem turned to writing folk monologues; and Hayyim Nahman Bialik reclaimed the biblical *massa* (oracle) to denote a "prophetic" poem of national exhortation. The folklore revival even inspired Bialik and his colleague Yehoshua Ravnitzky to reread the Babylonian Talmud in search of Jewish legend and lore. Thus was born their *Sefer ha-aggadah* (1909), the Jewish answer to the Brothers Grimm.

This dialectic of tradition and revolution—the third characteristic of Jewish culture—was to be replayed again and again, in the graphic arts (one thinks of Marc Chagall) and music (the current revival of klezmer music), but especially in literature. Moreover, many a career was marked by an ongoing tension between storytelling and the novel, between traditional and overtly secular forms of self-expression. It is perhaps not coincidental that two of the four Jewish Nobel Prize laureates in literature—Shmuel Yosef Agnon (1966) and Isaac Bashevis Singer (1978)—are exemplars of the "revolutionary traditionalist."

There are many other writers, however, and their number is ever growing, who do not fit this mold. As modern Jewish culture enters its third century, one must increasingly ask: What *is* Jewish literature? Why is it that of the two Jewish writers who most influenced the course of modern Jewish writing—Heinrich Heine and Franz Kafka—one was a convert to Christianity, and the other never once mentioned the word "Jew" in his fiction, and both wrote exclusively in German? By what logic can one place the Hebrew novels of the Israeli Arab novelist Anton Shammas alongside the writing of Galician-born Shmuel Yosef Agnon, born Czaczkes? Shall I. B. Singer be considered an American writer to the extent that he himself collaborated in the translation of his later work and insisted that all subsequent translations be made from the English, instead of the Yiddish original? Is it the very condition of exile, exterritoriality, linguistic displacement, and marginality that defines what is Jewish, as some contemporary critics have argued? Or shall one say, with the Russian Formalists, that just as the center and periphery of any literary "system" are in a constant state of flux, so will modern Jewish writing continue to exist in the tension between home and homelessness, innovation and reclamation?

Perhaps the identity crisis now facing so many national literatures across the globe can profitably be studied through the prism of modern Jewish writing, which seems to thrive on a permanent state of linguistic, ideological, and historic-geographic tension. To test this approach, I offer the following overview, arranged not by period or by author but according to literary genre.

Autobiography

Rousseau's *Confessions* (1778) stand at the juncture between two literary traditions: the plot of a religious conversion experience as laid out in *The Confessions* of Saint Augustine (354–430) and the modern autobiography. Neither model has yet taken root in Jewish culture. Although the narrative of a writer baring his soul has become commonplace in the Christian West, neither the *auto* nor the *biography* enjoys automatic citizenship in the republic of Jewish letters. To be sure, Solomon Maimon produced a *Selbstbiographie* (1793) to rival Rousseau's, but Maimon's was written for a German audience precisely to mark the distance traveled from the medieval backwaters of Jewish Eastern Europe, and nothing comparable was to appear among the Jews for almost a century. In 1876 Moses Leib Lilienblum published *Sins of Youth (Hattot neʿurim)*. It told the true-life story of a *maskil* from Lithuania, code-named Zelophehad (from the book of Numbers), whose search for love and secular learning foundered on the shoals of rigid Jewish legalism, medievalism, and patriarchy. Many a young Jewish male was to relive the "days of apostasy, crisis and renunciation" described so vividly by Lilienblum. Still, the precise form of the literary confession had few imitators.

Quite the opposite. As Jewish writers became public figures, they were expected to write an autobiography that would reflect not their true selves but their literary personae. Abramovitsh obliged by portraying the future artist *Shloyme Reb Khayims* as a true son of the shtetl K. (the White Russian market town of Kapulie). Only in the preface did he playfully reveal that "Mendele the Bookpeddler" was not to be confused with Reb Shloyme the Maskil. Abramovitsh's chief disciple, Sholem Aleichem, played an even more elaborate game. "Sholem Aleichem the writer," he announced in the preface to *Funem yarid* (From the Fair), would recount "the true-life history of Sholem Aleichem the person." Neither, of course, bore any resemblance to the "real" Solomon Rabinovitsh, a onetime member of the Kiev bourgeoisie in whose home Russian, not Yiddish, was the everyday language.

The rebellion and apostasy that accompanied the lives of every professional Jewish writer and artist were best kept hidden from a readership hungry for new folk heroes. Besides, Jewish history itself soon provided a narrative of rupture, as millions of Jews left their small towns for the metropolis, the Old Country for the New. In America, where "the pursuit of happiness" is considered a constitutional right, the Jewish autobiography finally came into its own. Hundreds of Jewish immigrants have produced autobiographical accounts in Yiddish, Hebrew, and English. Among the first was Abraham Cahan's *The Rise of David Levinsky* (1913). Written, like Maimon's *Selbstbiographie*, for Gentile readers and based on a non-Jewish literary model, this fictional autobiography stands the American "success story" on its head. Cahan himself apparently viewed this novel as so "un-Jewish" that he himself never translated it into Yiddish. By contrast, Cahan's five-volume *Bleter fun mayn lebn* (Pages from My Life, 1926–1931) is a straightforward account of his public life as a revolutionary, labor leader, journalist, and editor. It is 90 percent biography, 10 percent "auto." The American-Jewish writer who used the autobiographical form to reveal the full extent of his self-betrayal *as a Jew* is Henry Roth. His multi-volume *Mercy of a Rude Stream* (1994–1997) traces the painful move of a Jewish immigrant from an ethnically homogeneous neighborhood in Brooklyn and Lower New York to East Harlem, and from there to the haven of the self-hating Jewish intelligentsia, Greenwich Village.

The rupture caused by immigration was nothing compared to the multiple catastrophes visited upon the Jews of the twentieth century: czarist pogroms, World War I, the Bolshevik Revolution, the Civil War that followed, the Arab riots, and the Shoah. These in turn, spawned a subgenre of Jewish autobiography that focused exclusively on the catastrophe itself. That the Jews of Eastern Europe experienced World War I as a holocaust can be seen from S. An-ski's four-volume *Khurbn Galitsye* (The Destruction of Galicia, 1914–1917). Based on a real diary that An-ski kept in Russian as he crisscrossed the occupied war zone, this chronicle of destruction suppresses the author's individual experience in favor of a broad historical canvas. Fighting on the opposite side and using a contrasting literary approach was Avigdor Hameiri, whose *Ha-shigaʿon ha-gadol* (The Great Madness, 1925) refracted the slaughter of trench warfare through the autobiographical consciousness of an urbane Central European Jewish intellectual. It compares very favorably with Erich Maria Remarque's *All Quiet on the Western Front*.

The same split between a collective and individual perspective on the catastrophe has become far more pronounced in the wake of the Shoah. In general, the survivors who continued to write in Yiddish endeavored to make their personal saga into a memorial for their community. Leyb Rochman's *Un in dayn blut zolstu lebn* (translated as *The Pit and the Trap*, 1949) is a model of this approach. Those who either adopted new languages after the war or who returned to a home devoid of Jews tended to embrace the existentialism then current in intellectual circles: the individual in his face-to-face encounter with death. A case in point is survivor-writer Elie Wiesel. His first autobiographical work was published in Yiddish as *Ven di velt hot geshvign* (When the World Was Silent, 1956), and it ended with a call to capture the Nazis still at large. The same work, which he recast into French as *La Nuit* (Night, 1958), omitted any appeal to a community of like-minded readers.

The growing fragmentation of modern Jewish culture is most evident in the autobiographical genre. Yiddish writers who escaped from Europe prior to the war spent their postwar years erecting memorials to a lost civilization. The very title of Yehiel Isaiah Trunk's seven-volume autobiography says it all: *Poyln/Poland* (1944–1953). In marked contrast, the so-called New Wave of Israeli fiction was inaugurated by Pinhas Sadeh in his autobiographical novel *Ha-hayyim ke-mashal* (Life as a Parable, 1958). Though himself a veteran of Israel's War of Independence, Sadeh proclaimed the absolute autonomy of the self, divorced from the claims of the collective and from the tragic history of the Jews. The figure of Jesus as the God of love looms very large in this work. And there are many explicit love scenes.

The Novel

Indeed, autobiographers and novelists alike have equated the frustrated desire for love and sexual freedom with the hero(ine)'s quest for personal autonomy. This goes back to the first modern novel, *Don Quixote*, by Cervantes, culminating in Flaubert's *Madame Bovary* and Tolstoy's *Anna Karenina*. Writers who wished to render Jewish life through the conventions of the realistic novel were thus faced with a serious problem: Can one write *"a roman on a roman"* (Yiddish for "a novel without a love story")? Here, as elsewhere, S. Y. Abramovitsh paved the way with his *Fishke der krumer* (Fishke the Lame, 1869, 1888), the story-within-a-story of a hunchbacked beggar who falls in love with a blind waif. The novel can be read as an indictment of Jewish family life among both the merchant and the lower classes, a life so enslaved to money and sex that it robs the individual of any chance of self-fulfillment. Less strident (and much less innovative) was Sholem Aleichem, who brought together two sensitive souls, the Jewish folk fiddler, Stempenyu, and the righteous daughter of Israel, Rokhele the Beautiful. But Rokhele is married, and the norms of Jewish society do not allow for adultery. So Rokhele rejects Stempenyu's advances, returns to her husband, and the two leave their stifling home environment for Kiev, where they live happily ever after!

Was it the ideal of romantic love or the novel form itself that was Jewishly unassimilable? For Sholem Aleichem, form was synonymous with content. He played out his comedy of dissolution, not in the neatly plotted novel, but in the messy, repetitive, cyclical, monological, and dialogical tale. Through a cycle of *skaz*, monologues within dialogues, creating the illusion of live narration, Sholem Aleichem pitted the patriarchal world of Tevye the Dairyman against the anarchic power of love, of sexual and political passions, of history itself. Through the zany letters of Menakhem-Mendl to his wife Sheyne-Sheyndl, Sholem Aleichem pitted the madness of capitalism against the paranoia and claustrophobia engendered by a medieval society in a state of collapse. Judging from the Yiddish and Hebrew novel in the twentieth century, romantic love remains an absolutely unattainable goal, not because of societal constraints and corruptions, but because of the emptiness, depravity, or neuroses of human existence. This holds true whether the novel is set in the small towns of Russia, Poland, or Galicia—as are Dovid Bergelson's *Nokh alemen* (When All Is Said and Done, 1913), Micah Yosef Berdyczewski's *Miriam* (1920), and S. Y. Agnon's *Sippur pashut* (A Simple Story, 1935)—or in Tel Aviv, as is Yaakov Shabtai's *Zikhron dvarim* (translated as Past Continuous, 1970).

Since its inception, the novel has been associated with the city, both for its subject matter and its most avid readership. Among Jewish novelists, some are irresistibly drawn to a particular urban landscape, usually the city of their youth: Lodz for Israel Rabon, Warsaw for I. B. Singer, Vilna for Chaim Grade, New York City for Henry Roth, Chicago for Saul Bellow, Newark, New Jersey, for Philip Roth, Jerusalem for Amos Oz, Haifa for A. B. Yehoshua, and Tel Aviv for Yaakov Shabtai. But Yiddish and Hebrew writers found equal scope for their imagination in the shtetl, the "Jewish" market town of Eastern Europe. If anything, the collapse of the shtetl as a self-regulating social organism made it that much more appealing as a fictional laboratory. Unlike the hero(ine) of a city novel, who was expected to strive for autonomy, the shtetl itself became a kind of collective hero—or antihero.

The image of the shtetl is perhaps the greatest single invention of modern Jewish fiction. What the Western is to American popular culture, the shtetl novel and novella are to the Jewish imagination. Its symbolic landscape is etched into the East European Jewish psyche. Main Street is dominated by the marketplace and is occupied solely by Jews. Instead of the saloon, there is the *besmedresh* (the house of study); instead of the church, the *shul*. The *kohol-shtibl* where the Jewish notables meet replaces the sheriff's office. And of course there is the train depot, either nearby or somewhat removed, through which unwelcome news and travelers come to town.

With this symbolic map firmly in place, the variations on the theme of the small town in a dangerous world were almost inexhaustible. I. M. Weissenberg's *A Shtetl* (1906) opens in the house of study with a scene of class warfare. Weissenberg's animus was partly fueled by Sholem Asch's *The Shtetl*, which appeared two years before. Whereas Asch had written the first of many ecumenical fantasies in which the prayers of Jewish and Christian believers ascended to the same God, Weissenberg charts the rising tide of anti-Semitism and political reaction that culminates with the czarist forces carting the shtetl revolutionaries off to prison at the novella's end. By 1909, the shtetl had become the scene of ennui and existential despair in Dovid Bergelson's *Arum vogzal* (At the Depot).

As World War I and the Bolshevik Revolution added the physical destruction of the shtetl to its earlier economic and social decline, Yiddish and Hebrew writers exploited the shtetl more and more as shorthand for Jewish collective survival. Lamed Shapiro (1878–1948) provided a detailed anatomy of violence in a masterpiece of literary impressionism ironically titled *Di yidishe melukhe* (The Jewish State, 1919). The holy community of Krivodov, first seen at prayer in the old synagogue on Yom Kippur, the holiest day of the Jewish calendar, is reduced by novella's end to a few traumatized survivors being led into exile by a senile woman named Slove. A year later, Oyzer Varshavski (1898–1944) portrayed the Polish shtetl in wartime as nothing more than a den of *Shmuglares* (Smugglers). Meanwhile, in the USSR, the shtetl itself was cast in the role of villain, as an "ugly anachronism inimical to the interests of the working class." To disarm the apparatchiks, novelist Itsik Kipnis (1896–1974) relived the *Khadoshim un teg* (Months and Days, 1926) of the pogrom in his native town of Sloveshne (Ukraine) through the eyes of a childlike adult, modeled on the characters of Sholem Aleichem. What survives the slaughter in Kipnis's scheme is love.

By the 1930s, the shtetl of modern Jewish fiction became not merely a Jewish community in miniature, but the microcosm of a whole civilization standing on the brink of destruction. Thus, Agnon set out to rescue the complex layers of Jewish custom, legend, and learning in a mock-epic novel set in early-nineteenth-century Galicia. *Hakhnasat kalah* (The Bridal Canopy, 1931) was followed by two novels set in the fictional town of Szibusz (an anagram of Buczacz, but also meaning "trifle," or "mix-up"): *Sippur pashut* (A Simple Story, 1935), which focuses on the marketplace as the seat of bourgeois conformity, and *Oreah nata lalun* (A Guest for the Night, 1939), which revisits the "old house of study" as the seat of all the spiritual values laid waste by World War I and the forces of secularization. The protagonists of both novels struggle with madness, and though both are able, finally, to awaken from the nightmare, no hope is held out for the creative survival of the shtetl per se. Meanwhile, in *Der sotn in Goraj* (Satan in Goray, 1933), I. B. Singer refracted the apocalyptic events of the 1920s and 1930s through the lens of Sabbatianism, a Jewish messianic movement in the seventeenth century. Singer's nihilism, as opposed to Agnon's Zionism, allows for no consolation. Possessed by a dybbuk and exploited by all, Singer's heroine is left to die, and only the artificial imposition of a moral order rescues the Polish shtetl of Goraj from self-destruction.

With Hitler's rise to power, Jewish novelists turned to the family saga, a genre that threw the question of continuity into the sharpest possible focus. What would destroy the family first, they asked, its own pathology or the forces of historical destruction? Set in Lodz, the Manchester of Poland, Israel Joshua Singer's *Di brider Ashkenazi* (The Brothers Ashkenazi, 1936) places the blame squarely on such historical forces as industrialization and anti-Semitism. Set in nineteenth-century Berdichev, Der Nister's *Di mishpokhe Mashber* (The Family Mashber, 1939–1941) pays lip service to Marxism by exposing the internal decay of the Jewish market economy, personified by the eldest Mashber brother, Moyshe. The real culprit in this masterpiece of Soviet-Yiddish literature, however, is the middle brother, Luzi, a religious anarchist and a prototype of a Bolshevik. (The final volume of this novel was seized by the NKVD. Der Nister perished in the Gulag.) True to his pessimistic outlook on life, I. B. Singer portrays the decline of *Di familye Moshkat* (The Family Moskat, 1945) as a process that cuts across generation and gender. For Singer, the destruction of Warsaw by Nazi bombs only completes an inevitable process of ethical, metaphysical, and societal crisis.

Hebrew novelists, in contrast, responding to a Zionist reading of history, have held out some hope that the family may be able to withstand even the crisis of Zionist ideology itself. Moving backward in time, from 1982 to 1848, and divided into five "conversations," A. B. Yehoshua's novel *Mar Mani* (Mr. Mani, 1990) radically challenges the Zionist enterprise in the light of human sexuality, neurosis, and family history. In much the same way as Yehoshua uses the insights and techniques of psychoanalysis to question all nationalist or ethnic schemes to harness the contradictions of human existence, Meir Shalev's *Roman russi* (translated as *The Blue Mountain*, 1988) revisits the generation of Russian-born *halutzim* (pioneers) in Palestine, using the "magic realism" of Latin-American novelist Gabriel García Márquez. Despite the great sacrifices demanded of these pioneers, and despite the terrible mess their Israeli-born offspring then make of their own personal lives, Shalev ends this tragicomical family saga with the birth of a third—and presumably happier—generation, and names them after their deceased grandparents.

Although Saul Bellow has never employed the family saga genre per se, his novels and novellas consistently argue for the importance of the family as the bedrock of memory and morality. Whether he describes Moses Elkanah Herzog (*Herzog*, 1964), whose overabundant love for family and friends makes him so vulnerable to defeat, or Holocaust survivor Artur Sammler of *Mr. Sammler's Planet* (1970), who learns the lesson of human responsibility, not from books, not from historical experience, but from his dying nephew, it is the family that affords them the best schooling for a degree of humane letters. Whether American- or European-born, moreover, Bellow's heroes are mostly Jewish intellectuals of a high order of intelligence and worldliness. Bellow himself was awarded the Nobel Prize for Literature in 1976.

Between the Real and the Fantastical

Bellow's work—scrupulously realistic, "old-fashioned" in its plotting, and maximal in its intellectual demands of the reader—stands as a secular humanistic bulwark against certain modernist trends in contemporary culture. The modernists have used the novel to challenge the rational and optimistic assumptions of bourgeois society. Everything is now called into question: character, plot development, authorship, morality, society, history, and, above all, the distinction between fiction and fact. The writer who almost single-handedly effected this shift was Franz Kafka (1883–1924).

Beneath the microscopically amplified details of everyday life in Kafka's novels and short stories lies the perception of reality as an unending series of grotesque miracles. The semblance of normalcy and civility, law and order, authority and rank, is constantly belied by the existence of irrational forces out to destroy the individual. Joseph K., the hero of *Der Prozess* (The Trial, 1915), is tried and executed without actually standing trial or even learning of his crime. Gregor Samsa, the hero of "The Metamorphosis" (1915), wakes up one morning to find that he has turned into a cockroach. Because his work is so precariously poised between the real and fantastical, Kafka has influenced modern Jewish writing in two opposite directions: backward toward a rediscovery of Jewish myths and archetypes; forward to confront the immanent nightmare of the Soviet and Nazi regimes.

Thanks to Kafka, it is now possible to trace the origins of modern Jewish culture not only back to the Enlightenment but also to the fantastically elaborated fairy tales of Rabbi Nahman of Bratslav (1772–1810). True, these thirteen tales told by a zaddik, a Hasidic master, who left no successor, remain a unique phenomenon. Rabbi Nahman was the first Jewish intellectual to place storytelling at the center of his work, and these tales remain a sacred—and esoteric—document for his Hasidim (called the "Dead Hasidim") until this very day. Alongside the traditional interpreters, however, who read these tales in the light of Scripture and kabbalah, each successive generation of modern Jewish writers has discovered Rabbi Nahman anew. Peretz was fascinated by the lonely figure of Reb Nahman struggling with messianic hope and personal despair. Der Nister, during his years as a Symbolist, brought Reb Nahman's complex plots, repetitive style, and personal symbolism to the height of aesthetic perfection. In our own day, Elie Wiesel and Pinhas Sadeh have both rewritten Reb Nahman's corpus in whole or part. But it is Kafka, above all, who broke down the distinctions between storytelling and the novel, gothic romance and realism, logic and paradox, and who forms the critical link between the mystical and modernist traditions. Inspired, in turn, by Kafka's parables, Agnon wrote *Sefer ha-maʿasim* (The Book of Deeds [or Exempla], 1932), modern-day tales that defy interpretation. The personal and highly eroticized mythology of Polish-Jewish modernist Bruno Schulz (1892–1942) is likewise attributable to Kafka—and to Kafka's bizarre portrayal of women.

In contrast, Danilo Kiš's novel *A Tomb for Boris Davidovich* (1978) takes Joseph K. for an almost surrealistic tour of Stalin's Gulag—from Siberia to Republican Spain. As Jewish nightmares became reality, Kafka's "The Penal Colony" (1919) would seem to provide an accurate blueprint of the Nazi death camps. The Hebrew novels of Holocaust survivor Aharon Appelfeld are similarly cast in a "Kafkaesque" mold.

Kafka as a literary figure, finally, has come to exemplify the paradigmatic Jewish artist: neither German nor Czech, neither ghetto Jew nor cosmopolitan, neither bourgeois nor bohemian, neither true son nor true lover. Contemporary American-Jewish novelists Philip Roth and Cynthia Ozick identify themselves with Kafka most strongly. Critic Irving Howe even used Kafka's interest in Yiddish to reconnect American-Jewish readers with their East European past.

Poetry: The Oracle

What Kafka is to Jewish modernist prose, Heinrich Heine (1797–1856) is to poetry. Heine was long dead, however, before he became the stepfather of modern Jewish poetry. The poets of the Jewish Enlightenment, who enjoyed easy access to the German language, did not take kindly to Heine's apostasy, his liberal politics, or his poetics. Heine's surface simplicity, overt eroticism, his pervasive irony and parody, were anathema to the neoclassicism of the Haskalah. Only in the 1890s, when European Decadence began to make inroads in Russia and Poland, and the Symbolist poets took up Heine's cause, did Hebrew and Yiddish poets claim Heine as one of their own, a soul brother.

This points to a peculiar feature of modern Jewish culture: that the impetus to reclaim pieces of the discarded Jewish past invariably comes, not from within Jewish culture itself, but from the culture at large. It was Heine's "Romanzero" that inspired I. L. Peretz to collect Yiddish love songs. It was Heine's love affair with the Sephardic culture of medieval Spain that sparked a similar interest in Bialik and David Frischmann. It was

Heine's use of the ballad that paved the way for the ballad revival in modern Yiddish poetry. Heine proved to this second generation of Jewish rebels and revolutionaries that one could invent a usable past with materials long since abandoned and rendered obsolete. Only those who had made a clean break with the tradition, however, were free to do so. Heine, in other words, became the progenitor of the "revolutionary traditionalist."

Heine's great champion in modern Hebrew culture was Hayyim Nahman Bialik (1873–1934). Like Heine, Bialik was unsparing in his criticism of what he deemed to be the dead weight of the past. "What did I get from the poetry of the prayer book?" asks Bialik in "Shirati" (My Song, 1901). Endless boredom and depression is the answer. What of the *zmires*, the Sabbath songs that he would sing at home along with his father? They represent the terrible poverty and psychic wounds of his childhood. The whole of Jewish tradition is reduced at poem's end to a spider in a dark corner of the house devouring the innards of the last fly.

From this poetic and spiritual impasse, Bialik turned to the prophetic oracle, the *massa*. Why, of all classical forms, did Bialik fix on the oracle? Why not a more lyrical form, like the Psalms? And why did he identify with the prophets instead of the priests? Because Bialik's point of departure was God's absence, not God's presence. Because prophecy was the form best suited to express one's rage at the nation, the People of Israel. Because the new Christian reading of the Bible turned the prophets and not the priests into the source of biblical monotheism. And because Pushkin had made the call to prophecy synonymous with the lonely fate of the poet.

Never was Bialik's anger at his people kindled more strongly than in the wake of the Kishinev pogrom, in the spring of 1903. Sent by Ahad Ha'am and the ad hoc Union of Hebrew Writers to record eyewitness accounts of the pogrom, Bialik made history by publishing instead a ferociously angry poetic reportage. He called it "B'ir ha-haregah" (In the City of Slaughter), but the czarist censor changed the title to "The Oracle at Nemirow," to suggest an historical chronicle about the Chmielnicky Massacres. More shocking than the poet's description of the murder, rape, and plunder was that the entire poem was written *in God's own voice*. It is God who leads the tour, God who calls on his prophet to strike out against the heavenly throne, the people, and the world. At its deepest level, the poem points to the absurdity of writing a Great Oracle when one no longer believes in God. At the time, however, the poem was understood to be a denunciation of Jewish passivity and a call for self-defense. It launched the thirty-year-old poet as the prophetic voice of his generation.

By translating this great poem from Hebrew into Yiddish, Bialik challenged all Jewish-language poets to respond accordingly in times of national catastrophe. And respond they did. In the very midst of World War I,

American-Yiddish poet Moyshe-Leyb Halpern (1886–1932) wrote "A Night," combining the personal and historical nightmares into one. Making explicit that which was only implicit in Bialik's poem, Halpern denied national and religious meaning to this catastrophe—and to all of Jewish history. Soviet-Yiddish poet Perets Markish (1895–1952) went further still in his oracular poem "Di kupe" (The Heap, 1921). Here it is the mound of pogrom victims of the Ukrainian Civil War that blasphemes against God and eclipses all sacred mountains, from Mount Sinai to Golgotha.

Who was to blame for the cycle of catastrophes? Expressionist poet Uri Zvi Greenberg (1895–1981) issued his own "Oracle to Europe" in 1926, which proclaimed that it was not the Jews with their passivity and their false messianic expectations but Christian Europe with its lust for Jewish blood. Greenberg prophesied that only in their own land would the spiritual unification of the Jews take place, to be led by King Ahasver, the Wandering Jew of Christian myth. Greenberg lived to see both parts of his prophecy fulfilled.

The last great outpouring of oracular poems occurred during the Holocaust proper. Within the Nazi ghettos Bialik was the poet most often cited, as every Jewish community, large or small, became a veritable "City of Slaughter." In a poem with the bitterly ironic title "Spring 1942," Simkhe-Bunem Shayevitsh (1907–1944) "invited" Bialik to visit the Lodz ghetto and be humbled by the sight of so much human suffering. Six months before the final liquidation of the Vilna ghetto, in March 1943, poet Abraham Sutzkever (1913–) took up Bialik's denunciation of Jewish passivity and moral bankruptcy in "Song for the Last." Making good on his anger, Sutzkever left the ghetto with a group of Jewish fighters and took up arms against the Germans. And in 1944, poet Yitzhak Katzenelson completed his *Song of the Murdered Jewish People*, which combined the epic sweep of Lamentations with the visionary sweep of Ezekiel and Isaiah. Soon thereafter, Katzenelson was shipped off to Auschwitz, where he and his eldest son Zvi were gassed upon arrival.

Poetry: The Lyric

Heine's last years in Paris (where he died of tuberculosis) were an early instance of the state of exile experienced by so many modern Jewish poets. Jewish poets, after all, were not sons of the nobility, like Pushkin, Byron, or Mickiewicz. At best, their fathers were small-town merchants who sometimes traveled to the Leipzig fair. Few were the Jewish poets, moreover, who died in their native land, and those who stayed behind (in Poland or the USSR) were murdered. Poetic language therefore became for many a surrogate home and homeland.

Heine's most enthusiastic reception was in America, where his English-speaking admirers unveiled a monument to him in 1899. That is because a new generation of Yiddish poets, all recent immigrants from Eastern Europe, found themselves, like Heine, uprooted from home, while refusing to accept the prevailing spirit of their new home: socialism and nationalism at one extreme, materialism at the other. Even as they were importing the aesthetics and the music of Russian Symbolism to Yiddish verse, these so-called Youngsters (Di yunge) learned to master the lyrical stanza by translating into Yiddish The Complete Works of Heinrich Heine (1918). Two of his greatest admirers, Moyshe Nadir and Moyshe-Leyb Halpern, ran a joint column in a Yiddish satire magazine in which they alternated their own poetry with their translations from Heine; the readers were invited to guess whose was whose! The first self-consciously modernist work of American-Yiddish poetry, Halpern's In New York (1919), was also the most Heinesque. It portrayed the tormented inner life of an immigrant through disparate poems of varying length and contrasting moods: an urban, twentieth-century counterpart to Heine's Buch der Lieder.

The first generation of Yiddish poets truly at home in America were the so-called Introspectivists, led by Jacob Glatstein (1896–1971). New York City was the ideal setting for their cosmopolitan worldview and for the "kaleidoscopic" quality of modern life that they wished to convey in their verse. Glatstein rendered "1919" as an apocalyptic mindscape. The high point of his modernism came in Yidishtaytshn (1929–1936), an extravagant celebration of "Yiddish in All Its Meanings." In response to Hitler and the imminent destruction of Polish Jewry, however, Glatstein discovered that language was fate, and the particular fate of the Jews made of him the greatest national poet in the Yiddish language—the heir of Hayyim Nahman Bialik. Glatstein's Gedenklider (Memorial Poems, 1943) is the first volume of verse on the Holocaust to have been written in any language. Like Bialik, Glatstein the nonbeliever found a way of addressing a diminished God, sometimes through the persona of Rabbi Nahman of Bratslav. When not assessing the fate of his beloved language, Glatstein cast a satiric glance at suburban Judaism in America.

The problem of finding a homeland was greatly exacerbated for those Yiddish poets who stayed behind in Europe. Yiddish folklore became the surrogate homeland for Romanian-born Itsik Manger (1901–1969). Manger felt so at home in his ballads and Bible Poems that he adopted the freewheeling lifestyle of a Yiddish troubadour. Expelled from Poland for lack of a proper passport, Manger survived the war in London, and he never fully recovered from the loss of his Yiddish-speaking folk.

Abraham Sutzkever's search for a homeland led him in yet a third direction. Not New York, and not the reimagined folklife of Yiddish-speaking Jews, but the forests outside Vilna provided the very young Sutzkever with his "world of a thousand colors." Rather than free verse or folk-verse, a profusion of rhymes and metrical schemes displayed the poet's virtuosity. Then came the Nazis, in 1941. With ghetto walls blocking all access to nature, survival itself became a nightmare ("How?"). And so the poet cast about for new analogies, new meaning, new rhyme, and he fashioned an epic of "The Lead Plates at the Rom Press" being melted down into bullets for the uprising to come. Fated to survive the Holocaust, Sutzkever made his way to Palestine in 1947, where he has translated the irreconcilables of natural beauty and human barbarity, of national destruction and rebirth, into tightly wrought lyrics of extraordinary power. In a sequence of metaphysical *Poems from a Diary* (1974–1981), Sutzkever brought together all the landscapes he ever inhabited, both in this world, where Yiddish poetry is read by very few, and in the world to come, where the dead make up his most loyal readership.

Russia, home to this century's greatest Hebrew poets, was cruel to the ones who stayed behind. Hayyim Lenski (1905–1942?) studied at the Hebrew Teacher's Seminary in Vilna before settling in Leningrad. By day he worked at producing iron, by night—at writing Hebrew sonnets and dramatic ballads. Arrested in 1934 for the latter crime, he spent most of his remaining years at hard labor in the Gulag, where he perished. No volume of Lenski's poetry has ever been published in his native land. In Israel he is considered a major voice of the post-Bialik generation.

Even those Hebrew poets who escaped underwent a difficult transition when they reached the Promised Land. That is because a new Hebrew culture had come into being that was militantly secular both in substance and in sound. The Ashkenazi accent used in study and prayer by all European Jews was abandoned in favor of the so-called Sephardic accent. Bialik, who settled in Palestine in 1924, was never able to make the transition, and today his regular meters simply do not scan. Compare these famous opening lines written in strict trochaic tetrameters with the irregular way they are likely to be read by the average Israeli student:

> *Ha'khneese'enee ta'has kno'feykh,*
> *Va'-hayee' lee ey'm ve-ah'oys,*
> *Vee'-hee he'ykeykh mi'klat ro'yshee,*
> *Ka'n-tfilo'ysay ha'-needo'hoys.*

(Take me under your wing, / to be my mother, my sister. /
Take my head to your breast, / my banished prayers to your nest.)

> *Hakhnise'enee ta'hat kenafe'kh,*
> *Va-haye'e lee e'm ve-aho't,*
> *Ve-yehe'e heke'kh mikla't roshe'e,*
> *Ka'n-tefilota'y ha-nidaho't.*

The insistent rhythm of the one gives way to the hesitant rhythm of the other. Meter and rhyme work together in the first and work against each other in the second. The *ey* and *oy* sounds, so crucial to the meaning of this plaintive love song, disappear entirely in its Sephardic rendering.

It is therefore all the more astonishing to consider the poetic career of Bialik's great contemporary, Saul Tchernichovsky (1875–1943): Not only did he arrive in Palestine at a later age (Tchernichovsky at 56; Bialik at 51) and make the transition to the Sephardic accent, but also he produced some of his major work in the last years of his life. Perhaps this difference has to do with the fact that Tchernichovsky was thoroughly at home in European culture and drew his main inspiration from nature. The only Hebrew literary past to which his early poetry alludes with any imaginative richness is the Bible. The pagan world exercised a continuing fascination over Tchernichovsky, and his translations of the *Iliad* and *Odyssey* are themselves considered classics. When responding most directly to the violence of the twentieth century, Tchernichovsky chose the most demanding neoclassical form, the sonnet corona—"To the Sun" (1922) and "On the Blood" (1923)—as he would later respond to the Holocaust using the ballad. In these works the poet tries to shore up his sense of beauty against the moral chaos around him with an artistic control that demands restraint, control, and balance. Abraham Sutzkever would later follow in Tchernichovsky's footsteps.

The Hebrew poets who succeeded Bialik and Tchernichovsky arrived in Palestine at a much earlier age and thus made an easier transition to its Hebrew idiom: Yehudah Amichai at twelve, Avraham Shlonsky at thirteen, Natan Alterman at fifteen, Dan Pagis at sixteen. Yonatan Ratosh was the rare instance of a European-born poet who already came speaking modern Hebrew. He then went on to found the neo-Canaanite movement, whose members tried to sever all cultural ties with the European and, particularly, European-Jewish past.

A bona fide Israeli poetry, as distinct from the Hebrew poetry of "Russia and Palestine," only came into being after the War of Independence. Immediately recognized as the voice of the new state, German-born Yehudah Amichai (b. 1924) made the theme of war central to his lyric muse. By including even his father's participation in World War I, Amichai created a continuity with the past. By stressing the eternal presence of war throughout this century, analogous to love, he has domesticated the subject of death, stripped it of its mythic—and political—significance. Unlike prior generations of Hebrew poets, who drew their inspiration from German and Russian poetry, Amichai has adopted the conversational tone and the understatement so typical of Anglo-American poetry. Though the actual setting of his verse is Jerusalem, the ironic sensibility is that of London and Berkeley.

Not surprisingly, it is women, once the guardians of the Jewish hearth and home, who have given the most poignant voice to a sense of home and homelessness. American-Jewish poet Emma Lazarus (1849–1887) composed the lines that greet every immigrant to America on its Statue of Liberty:

> . . . *Give me your tired, your poor,*
> *Your huddled masses yearning to breathe free,*
> *The wretched refuse of your teeming shore.*
> *Send these, the homeless, tempest-tossed to me,*
> *I lift my lamp beside the Golden door!*

German-Jewish poet Else Lasker-Schüler (1869–1945) considered her *Hebräische Balladen* (Hebrew Ballads, 1913) to have contributed to the building of Palestine. Kadya Molodowsky's cycle of "Women's Songs" (1924) examined the modern legacy of the Biblical Matriarchs; her children's verse turned the Warsaw slums into a place of everyday miracles. In *Erd* (Earth, 1928), Rokhl Korn (1898–1982) reclaimed Galicia as the home of love, labor, and longing for both Jew and Gentile. Casting a harsher light on both the ancient and the more recent past was American-Yiddish poet Anna Margolin (1887–1952). It was in the face of Nazism that Nelly Sachs (1891–1970) returned to her Jewish roots, even as she was forced to flee from Germany. From her Swedish exile Sachs eulogized her people Israel, of whom there remained only the sand of their plundered shoes, now mingled with the sands of the Sinai. Sachs was awarded the Nobel Prize for Literature in 1966 along with S. Y. Agnon.

Israeli women poets, like their male counterparts, are less likely to touch on historical themes. Lea Goldberg (1911–1970) returned to the sonnet. Zelda (1914–1984) was a contemplative poet who drew directly from the rabbinic and Hasidic imagery of her orthodox upbringing. Dalia Ravikovitch (b. 1936), in contrast, combined a sexually explicit thematics with elements of pure fantasy. More often than not, the speaker in Ravikovitch's poems is homeless within her own body.

Jewish Drama and the Search for a Usable Past

Jewish culture has yet to produce a major dramatist. There is as yet no Jewish Ibsen, Strindberg, or Chekhov. Rather, the cultural legacy of the Jewish drama lies in its having greatly expanded the fund of Jewish collective memory. That is all the more significant given the extreme paucity of historical novels on Jewish themes. Jewish readers who hunger for a broad historical canvas must turn to Tolstoy. For portraits of famous men they must read Lion Feuchtwanger (a German Jew) on Nero or Napoleon. Whole millennia of Jewish history remain untapped by writers of prose fiction or by poets.

This problem became the more acute with the rise of nationalism throughout Europe, when the Jews were suddenly thrust into competing for national legitimacy. To qualify as a nation, the Jewish intellectuals understood, the Jews would need not only a bona fide folklore and high literary art, but also a full-blown, secular history. And so, with their wives dutifully serving them tea, the Odessa Circle of Simon Dubnow, Mordechai Ben-Ami, and Ahad Ha'am convened in the salon of Sholem-Yankev Abramovitsh to prevail upon the crotchety old gentleman to finally write his memoirs.

"Our people have no memory of past experience," says the anonymous guest who espouses Dubnow's position:

> and even events in our own times disappear into oblivion like a dream. Many things have happened in our lifetime that have not been recorded in any book only because of the foolish belief held by many people that nobody but the historians of the next generation can properly ascertain the true facts and form a correct and balanced picture. By that time, many of the events of our age will have been forgotten. (from the "Introduction" to *Shloyme Reb Khayims,* or *Bygone Days*)

But "Reb Shloyme" (i.e., Abramovitsh) can give as good as he gets. In his lengthy and acerbic rebuttal, he shows the absurdity of holding up Jewish corporate existence in Russia-Poland to Western criteria:

> None of us ever did anything to set the world on fire. Dukes, governors, generals, and soldiers we were not; we had no romantic attachments with lovely princesses; we didn't fight duels, nor did we even serve as witnesses, watching other men spill their blood; we didn't dance the quadrille at balls; we didn't hunt wild animals in the fields and forests; we didn't make voyages of discovery to the ends of the earth; we carried on with no actresses or prima donnas; we didn't celebrate in a lavish way. In short, we were completely lacking in all those colorful details that grace a story and whet the reader's appetite.[1]

Devoid of political history, bereft of individual acts of heroism or treason, all the Jews could offer was an unbroken and utterly banal record of collective suffering.

Three schools of historical thought developed out of this debate. The first, represented by Abramovitsh and Sholem Aleichem, asserted that only social history was worth recording, not the nonsense of legends, fairy tales, and sentimental romances. The historical record of how the Jewish family and community collapsed or were severely challenged in the face of modernity was the stuff of the realistic "Jewish novel," which they had introduced. The second school went back to Abraham Gold-faden (1840–1908), the father of the modern Yiddish theater. Goldfaden divided his repertory clean down the middle between satires set in the here-and-now and historical melodramas set in the time of Bar Kokhba and the biblical Shulamit. Almost single-handedly, Goldfaden created a Jewish heroes' gallery closely aligned with "dukes, governors, generals, or soldiers" or who otherwise performed deeds of true historical import and engaged in "romantic attachments." Goldfaden's heirs were soon to (re)discover the heroic saga of the Ger Tsedek, Count Valentin Potocki, who was burned at the stake for having converted to Judaism; the tragedy of Jacob Frank, the Polish Jew who claimed to be the Messiah; and most suggestive of all, the marriage of King Kazimir the Great to his Jewish consort, Esterke.

The third school owed its existence to Nietzsche and celebrated the visionary leaders who transcended historical exigency. And that is how the rabbis and mystics, who had led their flock for close to two thousand years but had been shunted aside by the cultural revolution, were finally brought back to center stage.

Early Hasidism served the poet and playwright I. L. Peretz (1852–1915) as the breeding ground for a true spiritual leader who could hasten the millennium by severing the bonds of historical determinism. Enter Reb Shloyme, the most famous zaddik in the annals of Yiddish literature, the first and most vital link in *Di goldene keyt* (The Golden Chain) of Jewish messianic struggle.

Reb Shloyme desires nothing less than the abrogation of Time. Calling for a race of spiritual giants, much as the reclusive Menakhem-Mendl of Kotsk (1787–1859) had cried out for "ten men of truth," Reb Shloyme's ecstatic vision of *shabbes-yontefdike yidn* (observant Jews) who would force God's hand by ushering in the messianic Sabbath is doomed from the start. Each of his successors likewise attempts a reversal of the natural order and faces defeat within his own Hasidic court, but for sheer poetic and psychological force, none can match Reb Shloyme's defiance of history itself.

The physical destruction of the Hasidic heartland in World War I followed by the Bolshevik seizure of power suggested the need for a more dramatic plot to eyewitness and chronicler S. An-ski. An-ski's *Between Two Worlds, or The Dybbuk* (1917) depicted the Jewish spirit struggling to maintain itself against forces of overpowering destruction. Thus, in each of the play's four acts, there is one figure who tries to reconcile This World with the Next: Khonon, the young kabbalist; Leah, his predestined bride; Reb Azrielke, the zaddik of Miropolye; and the town rabbi, Reb Shimshon. The play ends tragically for all concerned.

An-ski had intended *The Dybbuk* to provide generations of Russian audiences with a window on the Jewish past. It was to have premiered in the Moscow Art Theater—where Stanislawski had an active hand in shaping the script. Instead, An-ski had to flee for his life across the Soviet-Polish border, and *The Dybbuk* became the single most popular play in the Yiddish theater. An-ski, a pioneer of Jewish ethnography, embellished his plot of star-crossed lovers with manifold layers of Hasidic and East European Jewish lore. As a result, the play has challenged costume designers to learn how the Jews of Eastern Europe once dressed. It has inspired choreographers to learn how they may have danced. It has taught directors how they spoke, prayed, and told stories. And it has shown actors how men behaved in the company of other men as opposed to how they behaved in the company of women; differently at study and on the street; differently during the workaday week and at wedding celebrations. Most exacting of all, An-ski's "dramatic legend" taught a few exceptionally talented actresses how to project their voice when possessed of an evil male spirit, or dybbuk.

Whereas *The Dybbuk* has become a classical guide to the semiotics of East European Jewish culture, H. Leivick's *The Golem* (1920) used Jewish historical legend as an allegorical cloak for the major upheaval of the twentieth century: the Bolshevik Revolution. Through the historical personage of the great Maharal, Rabbi Judah Lowe ben Bezalel (1525–1609), who fashioned a clay figure to protect his people from imminent harm, Leivick explored what happens when brute force is unleashed in the service of spiritual, messianic, ends. What happens is that the Golem turns against the Jews of Prague. A verse drama of enormous power, *The Golem* was unfortunately beyond the physical means of the Yiddish theater and was most successfully staged in Polish translation (1928).

The important role played by Jewish historical drama in the process of nation building can be seen most clearly in the case of the Hebrew stage. The premiere production of the Habimah Theater, founded in Moscow, was *The Dybbuk*, in a masterful translation by Bialik (1922). The expressionist staging of the play by the Armenian director Vakhtangov turned the play into a revolutionary protest against the constraints of bourgeois society. Meanwhile, in Palestine, a group of young pioneers staged the play in the stone quarry where they worked. One of their number had just committed suicide, and it was hoped that the play's performance would help exorcise the demon of his death. On the occasion of the Habimah production in Palestine in 1926, however, *The Dybbuk* was "brought to trial" by leading members of the Zionist intelligentsia and "convicted" of being a pastiche of "legendary, realistic and symbolist elements." Yet the jury was forced to admit the play's tremendous audience appeal and expressed the hope that "the new life in the Land of Israel" and the awakening of a Hebrew secular culture would someday do the same. That day lay far in the future: The Habimah's second most popular production was Leivick's *The Golem*.

As long as Zionism was viewed as a national liberation movement, the Hebrew theater reread the struggle for the Land and for political sovereignty in the light of Jewish symbols and historical themes. With the War of Independence, the fledgling state finally had a contemporary theme worthy of the stage, and the native-born playwrights Moshe Shamir and Yigal Mosonzon turned that bloody conflict into Zionist melodramas. Soon thereafter a disenchantment with Zionism and the state set in, reinforced by postwar European trends such as the Theater of the Absurd. When Israeli playwrights, who now favor a minimalist stage design and ordinary dialogue, turn to historical themes, they do so in the name of leftist politics.

In its militant secularism, Israeli drama contributes to the deep split between the religious and secular. The portrayal of rabbis ranges from the laughable to the grotesque. Outside of Israel, where Jewish plays are staged mostly for reasons of nostalgia, the portrayal of the past can likewise produce comical results. In 1993, I. B. Singer's *The Magician of Lublin* was adapted into a musical on the Warsaw stage. The Polish actor chosen to play the rabbi studied for his part by attending performances at the state-run Yiddish theater (a legacy of the Communist regime). There he saw the veteran member of the troupe, a man in his eighties, moving in a strange manner. Having never seen a rabbi in the flesh, his Polish understudy concluded that a rabbi always shuffled when he walked. And that is how a Yiddish actor's infirmity became enshrined in the Polish theater!

A Literature in Translation and Transition

Modern Jewish literature, born to explain the Jews to the world and the world to the Jews, has now moved far beyond its original mandates. It is international and multilingual in scope, and thanks to the rapid pace of translation, anyone can eavesdrop on this new form of Jewish discourse. Even writers who write only in Hebrew do so with an eye to their translators, and it is not uncommon for a Hebrew novel to appear in English before being published in the original. Some writers, of course, translate more readily than others. Aharon Appelfeld's spare Hebrew style loses next to nothing in translation. Agnon's richly allusive style loses almost everything. Amichai's poetics travel much more easily than do Sutzkever's. I. B. Singer has a much larger following in Polish and Italian than he does in either Yiddish or Hebrew. Whereas once upon a time, a person had to master a rigorous Judaic curriculum in order to decipher the main works of the canon—the Bible, midrashim, *piyyut,* the Babylonian and Palestinian Talmuds, the commentaries and responsa—today the main interpretive tools for a proper understanding of Jewish literature are the same as for the study of any other literature: bibliography, biography, history, aesthetics, stylistics, folklore, philosophy, psychology, and literary history. As Heine said, "So wie es christelt zich, so jüdelt zich" (As it is among the Christians, so it is among the Jews).

And yet. The ability of so many Jewish writers to straddle more than one culture; the unbroken bond between Jewish religion and nationhood; the rebirth of the Hebrew language and the return of a dispersed people to its land; the vast and unprecedented array of possible Jewish identities; the coexistence of traditional and modern, sacred and secular forms of Jewish self-expression; and the stubborn refusal of Jews to be defined out of their particular existence—all this and more have given rise to a modern literature worthy of a people whom Muhammad called the People of the Book.

Notes

1. Ruth Wisse, ed., *A Stetl and Other Yiddish Novellas,* trans. R. P. Scheindlin (Detroit: Wayne State University Press, 1986).

Suggested Readings

Alter, Robert. *After the Tradition: Essays on Modern Jewish Writing.* New York: Dutton, 1971.

Miron, Dan. *A Traveler Disguised: The Rise of Yiddish Fiction in the Nineteenth Century,* 2nd ed. Syracuse: Syracuse University Press. 1996.

Roskies, David G. *A Bridge of Longing: The Lost Art of Yiddish Storytelling.* Cambridge, Mass.: Harvard University Press, 1995.

Sandrow, Nahma. *Vagabond Stars: A World History of the Yiddish Theater,* 2nd ed. Syracuse: Syracuse University Press. 1996.

Wirth-Nesher, Hana, ed. *What Is Jewish Literature?* Philadelphia: Jewish Publication Society, 1994.

Zinberg, Israel. *History of Jewish Literature,* 12 vols. Trans. & ed. Bernard Martin. Cleveland and New York: Ktav Publishing House. 1972–1978.

About the Editors
and Contributors

Albert I. Baumgarten is professor in the Department of Jewish History, Bar Ilan University, Ramat Gan, Israel, where he is also the director of the Jacob Taubes Minerva Center for Religious Anthropology. He specializes in the history of the Second Temple Period, as well as in the times of the Mishnah and Talmud. His most recent books include: *The Flourishing of Jewish Sects in the Maccabean Era* (1997) and *Self, Soul and Body in Religious Experience* (1998), which he coedited with J. Assmann and G. Stroumsa.

Robert Chazan is the Scheuer Professor of Hebrew and Judaic Studies at New York University. His most recent books are *Barcelona and Beyond* (1992), *In the Year 1096 . . . : The First Crusade and the Jews* (1996), and *Medieval Stereotypes and Modern Antisemitism* (1997). Prof. Chazan serves currently as president of the American Academy for Jewish Research.

Shaye J. D. Cohen is Ungerleider Professor of Judaic Studies at Brown University and director of the Judaic Studies program there. He is author of *Josephus in Galilee and Rome* and *From Maccabees to Mishnah* as well as editor of a number of scholarly volumes.

David E. Fishman is associate professor of Jewish history at the Jewish Theological Seminary (JTS) and senior research associate at the YIVO Institute for Jewish Research. He is coeditor of this volume and author of *Russia's First Modern Jews, Dimensions of Yiddish Culture*, and other studies on the history and culture of East European Jews. In addition, Fishman is editor-in-chief of *Yivo Bletter* and director of Project Judaica, a joint program of the Russian State University for the Humanities, Moscow, with JTS and YIVO.

Zvi Gitelman is professor of political science and Preston R. Tisch Professor of Judaic Studies at the University of Michigan, Ann Arbor, where he is also director of the Frankel Center for Judaic Studies. He is the author, editor, or coeditor of nine books and more than eighty articles in scholarly journals. The most recent work is *Bitter Legacy: Confronting the Holocaust in the Soviet Union* (1997).

255

Warren Zev Harvey is professor of medieval Jewish philosophy at the Hebrew University of Jerusalem. He is author of *Ḥasdai Crescas' Critique of the Theory of Acquired Intellect* and is a frequent contributor to scholarly journals.

Ora Horn Prouser is visiting assistant professor of Bible at the Jewish Theological Seminary. She is author of *The Phenomenology of the Lie in Biblical Teaching* and is a regular contributor to scholarly journals on such topics as literary approaches to biblical study and feminism and gender issues.

David G. Roskies is professor of Jewish literature at the Jewish Theological Seminary. He is author of two books on Jewish responses to catastrophe—*Against the Apocalypse* (1984) and *The Literature of Destruction* (1989)—and two on the return to folklore in modern Jewish culture: *A Dybbuk and Other Writings by S. Ansky* (1992) and *A Bridge of Longing: The Lost Art of Yiddish Storytelling* (1995). His latest book, *The Jewish Search for a Usable Past*, was published in 1999. Roskies is cofounder and editor of *Prooftexts: A Journal of Jewish Literary History*, established in 1981.

Raymond P. Scheindlin is professor of medieval Hebrew literature at the Jewish Theological Seminary. He is author of many books, including *201 Arabic Verbs, A Short History of the Jewish People*, and *Wine, Women and Death*.

Burton L. Visotzky holds the Appleman Chair of Midrash and Interreligious Studies at the Jewish Theological Seminary. He is coeditor of this volume and author of many scholarly articles and books, including *Reading the Book, The Genesis of Ethics*, and *The Road to Redemption*.

Index